LANGUAGE AND LITERACY SERIES

Dorothy S. Strickland and Celia Genishi, SERIES EDITORS

The Complete Theory-to-Practice
Handbook of Adult Literacy:
Curriculum Design and
Teaching Approaches
RENA SOIFER, MARTHA E. IRWIN,
BARBARA M. CRUMRINE,
EMO HONZAKI, BLAIR K. SIMMONS,
and DEBORAH L. YOUNG

Literacy for a Diverse Society:
Perspectives, Practices, and Policies
ELFRIEDA H. HIEBERT, EDITOR

The Child's Developing Sense of
Theme: Responses to Literature
SUSAN S. LEHR

The Triumph of Literature /
The Fate of Literacy: English in the
Secondary School Curriculum
JOHN WILLINSKY

The Child as Critic:
Teaching Literature in Elementary
and Middle Schools, THIRD EDITION
GLENNA DAVIS SLOAN

Process Reading and Writing:
A Literature-Based Approach
JOAN T. FEELEY,
DOROTHY S. STRICKLAND,
and SHELLEY B. WEPNER, Editors

Whole Language Plus:
Essays on Literacy in the
United States and New Zealand
COURTNEY B. CAZDEN

Literacy Events in a
Community of Young Writers
YETTA M. GOODMAN
and SANDRA WILDE, Editors

Inside/Outside:
Teacher Research and Knowledge
MARILYN COCHRAN-SMITH
and SUSAN L. LYTLE

The Politics of Workplace Literacy:
A Case Study
SHERYL GREENWOOD GOWEN

The Social Worlds of Children
Learning to Write in an Urban
Primary School
ANNE HAAS DYSON

Partners in Learning: Teachers and
Children in Reading Recovery
CAROL A. LYONS, GAY SU PINNELL,
and DIANE E. DEFORD

The Languages of Learning:
How Children Talk, Write,
Dance, Draw, and Sing Their
Understanding of the World
KAREN GALLAS

Dramatizing in Literature in Whole
Language Classrooms, SECOND EDITION
JOHN WARREN STEWIG
and CAROL BUEGE

When Children Write: Critical
Re-Visions of the Writing Workshop
TIMOTHY LENSMIRE

Nonfiction for the Classroom:
Milton Meltzer on Writing, History,
and Social Responsibility
Edited and with an Introduction by
E. WENDY SAUL

Unequal Opportunity:
Learning to Read in the USA
JILL SUNDAY BARTOLI

No Quick Fix: Rethinking
Literacy Programs in America's
Elementary Schools
RICHARD L. ALLINGTON and
SEAN A. WALMSLEY, Editors

NO QUICK FIX

*Rethinking
Literacy Programs
in America's Elementary Schools*

Edited by
Richard L. Allington
and
Sean A. Walmsley

International
Reading
Association

Teachers College
Columbia University
New York and London

Published simultaneously by Teachers College Press, 1234 Amsterdam Avenue, New York, NY 10027 and the International Reading Association, 800 Barksdale Rd., Newark, DE 19714

Copyright © 1995 by Teachers College, Columbia University

Library of Congress Cataloging-in-Publication Data

No quick fix : rethinking literacy programs in America's elementary
   schools / edited by Richard L. Allington and Sean A. Walmsley.
       p.   cm. — (Language and literacy series)
   Includes bibliographical references and index.
   ISBN 0-8077-3389-X (cloth : acid-free paper). — ISBN
   0-8077-3388-1 (paper : acid-free paper)
       1. Language arts (Elementary) — United States.   2. Socially
   handicapped children — Education (Elementary) — United States —
   Language arts.   3. Reading (Elementary) — United States.
   4. Educational change — United States — Case studies.   5. English
   language — Composition and exercises — Study and teaching
   (Elementary) — United States.   I. Allington, Richard L.
   II. Walmsley, Sean A.   III. Series: Language and literacy series
   (New York, N.Y.)
   LB1576.N8   1995
   372.6'0973 — dc20   94-29705

ISBN 0-8077-3388-1 (paper)
ISBN 0-8077-3389-X (cloth)
IRA Inventory Number 155

Printed on acid-free paper
Manufactured in the United States of America
02   01   00   8   7   6   5

Contents

A Conversational Preface

Sean: When I first came to the United States in the early 1960s, I was trained in Orton-Gillingham remedial techniques, and worked for several years with dyslexic children. I was convinced that children's learning disabilities would be solved by these teaching techniques, if only we could persuade everyone to adopt them. It was several years later that I began to realize that not everyone saw the world the same way I did, and several years after that that I began to acknowledge the legitimacy of different ways of teaching at-risk children. I have long since abandoned Orton-Gillingham's rather narrow focus on decoding skills, in favor of a broader, more literature-based philosophy. My own metamorphosis from one end of the literacy continuum to the other reminds me of how important it is to accept the reality of different ways of thinking about what "at-risk" means, and that there will always be debates about how best to meet the needs of children who find it difficult to acquire literacy. I am secure in my current beliefs about how I would define what it means to be "at-risk," and how I might help children with literacy difficulties, but I'm more tolerant than I used to be of beliefs and approaches that differ from my own. We are all in transition with respect to these notions, and until we find approaches that work with all children under all circumstances, we will have to remain in transition.

Dick: Well, twenty-five years ago I too was much surer about precisely what needed to be done than I am today. I had grown up, academically speaking, in a behavioral psychology world with an emphasis on mastery of sequential skills and precision teaching. I too was a reading specialist, working in Title 1 programs for children then labeled "disadvantaged." A few years later I was training remedial reading and special education teachers to focus on specific skill deficiencies and, then, one day I noticed that virtually no child was ever observed reading in our university-based clinic tutorials. Next, I noticed hardly anyone was reading in remedial reading and special education classes. Finally, I noticed that children in the lowest-achieving reading group had little opportunity to read during their reading lessons. In every case the children spent most of their time doing skill work of one sort or another and had little opportunity to read, to hear a skilled reader read, or to select things to read themselves. I had, as they say, an Aha! moment around that same time. "Aha!", I said, "We seem to have left the reading out of reading lessons." Well, that event altered my research, my teaching, and made me rethink most everything I had ever recommended as a solution to the problems some children experience with learning to read and write (actually the writing part of this rethinking came later, after Sean forced me to read some things on writing and reading/writing relationships.)

The past fifteen years or so have been wonderfully disturbing times. Wonderful because it seems that many others are also rethinking elementary schools and the reading and language arts instruction they offer. Disturbing because I had been much more comfortable being quite sure of what needed to be done than I was puzzling about what else we might try. One thing I have learned is the virtue of patience. Change is hard and change is always slower than I'd like. But change is occurring in our elementary schools. I've learned to notice and appreciate evolutionary change and not to expect revolutionary change. Like Sean, I've learned to listen more and advise less. I've learned to watch good programs and see how they work.

Sean: The other thing I have learned about reforming elementary schools to better meet the needs of low-achieving children is that schools are political as well as academic institutions; they reflect the values, attitudes, and knowledge of both their communities and society at large. A good remedial approach that ignores or rides roughshod over political realities will not last long. Good ideas need good politics to help them get initiated, and even better politics to keep them going. On the other hand, programs that are politically aware but have no academic substance can do enormous harm to children.

Dick & Sean: We have both learned that there is no quick fix that will solve the problems that some children face in our schools, even though many such fixes are routinely touted. Almost no school (or district or state or federal agency) has any sort of comprehensive, long-term plan for improving the schools in substantial ways. Very few even have a vision of what the school might be. Almost no school has any long-term plan for funding such an effort. Most rely on one-time grants or allocations. Most expect the quick fix. But we have also discovered schools—some we have worked with directly, others we've read about in the literature, or heard about at professional conferences—that have restructured themselves to benefit at-risk children. That's how this book came about. We had written a chapter about some of our own experiences in reforming elementary programs for at-risk children, but the book we wrote it for never materialized. So we decided to write the book ourselves. We tapped colleagues in different parts of the country whose work we admired, and asked them to write up case studies of their efforts. We asked that these case studies take a developmental approach describing the evolution of their programs across time, and deal with what went wrong as well as what went right. We put these case studies in the second section of the book. In the first section, we present chapters that summarize what we think are some of the most important issues facing schools determined to better serve at-risk children. This collection of papers is an attempt to foster further rethinking and restructuring of our elementary school literacy programs. The chapters do not provide a blueprint, but they do offer good evidence that we can change schools in ways that enhance the benefits to children.

P.S. We owe a debt of gratitude to many folks, but especially to those colleagues who contributed chapters to this book and to the teachers and students in the schools they have written about. We hope their insights will reach a wider audience through this book, and that others will profit from their experiences.

Introduction

Literacy Lessons in the Elementary Schools: Yesterday, Today, and Tomorrow

RICHARD L. ALLINGTON
State University of New York at Albany

If we could spend a year visiting elementary schools across the United States, we would find rather few surprises. Elementary schools in Wisconsin, Mississippi, New York, Texas, and Oregon are remarkably similar when one considers that no compulsory national educational curriculum exists. There has been a national consensus, it seems, a sort of conventional wisdom, about how elementary schools should be organized and what should occur in those schools.

However, that conventional wisdom is being challenged on a variety of fronts: professional, political, and public. While high schools have taken the brunt of the impact of criticism and reform efforts in recent years, the focus is shifting to rethinking the nature of American elementary schools. Much of the impetus comes from a clearer understanding of how early in the schooling process the educational die is cast and a growing recognition that our schools, elementary and secondary, must provide all students with the knowledge, skills, and strategies that until now have been targeted only to some.

Our schools have been described as "sorting machines" (Spring, 1989), designed to separate children into ability groups. Once sorted, children are offered a curricular experience that has been deemed "suitable" to their ability. For some children this means a reasonably demanding set of curricular expectations and, ultimately, preparation for college study. For others the curricular experiences have been less demanding, and the expectation is high school completion followed by employment. Finally, there have been "minimal skills" curricula targeted to the remaining children. The expectation is that many of these children will never complete high school, especially if held to traditional standards, and will enter relatively unskilled employment in the mills and factories that once dominated our manufacturing economy.

The widespread and long-standing elementary school practice of organizing first graders into three reading groups could be considered the initial sorting of children, except that the sorting criterion is not ability (or raw aptitude) as much as it is experience with print, with books, with stories, all before entering school. This sorting is done, it is generally argued, in an attempt to meet the needs of all children, regardless of which group they might be assigned to. But even the best of intentions at times go astray and such seems to be the case here. Assignment to a group predicts future educational outcomes with alarming accuracy. Most children placed in high-ability groups remain in those groups and go on to college. Most children placed in the low-achievement group remain there and are far more likely (1) to leave school before graduating, (2) to fail a grade, (3) to be placed in special education, (4) to become a teenage parent, (5) to commit a juvenile criminal offense, and (6) to remain less than fully literate.

It is distressing to think that our schools are so ineffectual with children who begin school with few literacy experiences that we can predict with horrifying accuracy what lifestyles different six-year-olds will attain when they reach adulthood. It is even more frightening to think that we may have adopted a conventional wisdom that creates elementary schools that literally work to deliver these results. Yet this is the message that has gradually emerged from an array of research on children's learning in elementary schools, especially their literacy learning. When we design elementary schools expecting that not all children will be able to develop as readers and writers with their peers, we should not be surprised that such a design produces precisely that result. However, we have good evidence that most children can become literate alongside their peers (McGill-Franzen & Allington, 1991). *Not just a majority of children, but virtually all. Not someday, but along with their peers.*

To make literacy for all children a reality and not just a slogan will require a dramatic shift in the conventional wisdom that has dominated the educational profession since the turn of the century—the era of the creation of the modern elementary school. But to reject the dominant conventional wisdom may require a better understanding of the roots of those beliefs and a clearer explication of beliefs that undermine attempts to make literacy for all an achieved goal.

ASSEMBLY-LINE ELEMENTARY SCHOOLS

Free compulsory elementary education became available to all children in the United States at the turn of the last century. This coincided with the "efficiency movement," as the nation shifted from an agrarian to a manufacturing economy, with assembly lines for efficient mass production of consumer goods. This same efficiency movement had an enormous impact on the design of educational programs. Small schools were combined so that whole classrooms could be filled with children of a similar age, ultimately eliminating the multiage classroom and one- and two-room elementary schools. During this period the concept of grade levels emerged and curricula became tied to those grade levels, a practice that survives today.

During this same period, standardized tests of intelligence were developed along with standardized tests of achievement. This was seen as an important step because the tests would allow an efficient sorting of children by aptitude. Not surprisingly, it became almost immediately apparent that there was a correlation between performances on these two types of tests. More often than not, children who were experiencing difficulty learning to read were also children whose performance on the paper-and-pencil intelligence tests suggested some limitations in intellectual ability. Of course, the intelligence tests typically tested information that was taught in school, and many of the tests also required children to read the test items. Middle-class children with print and book experiences before entering school scored well on both tests.

Children of poor and less well-educated parents typically fared poorly on these "intelligence" tests. This outcome fit the prevailing notion that "innate stupidity" was the primary cause of poverty. The hereditability of intelligence was, by and large, assumed, and research evidence was manipulated to bolster that position (Gould, 1981). Ultimately a conventional wisdom emerged that (1) intelligence is an inherited, generally fixed trait, (2) young children's intelligence can be measured accurately with paper-and-pencil tests, and (3) this measured intelligence predicts what a child can learn.

It did not take long for educators to suggest different educational goals for children who demonstrated different aptitudes on standardized assessments. In his classic treatise, *Laggards in Our Schools*, Leonard Ayres (1909) argued eloquently that it was unfair to hold all children to the same standard, since only some had the intellectual ability to perform at grade-level proficiency. He reported that fully one-third of all children were failing first grade as a result of attempting to hold all children to the grade-level standard. Like many others of the era, he argued for accepting differential outcomes based on an analysis of each child's aptitude and manner.

This argument led to the conventional wisdom of the necessity of three reading groups in each classroom. Children were to be grouped homogeneously by reading achievement within classrooms or sorted by achievement and placed in separate classrooms according to their achievement levels. It was assumed that three groups of high-, middle-, and low-achievement students would result in differentiated instruction that better met the children's needs. While reading achievement was the qualifying criterion, this grouping pattern came to be called "ability" grouping. There is an important distinction between achievement and ability. A child's current achievement level can be seen as a temporary condition, and one easily imagines the child enhancing that achievement level with new learning. Ability, on the other hand, is more often viewed as fixed and permanent. When we talk of low achievement, we leave room for optimism that the situation can be improved, but when we talk of low ability (or low intelligence), we are necessarily more pessimistic. In fact, when we talk of low-ability groups we may be communicating reduced expectations for the children in those groups even though no thorough assessment of aptitude or intelligence has been conducted.

By 1930 the concept of the "slow learner" was emerging in American education. Standardized achievement and aptitude tests provided educators with "objective" assessments for identifying which children were "slow" and which were not. It was felt that these students needed not just different goals but different instruction as well, since so many failed to profit from classroom programs. The most common recommendation was to slow the pace of curriculum introduction and to provide more concrete instruction. This "slow it down and make it more concrete" approach (Allington, 1991) was characterized by covering one basal story every two weeks instead of one week, for instance. Substantial amounts of repetition and drill were seen as necessary for slow children. Dolch (1931) described what he felt was necessary for these slow learners:

> Methods of word recognition that other children pick up by themselves must be taught to these slow minds. Attention to individual letters amounting almost to a spelling method may be necessary. Reading material must remain very simple and childlike. (p. 248)

It was also during this era that reading curricula came to be described in terms of skills hierarchies. What began around 1940 with quite simple schemes separating decoding from comprehension goals and first grade goals from fourth grade goals ultimately blossomed, by 1970, into complex listings of hundreds of reading and language arts objectives to be mastered. School readers shifted from collections of stories loosely organized by difficulty to "scientifically" created textbooks with strict vocabulary control guidelines, skills lessons, workbooks, and mastery tests (Langer & Allington, 1992).

The development of skills hierarchies fit well with the test developers' ambitions for increasingly precise assessment of children's reading achievement. When reading is viewed as a complex hierarchy of sequential skills to be acquired across the elementary years, then developing tests to identify the skills that children have not yet mastered makes sense. But skills hierarchies dissected literacy learning into so many parts that in both testing and teaching we lost sight of the forest by focusing on individual trees. Nonetheless, the decade from 1970 to 1980 probably represented the pinnacle of the skills mastery view of learning to read. This era also saw the development of minimum competency standards and the "back to basics" movement in American elementary schools.

Accompanying these changes was the rise of the specialist teacher and special programs between 1970 and 1990. The civil rights movement and the War on Poverty produced the first large-scale federal programmatic involvement in American education. With the advent of Title I of the Elementary and Secondary Education Act (ESEA) in 1965, large numbers of special reading teachers appeared in elementary schools. With the passage of PL 94–142, the Education of Handicapped Children Act (EHA) of 1975, elementary school special education programs doubled, then tripled, and finally quadrupled in size, sending large numbers of special education teachers into schools. (The concept of "learning disabilities" was codified into law at this time, and today over half of all handicapped students are identified as learning disabled.) Soon, children in some schools who were having difficulty learning to read received all or most of their reading instruction from a special teacher who employed a diagnostic–prescriptive plan emphasizing skills mastery.

Six beliefs about teaching reading in the elementary school have emerged since the early 1900s and now dominate our thinking about children who find learning to read difficult:

- Not all children can achieve literacy with their peers.
- We can measure children's aptitude for learning to read.
- Children learn best in homogeneous age and achievement groups.
- Reading is best defined as a hierarchy of increasingly complex skills.
- Children who find learning to read difficult need slower-paced lessons featuring repetition, concrete experience, and a single-skill focus.
- Special teachers and special programs are the best way to address the needs of children who find learning to read difficult.

Each of these beliefs impedes efforts to change American elementary schools, but they are powerful and difficult to alter. There is, however, growing recognition that these beliefs are, by and large, simply wrong.

RETHINKING THE CONVENTIONAL WISDOM
OF ELEMENTARY SCHOOLS

In order to fundamentally and permanently change American elementary schools, we must challenge the conventional wisdom that supports current school organization and instructional practice. While many of the remaining chapters in this volume address the problems associated with many of these conventions, directly or indirectly, below a brief summary of an alternative wisdom is offered.

Conventional Wisdom #1: Not All Children Can Become Literate with Their Peers

There is an enormous range of differences in children when they begin school. This suggests that the quantity, quality, and intensity of instruction needed for children to become literate with their peers will differ. We need to think of individual differences less as indicators of how much or how little children might learn, and instead think of them as indicating how much intensive instruction will be needed to accelerate their literacy development and move them alongside their peers. As long as we believe that not all children can learn to read on schedule, we will fail to embrace instructional programs that demonstrate how wrong that tradition is.

Conventional Wisdom #2: We Can Measure Children's Literacy Aptitude

While we can predict with alarming accuracy which children will have difficulty learning to read, this seems to say more about the instruction offered to them than about any innate literacy learning ability. We have good evidence that children with low scores on readiness assessments can learn to read along with their peers, but only when provided substantially larger amounts of more intensive instruction than is normally available. It is also the case that family wealth predicts reading achievement—children from wealthy families are more likely to learn to read better than children of poorer families. But wealthier families have more financial resources to purchase extra instruction when it is needed. Parents in these families are more likely to be better educated and have acquired higher levels of literacy themselves and, thus, are more able to assist their children in literacy learning. It is not that children from wealthier families have enhanced aptitudes for literacy learning, even though they may score higher when tested, but rather that they have instructional resources and options that typically are unavailable to children from poor families.

While we are able to predict which children will benefit from larger amounts of more intensive instruction, too often we have used this knowledge not to provide that instruction but to categorize and label children. We must move beyond thinking about predictive tests as indicating which children can learn and which cannot and use such indicators to predict how much of what kind of instruction will be needed to develop the literacy of all children.

Conventional Wisdom #3: Children Learn Best in Homogeneous Groups

The majority of children seem to learn best in classrooms with children of a range of achievement levels. We know that children who have difficulty learning to read achieve more in heterogeneous settings. Grouping all the lowest achievers together is simply deadly for those children. Instruction is often slower-paced and less well focused than in other groups. Placing together all the children experiencing literacy learning difficulties, with all the concomitant motivational and behavioral difficulties, creates an instructional group that has few successes, few role models, and few peer coaches.

While homogeneous groups may seem like a logical idea at first glance, such designs are simply characteristic of a "dumping ground" mentality, supported by low expectations that these children will ever learn and a concern that their difficulties will impede the learning of other children. Such groupings may seem to make teaching easier, but even this has to be questioned in the case of groupings of low-achieving students. However, even if teaching were easier with homogeneous groups, the negative effects on children's learning make such a practice untenable. The conventional wisdom about homogeneous instructional groups is simply misguided.

Conventional Wisdom #4: Reading Is a Hierarchy of Increasingly Complex Skills

This element of the conventional wisdom gave us detailed scope and sequence charts of supposed subskills that were to be mastered in a specific order by children. However, researchers were never able to verify the existence and sequencing of these hierarchies. In addition, these subskill curricula contained so many isolated skill activities—usually of a paper-and-pencil variety—that researchers noticed children spending little time actually reading and writing during school literacy lessons (Allington, 1980). Also, the time spent in skill and drill did not increase reading achievement—the time spent actually reading was the best instructional predictor of who read best (Leinhardt, Zigmond, & Cooley, 1981).

What seemed so logical—identifying component parts of the reading process and focusing instruction on those that were not yet mastered—was revealed in practice to be seriously flawed. It is not that children do not need to learn important literacy skills and strategies, but that reading and writing activity need to drive the instruction (Walmsley, 1991). When arbitrary skills sequences—and they are all arbitrary—drive instruction, we fail to watch children carefully. We fail to note which understandings and strategies they have acquired, which they have not, and which they need help acquiring to succeed in their reading and writing.

Conventional Wisdom #5: Some Children Need Slowed-Down and More Concrete Instruction

Slowing down the pace of instruction ensures that children will always remain behind other children whose instruction proceeds at a normal pace. If we design instruction so that one group of first graders completes only the preprimer and primer levels of a reading series, we should not be surprised when the scores of these children on achievement tests fall below grade-level standards. If we have fourth grade students whose pace of instruction has been slowed to the point that they are still reading only easy-to-read trade books series, we again should not expect demonstrations of literacy proficiency comparable to peers who are reading more complex texts.

While the conventional wisdom has often recommended slowing instruction down, there is an alternative that involves accelerating the instruction offered. Acceleration of instruction means that we offer children larger amounts of more intense teaching in order to enhance the pace of literacy development (Clay, 1985). Children who begin school with fewer experiences with literacy need not remain behind their more advantaged peers throughout their school careers. In fact, designing schools that offer instruction that accelerates development early, in kindergarten and first grade, must become our priority. The longer we allow children's development to lag behind that of their peers, the more difficult it becomes to accelerate their learning and the less likely it is that these children will ever develop full literacy.

Conventional Wisdom #6: We Should Use Special Teachers to Meet the Needs of Some Children

Fifty years ago there were no reading teachers, no special education resource room teachers, no speech therapists, no ESL teachers, and no school psychologists in schools. Even twenty-five years ago few schools employed such personnel, but with the passage of the ESEA of 1965 and the EHA of 1975 schools scrambled to add these extra staff members. In most cases these additional positions were funded from federal or state educational improvement programs. Federal and state educational policy experts felt that it was more cost-effective to add a few specialized personnel instead of upgrading the expertise of the many classroom teachers (Allington, 1994).

As detailed in the next chapter, this conventional wisdom resulted in an array of special programs and specialist teachers. Unfortunately, these programs gave children highly fragmented educational experiences. Soon the regular education programs reneged on their responsibility to educate all children and instead focused on serving only those children with no difficulties in academic learning. A series of large-scale program evaluations found much evidence that the addition of these special programs had not improved educational experiences for low-achieving children, and the few achievement gains found were disappointingly small (see Walmsley & Allington, this volume).

ELEMENTARY SCHOOLS IN THE INFORMATION AGE

The American economy is no longer driven by manufacturing but by the creation, manipulation, and communication of information. We are rapidly losing the blue-collar assembly-line jobs central to the economy for most of this century. At the same time, new jobs are being created in robotics, information technology, genetic engineering, electronic communication, computer-aided design, and so forth. Even the old jobs remaining in the service industry, sales, transportation, and manufacturing are already requiring different sorts of literacy and occupational skills. Fast food restaurants are today largely computer driven, as is the leisure and travel industry; manufacturing is becoming more automated; increasingly, professions that used to focus narrowly (e.g., banks offering only banking services) now offer a wide range of services with the same or even fewer staff. In the future, we will have fewer of the old jobs, however, and the newly created jobs will require higher levels of education:

> Projections for the year 2000 . . . are that new jobs will require a workforce whose median level of education is 13.5 years. That means, on the average, that the workers who will fill these jobs will have to have some college training. Not to be the boss, mind you, but just to bring home a paycheck. (Smith & Lincoln, 1988, p. 2)

There will be no increase in assembly-line occupations in the foresee-able future. Schools created to produce assembly-line workers are already out of date. If this is so, what kinds of schools are needed and what kinds of students should these schools produce?

Rexford Brown (1991) writes of "thoughtful literacy," contrasting it with basic, or functional, literacy. We have just survived the "Back to Basics" era, which focused our attention on developing minimal compe-tency in reading and writing in all children. In fact, it is these minimal standards that seem to have become the de facto national standards for elementary schools. While our efforts did seem to reduce the number of children who were functionally illiterate and closed the achievement gap between more and less advantaged students, there is little evidence that many children are reading and writing as well as they need to if they are to become contributing members of American society.

The present minimal competency levels are simply insufficient in to-day's world. Thus, we have seen high school graduation standards ratch-eted upwards, and this tightening of standards can be expected to continue for some time. At the same time, little has been said about the role of the elementary school in facilitating student attainment of these standards. Elementary schools will need to change so that all students are well pre-pared to meet the increasing standards for high school graduation. The elementary-age children of today will comprise the high school graduating classes after the year 2000. Are all of today's second and third graders on schedule for successfully completing four years of mathematics, including algebra, geometry, and trigonometry? For mastering a foreign language? For four years of science, including biology, chemistry, and physics? Are they ready for four years of study of American, British, and foreign litera-ture? Ready to complete independent research in social studies, govern-ment, or ecology? These are but a few of the standards already in place in some states and widely agreed upon by various business and political leaders.

Central to accomplishing such goals will be elementary schools where all students succeed in a curriculum substantially different from that in place today. Elementary schools must be created where all students develop high levels of literacy. This is not just a matter of raising test scores to grade level for all children. The target is the "new literacy" that Willinsky (1990) writes about, the "thoughtful literacy" that Brown proposes. It is about effective reading, writing, and thinking. Today, classrooms are character-ized by teacher interrogation of children after reading, not by discussion, reflection, revision, or analysis. We are still by and large a fill-in-the-blank operation. Writing is still an assignment that is corrected more for grammar and spelling than for the quality of the thought that went into composing it. For instance, consider the following verse composed by a sixth grader:

> I saw a doe hit by a car,
> the doe was bloody and grinning
> I got out, thought it was dead
> but still alive, quivering and shivering
> from the surprise,
> it had to be put out of its
> misery.

M.M.A.

The teacher had used red ink to place two periods after second and fifth lines and jotted the following comments: "Avoid run-on sentences. Should be 8 or more lines." There was no comment on the incident, nor a query as to why the student selected this topic to write about. No conference took place to discuss this composition or any of the others in the assignment. What the child thought was, "I guess he didn't like it." This verse could have been a powerful piece for public or private discussion. It could have been a point of departure for thoughtful revision or extension. Instead, it was simply marked in red and graded (78).

This and similar episodes are repeated hundreds of thousands of times each day in our elementary schools. Children work, teachers correct and grade, and no one ever discusses the work, the content, the thought, or the response. Thus, a first order of change in elementary schools must be in the kind of work that both teachers and children do. To create thoughtful readers and writers, we must focus on topics worth knowing and evaluate understanding, not remembering. To create thoughtful readers, children must spend large parts of the school day engaged in reading and writing. Thoughtful schools focus children's attention on understanding and communicating information and ideas to each other.

We must create schools that provide children who need more and better instruction with that instruction. But to create such schools will require that we reject much of the conventional wisdom that has dominated our thinking about schools, teaching, children, and literacy learning. We must accept that all children can become literate before we design schools to achieve that end. Schools are, primarily, collections of classrooms staffed by teachers. It is the teachers who are the key to rethinking our elementary schools.

Teachers plan their lessons based on beliefs about what is expected of them by the community and school administrators and beliefs about children, learning, and literacy. It is difficult to find teachers who plan lessons that routinely violate these constraints. The charge to those who wish to change elementary schools is to confront two conventional wisdoms: (1) the bureaucratic and societal conventional wisdom about what elementary schools should do and how they should be organized, and (2) the professional conventional wisdom about literacy lessons and learning.

ABOUT THIS BOOK

Change is never easily accomplished, no matter what the venue. Educational practice has been enormously resistant to any sort of fundamental changes across the last century (Cuban, 1989; Fullan, 1991; Sarason, 1991). To have any hope of achieving systemic changes, we must accept four principles:

- Change comes from within, not afar.
- Change will not necessarily cost more money.
- There are no quick fixes.
- There is no one best way.

In this book you will find a collection of chapters that implicitly, at least, support the validity of these four principles. The first part of the book includes chapters that expand the argument about the need for change in our elementary schools. Remedial and special education programs have become pervasive in elementary schools as the major strategy for addressing the needs of at-risk children. In Chapter 1, "Redefining and Reforming Instructional Support Programs for At-Risk Students," Walmsley and Allington present a brief history of the development of instructional support programs in the United States, and review the evidence on the effectiveness of these programs. They then set out principles for the redesign of instructional support programs and give suggestions as to how school districts might begin the process of reforming their instructional support services.

In Chapter 2, "Flunking: Throwing Good Money After Bad," Allington and McGill-Franzen examine the issue of retention in grade. Despite evidence of the long-term negative effects of keeping children from being educated with their peers, the authors find that retention is still widely practiced as a strategy for dealing with children who find it hard to become literate. The authors argue that retention is not cost-effective and suggest a procedure for schools to examine the long-term effects of their own retention practices.

In Chapter 3, "Estimating Cost-Effectiveness and Educational Outcomes: Retention, Remediation, Special Education, and Early Intervention," Dyer and Binkney expand on the issue of cost-effectiveness and present a procedure for calculating the cost benefits of various instructional support approaches.

In Chapter 4, "Portfolios in the Classroom: What Happens When Teachers and Students Negotiate Assessment?," Stowell and Tierney present an argument for making changes in traditional assessment practices; they propose portfolio assessment as a viable alternative to traditional measures. Portfolios, they suggest, offer the potential for enhancing student involvement and ownership in the assessment of their learning. Such a shift offers particular advantages to at-risk students, who are the least well served by traditional measures, and least often motivated to do well on school assessments.

The second part offers case studies of change in elementary school literacy programs. In Chapter 5, "Literacy Partnerships for Change with 'At-Risk' Kindergartners," Morrow and O'Connor describe a university-school partnership to address the literacy needs of kindergarten children. They were successful in reforming a traditional "readiness" kindergarten into an approach that incorporated the findings of the research on emergent literacy.

In Chapter 6, "Reducing Retention and Learning Disability Placement Through Reading Recovery: An Educationally Sound, Cost-Effective Choice," Lyons and Beaver discuss the implementation of Reading Recovery in two Ohio school districts. What they found was that Reading Recovery significantly reduced the number of first grade retentions and referrals to special education and the number of students assigned to long-term remediation.

In Chapter 7, "Eliminating Ability Grouping and Reducing Failure in the Primary Grades," Hall, Prevatte, and Cunningham describe an approach to first grade classroom literacy instruction in two schools in North Carolina, in which ability grouping is replaced with a flexible program based on current research findings. A major component of the approach is reorganizing the daily classroom instructional routines.

In Chapter 8, "First Grade Teachers Provide Early Reading Intervention in the Classroom," Taylor, Short, Shearer, and Frye describe the development and implementation of their early intervention program in three school districts in the Midwest. This program also provides classroom teachers with strategies for adapting their instruction to meet the needs of the lowest-achieving first graders.

In Chapter 9, "Scoring Well on Tests or Becoming Genuinely Literate: Rethinking Remediation in a Small Rural School," Walp and Walmsley describe a long-term reform of the elementary literacy curriculum, with accompanying restructuring of the remedial program. Major principles guiding these reforms include establishing a schoolwide integrated, literature-based language arts program, remedial services closely coordinated with the regular classroom, and a shift toward more authentic assessment of children's growth in literacy.

In Chapter 10, "Improving Early Literacy: Vermont Stories of Educational Change from the Bottom Up and the Top Down," Biggam, Teitelbaum, and Willey describe a statewide effort focused on enhancing the capacity of schools to better address the needs of at-risk children in the primary grades. Their approach emphasizes staff development, in which teachers, administrators, and state education department staff collaborate on reform strategies.

In Chapter 11, "Change in Urban Schools with High Concentrations of Low-Income Children: Chapter I Schoolwide Projects," Winfield discusses educational reform in large inner-urban schools. Taking advantage of the opportunities provided by the federal Chapter I schoolwide projects initiative, she describes some substantial changes in programs for at-risk children in a major eastern city. Two strategies, using federal funds to reduce class size or extend the school year, were found particularly effective, but making change happen in highly centralized districts presents a formidable challenge.

In Chapter 12, "The Implementation of the Accelerated School Model in an Urban Elementary School," Knight and Stallings describe a systemic reform effort in a Southwestern urban setting. Site-based management, a fast-paced curriculum, and high expectations characterize their approach. The program aims to have all children "caught up" by the end of fifth grade.

In the Afterword, "No Quick Fix: Where Do We Go from Here?" Allington and Walmsley address the lessons to be learned from these reform efforts and suggest a framework that elementary schools might profitably employ as they come to grips with the needs of their own at-risk students.

These case studies represent no single change process or product. While each school accomplished some fundamental changes that resulted in far larger numbers of successful students, each change effort was crafted to fit the particular characteristics of the local community. Teachers were central to these efforts, and changes in teachers' perspectives on children and literacy learning were an important outcome. School administrators often supported the reforms, but they did not always lead them. Perhaps they were "leading from behind." The projects were not run by the stereotypical strong-armed manager who constantly monitored the efforts for indicators of excellence—more often they were characterized by an almost bumbling, stumbling approach, until things fell into place. These case studies represent discovery and reflection on the part of the teachers who created the initiatives.

This book, then, is not intended as a cookbook containing the secret recipe for changing America's elementary schools. Rather, it is a sourcebook for ideas and an inspiration for those who would challenge the status quo.

REFERENCES

Allington, R. L. (1980). Poor readers don't get to read much in reading groups. *Language Arts, 57,* 872–877.

Allington, R. L. (1991). The legacy of "slow it down and make it more concrete." In J. Zutell & S. McCormick (Eds.), *Learner factors/teacher factors: Issues in literacy research and instruction* (pp. 19–30). Chicago: National Reading Conference.

Allington, R. L. (1994). The schools we have. The schools we need. *Reading Teacher, 46,* 2–16.

Ayres, L. P. (1909). *Laggards in our schools.* New York: Russell Sage Foundation.

Brown, R. G. (1991). *Schools of thought: How the politics of literacy shape thinking in the classroom.* San Francisco: Jossey-Bass.

Clay, M. M. (1985). *The early detection of reading difficulties: A diagnostic survey with recovering procedures* (3rd ed.). Exeter, NH: Heinemann.

Cuban, L. (1989). Reforming again, again, and again. *Educational Researcher, 19,* 3–13.

Dolch, E. W. (1931). *The psychology and teaching of reading.* Boston: Ginn.

Fullan, M. (1991). *The new meaning of educational change.* New York: Teachers College Press.

Gould, S. J. (1981). *The mismeasure of man.* New York: Norton.

Langer, J. A., & Allington, R. L. (1992). Curriculum research in writing and reading. In P. Jackson (Ed.), *The handbook of curriculum research.* New York: Macmillan.

Leinhardt, G., Zigmond, N., & Cooley, W. (1981). Reading instruction and its effects. *American Educational Research Journal, 18,* 343–361.

McGill-Franzen, A., & Allington, R. L. (1991). Every child's right: Literacy. *Reading Teacher, 45,* 86–90.

Sarason, S. B. (1991). *The culture of the school and the problem of change.* Boston: Allyn & Bacon.

Smith, R. C., & Lincoln, C. A. (1988). *America's shame, America's hope: Twelve million youth at risk.* Chapel Hill, NC: MDC, Inc.

Spring, J. (1989). *The sorting machine revisited.* New York: Longman.

Walmsley, S. A. (1991). Literacy in the elementary classroom. In A. C. Purves & E. M. Jennings (Eds.), *Literate systems and individual lives: Perspectives on literacy and schooling* (pp. 139–164). Albany: State University of New York Press.

Willinsky, J. (1990). *The new literacy: Redefining reading and writing in the schools.* New York: Routledge.

Part I

A FRAMEWORK FOR CHANGE

CHAPTER 1

Redefining and Reforming Instructional Support Programs for At-Risk Students

SEAN A. WALMSLEY
RICHARD L. ALLINGTON
State University of New York at Albany

Instructional support programs are those many and varied efforts to intervene when learning difficulties become apparent. Failure to maintain an on-schedule pace of reading acquisition is the most frequent basis for referral to an instructional support program. In the United States, as in many other nations, such programs can be broadly categorized as either remedial or special education (though remedial programs are often considered *compensatory*—compensating for, say, economic disadvantage). While remedial and special education are often viewed as two separate educational streams, in this chapter we consider programs of either type as *instructional support programs*, for reasons we detail later.

In the four sections that follow we (1) present a brief history of the development of instructional support programs in the United States; (2) review the evidence on the effectiveness of these programs; (3) set out principles for the redesign of instructional support programs; and (4) give suggestions as to how a school district might begin the process of reforming its instructional support services.

A BRIEF HISTORY OF PROGRAM EVOLUTION IN THE UNITED STATES

Until the arrival of compulsory and universal schooling in the twentieth century, failure to learn to read was not considered at all noteworthy; in fact, learning to read was viewed as a particular accomplishment for all but a privileged class. The notion of reading difficulties emerged as an issue during the 1920s. While a few articles had appeared in the previous decade, the notions of remedial reading instruction and of diagnosis were expounded and refined between 1920 and 1950 (Pelosi, 1977). The most common explanation for reading difficulties seemed to center around the concept of the "slow learner," and textbooks of that period described special instructional techniques for students of limited intellectual capacity (e.g., Dolch, 1931; Kirk, 1940). The primary recommendations were to slow the pace of instruction, offer more frequent repetitions and practice, and move in small steps. At the time, remedial and special education were not typically separated, at least not for those children who were to come to be called the "mildly handicapped" over the next three decades (1950–1980).

As the baby-boom generation went to school during the 1950s, the most common explanation for reading difficulties was impaired intellectual functioning. Children with reading difficulties were still referred to as slow learners (Johnston & Allington, 1991); remedial efforts were primarily a responsibility of the local schools. Classes for slow learners expanded, as did the number of articles and texts on instructional techniques for intervention and the number of tests and techniques designed to facilitate diagnosis. Within a decade, however, the concepts of educational disadvantagedness and cultural deprivation emerged as alternative explanations for the high incidence of reading difficulties among poor and minority populations.

McGill-Franzen (1987) traces the evolution of assumptions about the etiology of reading difficulties from the 1960s to the present. She presents a variety of evidence illustrating changes in societal and professional understandings of the source of reading difficulties and the governmental responses. For instance, professional journal articles that had reading difficulties as the topic shifted dramatically from a disadvantaged to a learning disability focus, reflecting the accelerating separation of remedial and special education. One indication of this separation is evident in the fact that reading difficulties of children became a topic more frequently discussed in special education journals than reading journals.

Governmental response also illustrates the changes. In 1965 the Elementary and Secondary Education Act (ESEA) was approved, and with it came the first substantial federal expenditures for education. The largest program under ESEA was Title 1, which provided additional funds for schools based upon the number of students who lived in poverty. In 1966, remedial services were provided under ESEA for 8.3 million students considered disadvantaged. By 1985 only 4.8 million disadvantaged students were served under this program, a decline of nearly half (McGill-Franzen, 1987). At the same time, the number of children identified as learning disabled was virtually nil in 1966 but grew to 796,000 by 1976, to 1.8 million by 1986, and to 2.2 million by 1990 (Singer & Butler, 1987; U.S. Department of Education, 1992). Similarly, federal support for the preparation of reading teachers to work with disadvantaged children shrank from 1965 to 1975 and was eliminated shortly thereafter, while support for the preparation of special education teachers increased during this period and expanded substantially between 1975 and 1985.

Central to these shifts in student and teacher categories was the passage of the Education of Handicapped Children Act of 1975 (EHA), which codified the rights of handicapped children and included learning disabled (LD) students as part of the handicapped population. Children identified as learning disabled were thought to have some neurological difference, deficit, or damage that impaired the acquisition of reading abilities, although demonstration of any specific neurological problem was not required. Between 1976 and 1986 the LD population more than doubled in size, growing from 1.8 percent to 4.7 percent of the total school population. Children identified as LD now represent the largest population of special education participants, accounting for over half of the special education population (U.S. Department of Education, 1992).

Over the past thirty years the conventional wisdom concerning the etiology of reading difficulties has shifted from discussions of limited intellectual functioning to environmental disadvantagedness to organically based impairment. These changes are illustrated in the enrollments in programs that serve students, the training of specialist teachers, the federal funding sources, the types of articles published in various professional journals, and the textbooks written about students who have difficulty acquiring reading abilities. Currently, there exist two large and separate instructional support programs for children who experience reading problems — remedial/compensatory and special education. The separation is largely complete, with different federal programs, different state regulatory agencies, different district administrators for each program, different certification for specialist teachers, different professional organizations, and little overlap in program participation by students (Allington & Johnston, 1989).

Thus we find that most schools offer remedial and special education programs and that difficulty in learning to read is a primary characteristic of children in both programs. Reading difficulty, however, is not the only characteristic that participants in these two programs share, and the identification of the shared similarities between remedial and mildly handicapped special education students (especially those identified as LD) has resulted in calls for a reexamination of the current separation. Reschly (1987) reviews the research and argues that there are no reliable indicators that discriminate between mildly handicapped students and children of poverty or low achievers in general. While disadvantagedness was associated with children living in poverty, Singer and Butler (1987) report that about half of the special education students were from poor homes. Children of poverty are the most likely participants in either remedial or special education programs, primarily because they have not been successful in acquiring reading ability or have not acquired it according to the schedule set by the school.

Not only is there no reliable method of identifying which children would be best considered remedial or mildly handicapped, there is also little evidence that the two programs, as currently offered, differ substantially in the intervention strategies commonly employed. Allington and McGill-Franzen (1989a) report the use of similar materials, tasks, and techniques in remedial and special education programs. However, a critical difference was identified (Allington & McGill-Franzen, 1989b) in the amount of reading instruction offered to the two groups of students. Mildly handicapped special education students received significantly less reading instruction than remedial students, and there is evidence that both groups actually received less reading instruction than better readers (Haynes & Jenkins, 1986; Vanecko, Ames, & Archambault, 1980). Similarly, studies of effective instructional intervention with special student populations (Larrivee, 1985; Lyons, 1989) suggest that there are no truly specialized materials or teaching strategies with demonstrated advantages over the best teaching available in regular education classrooms. In short, it seems that while we have two broad program types and routinely separate low-achieving students into one of these two strands, there is little evidence that such assignment is carried out in a reliable manner, or that the instructional interventions offered in the two programs differ from each other.

Currently, the design of instructional support programs for children who have not found learning to read easy is more likely to reflect minimal compliance with federal and state program regulations than to reflect the best evidence on how best to accelerate reading and writing development (Birman et al., 1987; Fraatz, 1987; Hyde & Moore, 1988; McGill-Franzen & Allington, 1990, 1993; Mehan, Hartweck, & Meihls, 1986). We know, for instance, that early intervention is more often successful than later intervention, and yet most participants in either remedial or special education are not referred until they have experienced several years of unsatisfactory school progress and often after they have been retained. In fact, retention (or transition room placement) seems to be the most common school response to early difficulty, even though evidence of the negative effects of this practice on children is overwhelming (Shepard & Smith, 1989, 1990).

We know that increasing the quantity of reading instruction provided is critical to acceleration of reading development, and yet participation in either remedial or special education is more likely to decrease the quantity of instruction, even though most school personnel assume that quantity is increased. We know that enhancing the quality of instruction is critical in accelerating reading development, but remedial and special education students spend substantially more time with minimally trained paraprofessionals than do children who experience no difficulties. We know that one-to-one tutorial instruction is powerful, yet it is virtually unavailable in current programs. We know that active involvement in actual reading and writing of texts is critical to accelerated development, yet remedial and special education students are the group least likely to be asked to read or write—in any sustained form—during instruction.

The design of current remedial and special education programs generally suggests that more attention is directed toward identifying and scheduling participants than to critical instructional issues. Some of this can be attributed to federal and state regulations, but not all—the regulations offer substantial flexibility that is either not known or, if known, routinely ignored. It is our position that school districts ultimately bear the responsibility for educating all children—not just those who are the easiest to teach. School districts bear the responsibility for the design of all instructional programs, regular, remedial, and special. It is, then, at the district level that change must occur. Changes in federal and state regulations may facilitate the process, and such change seems likely in the near future, as federal and state education agencies continue to deregulate the various categorical programs.

THE EFFECTIVENESS OF REMEDIAL
AND SPECIAL EDUCATION

As might be predicted from the brief review of critical instructional issues above, the evidence of effectiveness is not generally heartwarming. Both Carter (1984) and Slavin (1991) provide large-scale analyses of the effects of Chapter I remedial programs, and both conclude that positive effects are at best small, often nonexistent. Glass (1983), Leinhardt and Pallay (1982), and Kavale (1988) review special education effects and conclude that little evidence exists of enhanced academic performance as a result of participation. However, in these large-scale analyses some programs in both categories did produce substantial effects. Unfortunately, these effects are generally negated in the analyses by programs that demonstrated little or no positive effects on student achievement, and as Slavin (1987) points out, little effort or energy has gone into identifying successful programs or studying them.

The disappointing lack of positive effects on student achievement in Chapter I programs stimulated the passage of the Hawkins–Stafford amendments to the Chapter I reauthorization in 1988. Basically, this legislation required changes in Chapter I programs. First, all programs had to produce achievement growth or undergo program review by state and federal officials. Second, the gains had to be sustained over time, and testing had to shift from a fall pretest and spring posttest to a fall-to-fall pre- and posttest. This assessed whether gains were sustained over the summer months. Finally, achievement gain was to focus on reading comprehension, not word recognition. Additionally, the language of the reauthorization bill required that Chapter I instructional support be designed to accelerate progress in the classroom and to support, extend, or reinforce classroom instruction. Thus, the Chapter I regulations were revised in several ways at the federal level in an attempt to improve the program. The most recent (1994) reauthorization continues these trends of further deregulation and moving the purpose of the program away from a focus on providing supplemental instructional support toward an emphasis on building the capacity of schools to serve at-risk children better. Perhaps because changes at the school level have often been quite slow, the effectiveness of Chapter I programs is only slowly improving.

Unlike Chapter I, special education programs have never been evaluated for academic effects at the national level. In fact, most states and school districts conduct no such evaluations on any regular basis (Gartner & Lipsky, 1987). While measuring the academic effects of special education programs presents problems, these are not sufficient to account for the wholesale neglect of outcomes (Kavale, 1988). Rather, something else seems to be at work here. McGill-Franzen (1987) notes that remedial efforts carry with them a sense that the learning difficulties can be remedied, but special education carries a sense of permanence in learning difficulties. However, as Kavale (1988) notes in his review, some of the participants in special education demonstrate substantially improved academic performance, with some mildly handicapped children (behaviorally disordered, learning disabled, and so forth) improving sufficiently to be declassified and returned to the regular education program.

Recently, federal authorities have begun to encourage declassification and instructional programs that will accelerate academic learning. Similarly, Singer and Butler (1987) note that the more severely handicapped (deaf, visually impaired, physically impaired, profoundly retarded) now often attain levels of academic learning that were rare just a decade ago. On the whole, however, there is insufficient evidence to support the assertion that special education programs generally and, especially those for the mildly handicapped, substantially enhance academic learning of participants.

None of this is to suggest that students with learning difficulties would be better served without remedial and special education programs. In fact, the impetus for the federal legislation was the low levels of effort most school districts put forth in educating such children prior to ESEA or EHA. In both cases the federal government, in the interest of educational equity, provided funds for the education of students who were considered hard to teach and in need of additional educational resources that few districts routinely provided. Also, it is not the case that no children benefit from participation in remedial and special education programs. In virtually every study the evidence indicates that some children seem to benefit enormously, but, unfortunately, these children are seldom in the majority. Our concern is the design of instructional support programs that alleviate, if not resolve, the reading difficulties of all participants.

REDEFINING INSTRUCTIONAL
SUPPORT PROGRAMS

It is clear from our review of the history of instructional support programs that in general these programs have not adequately met the needs of students assigned to them. That they have been unsuccessful may be in part an unfortunate by-product of their existence, namely, that once programs have been established to meet the needs of students with learning difficulties, regular classroom teachers excuse themselves from responsibility for the education of low-achieving students. Yet remedial and special education students spend more time in regular education instructional settings than in the support program, unless enrolled in self-contained special education rooms, which is an increasingly infrequent placement under the "least restrictive environment" requirement of EHA. Thus we have a situation in which students who are in most need of instructional support may actually receive less of it in the regular classroom, where they spend most of their school day, because classroom teachers do not consider it their responsibility to provide such support. Furthermore, classroom teachers may not actually know how to provide this support, even if they wanted to.

It is also clear from our review that there are not sufficiently well defined categories of reading, writing, and learning disabilities to justify separate funding, separate diagnoses, and separate instructional materials and techniques for students who basically are all having difficulty in learning to read and write on schedule. We do not deny that there are many causes and many manifestations of learning difficulties: current classification schemes (including referral procedures, testing, and remedial instructional approaches), however, do not discriminate adequately between the various manifestations, and in practice—which is the acid test—a child is more likely to be in one program or another, being treated by one approach or another, as much by chance (e.g., to whom the child was initially referred) or by availability of funding as by accurate and appropriate diagnosis followed up with appropriate remediation.

As we think about redesigning instructional support programs, we need to differentiate between long- and short-term reforms. We do not underestimate the difficulties in reforming approaches to remediation that have become such enormous bureaucracies at both the federal and state levels, and so institutionalized in both universities and school districts. The process of change inevitably will be slow, and because it involves professional "turf," it will also be vigorously challenged. Thus we offer some principles to guide both long-term and short-term reforms of instructional support programs.

Principle #1: All Staff Are Responsible for the Education of All Students

There are a number of reasons why many teachers and specialists currently do not accept responsibility for the education of all students. With the increase in specialization over the past fifteen years has come the notion that the education of children with special needs (e.g., gifted and talented, remedial and special education) requires teachers specifically trained to deal with these needs (Allington, 1994). Presumably classroom teachers do not have this specialized training, and therefore are not able to offer specialized instruction. Moreover, conventional wisdom has supported the traditional belief that there are three groups of learners—fast, average, and slow—and that teachers should teach each of these groups differently (often even using different materials). Because we have done little to accelerate the reading development of the low-achieving students, classrooms often have a wide range of reading abilities. This, in turn, results in classroom teachers finding it harder to match their instructional materials with the wide range of reading abilities of their students, and so finding it convenient and appropriate that children at either end of the spectrum should be taught language arts (or at least a significant part of it) by someone else, leaving the classroom teacher with a more manageable—and more homogeneous—group of readers. This arrangement, as Fraatz (1987) points out, "helps to reduce the professional uncertainty they [classroom teachers] experience in trying to meet children's needs" (p. 73), and it certainly eases the classroom teacher's administrative burdens, but it also has the effect of transferring responsibility for the poor readers' literacy instruction from the classroom teacher to the remedial specialist.

The same is true with children with exceptional talents in reading or writing; once these children spend even small amounts of time with a gifted and talented specialist working on language arts–related projects, the classroom teacher often begins to let go of her responsibility for these children's literacy instruction.

Essentially, this abrogation of responsibility stems either from a classroom teacher's belief that it "can't be done" (i.e., the children's abilities or lack of them are such that the classroom program is inappropriate to their needs), or from a belief that it "isn't my job" (i.e., the responsibility for the literacy instruction of remedial or gifted students properly belongs to the remedial or gifted specialist, respectively). We would point out that except in very unusual circumstances, both remedial and gifted students spend less than 10 percent of their instructional time in "specialist" programs, and so most of their literacy instruction has to take place in the regular classroom anyway. If the classroom teacher has "signed off" on a child's literacy education, it almost certainly follows that the child will receive inadequate literacy instruction, because the specialist will not be able, in the 10 percent of instructional time available, to compensate for the lack of literacy instruction in the other 90 percent of time available. We are also greatly concerned about the more subtle, long-term effects of a "can't be done" or "isn't my job" attitude toward children with special needs; these attitudes convey to the children lowered expectations, especially in the classroom, and—in contrast to children for whom the classroom teacher does accept full responsibility—less attention to the children's literacy needs and less nurturing of their literacy growth (Winfield, 1986). These children need additional attention and nurturing, not just the same as the others, and certainly not less.

What we propose here is a shift toward an attitude of "it *can* be done" and "it *is* my job" on the part of *all* the professional staff in a school. We would place a particular emphasis on the classroom teacher here. Thus children with special needs regularly receive the message that "it *can* be done" from everyone they come into contact with, not just the specialists. They also receive assistance, when they need it, from any and all faculty members, but especially from their classroom teacher. One of the dangers of sharing responsibility in this manner is that once everyone has responsibility, no one individual has, and so the child might be worse off in this situation than before. In the past, at least, the student could rely on the specialist as a primary source for assistance, assuming, of course, that the specialist teachers accepted this responsibility. Nevertheless, we would return the primary responsibility for educating the child to the classroom teacher.

Principle #2: All Children Are Entitled to the Same Literacy Experiences, Materials, and Expectations

Over the years, and for a variety of reasons, poor readers and writers have routinely been denied access to the literacy experiences and materials afforded to better readers and writers. On the surface, it seems only proper that children who experience difficulty acquiring literacy should be provided with instruction suited to their level of proficiency, even if it differs from that provided for normal-achieving readers and writers. Further, a view has developed among many teachers that it is appropriate to lower the expectations of low-achieving students so as to help them make more realistic choices about their immediate and future academic studies. For example, these teachers ask: Why embarrass a poor reader by insisting he or she read a book whose difficulty level exceeds by two grades or more the child's reading ability? How can a poor reader engage in the reading of full-length literature if he or she has not yet mastered sufficient comprehension and vocabulary skills?

Traditionally, the remedial curriculum has been based either on the results of reading tests administered to students thought to be "at risk," or upon what reading specialists feel is an appropriate remedial curriculum. The former restricts the curriculum to a few reading "skills," while the latter typically results in a curriculum with different philosophical assumptions, different emphasized skills and strategies, and different content than that of the regular classroom (Johnston, Allington, & Afflerbach, 1985). This use of different curricula in the two settings was often planned, based upon either a misunderstanding of federal program regulations (Allington, 1986) or an adherence to the differential teaching hypothesis (i.e., the notion that children with reading difficulties need a different approach or curricula in order to learn to read successfully). In the first case, federal regulations have not required different materials in support programs, although this was an early confusion under ESEA.[1] In the latter case, Johnston et al. (1985) argue that no empirical or theoretical evidence supports the differen-

---

[1]Federal regulations prohibit the use of Chapter I funds to "supplant" the regular curriculum — the funds could only be used to "supplement" the existing program. In order to ensure that their Chapter I programs avoided even the appearance of supplanting the regular program, specialists would often make sure that the regular and remedial programs used different materials. From this practice came the assumption that Federal regulations demanded that different materials be used.

tial teaching hypothesis. While the differential teaching hypothesis has a long tradition in remedial and special education, they suggest that it is time it be laid to rest.

The instructional tasks that learners are assigned are another critical dimension of effective instructional programs. The tasks represent the experienced curriculum and delimit the range of learning. Poor readers have historically experienced a curriculum quite different from that experienced by better readers (Allington, 1983; Collins, 1986; Hiebert, 1983). Low-achieving readers are more likely to be asked to read aloud than silently, to have their attention focused on word recognition rather than comprehension, to spend more time working alone on low-level work sheets than on reading authentic texts, and to experience more fragmentation in their instructional activities. Instructional tasks, then, differentiate the experiences of children who have little difficulty acquiring reading and writing abilities and those who have some or much difficulty. Much of the difference in reading strategy between high- and low-achievement readers can be explained by the differences in the instructional tasks emphasized.

If it is true that the major differences between the literacy strategies of better and poorer students can be explained by differences in curriculum, opportunities, and instructional tasks, then there should be no barriers to entitling all children to the same literacy experiences and expectations. Convincing regular classroom teachers and specialists to afford all children these opportunities is a major task, however, in light of the long history of disentitlement.

Principle #3: Children Should Be Educated with Their Peers

Over the past quarter-century, at-risk children have become increasingly segregated from their more successful peers. As we have expanded the number of special teachers and special programs available to attempt to address the needs of children who find learning to read difficult, we have pulled more and more children out of the regular classroom for instructional support. As we have increased the accountability pressure on public schools, there has been an increase in retention and identification of children as handicapped, especially in the primary grades (McGill-Franzen & Allington, 1993).

Each of these trends increases the segregation of some children from their peers. Yet increasing evidence suggests that segregation, be it the result of flunking, or placement in a special education classroom, or even participation in remedial or resource room programs, stigmatizes children to a far greater degree than educators ever realized. It is this evidence that has fostered the movement toward "inclusionary" education. While much of the current emphasis is focused on returning handicapped students to the regular classroom of their neighborhood schools, inclusionary education is not just the realm of special education. Witness, for example, the calls for ending the practice of retaining students, based on evidence of little academic benefit and substantial loss in self-esteem in retained children. Or the push for special programs to provide in-class consultant teacher services in lieu of the traditional pullout instructional model (Gelzheiser, Meyers, & Pruzek, 1992).

In the case of handicapped students inclusion is being argued as a civil right, with references to "separate is never equal" court decisions. In a similar vein, the National Center on Educational Outcomes (1993) calls for national standards to be established for all students, not separate standards for students identified as handicapped. There are increasing calls from regular educators to end—or at least severely limit—pulling students from their classrooms for special programs. There are a variety of arguments for redesigning special programs to increase the inclusionary emphasis, but one often overlooked argument is the disabling effect that segregated program models have on the classroom teacher's ability to properly serve at-risk children.

One teacher took the pullout special program to task for perpetuating the assumption that classroom teachers were incompetent to instruct at-risk children effectively. This second grade teacher said,

> Every time one of my kids leaves the room for help it says to me, "We think you are incompetent. We don't think you can help this kid." Every time a kid leaves my room it tells the kid that there is something so seriously wrong with him that even I can't help him. It really irks me to be treated this way. No one in this building knows these kids better than me. No one knows more about what they need. But every day I'm told I'm incompetent, they're told I'm incompetent. Just leave us alone and the kids will be fine.

Segregating some children from their peers in an attempt to provide needed instructional support undermines the responsibility of the regular education program to educate all children. Segregated settings undermine classroom teachers and seem to have a negative impact on children's self-concept. Segregated instructional support models foster curricular fragmentation and may hinder children's access to the rich core curriculum all children should experience. However, short-term segregation (3 to 12 weeks) in some instances, primarily where the goal is intensive, personalized instruction designed to rapidly accelerate achievement and return the child shortly to his or her regular classroom better able to handle the demands of the core curriculum, does seem justified.

Principle #4: We Need to Define What Counts as the Literacy Curriculum

For the majority of children with poor literacy skills, the literacy curriculum comprises a very narrow sampling of the broad range of activities and materials that should make up a language arts curriculum. It is not unusual for remedial reading or special education programs to emphasize isolated reading (e.g., comprehension, vocabulary, word attack, study skills) and editing (e.g., spelling, grammar, punctuation/capitalization, handwriting) skills. At the very minimum, the literacy curriculum for all children should include reading skills and the reading of full-length material. This full-length material should include books, magazines, newspapers, and documents. In each of these categories, students need to read widely and deeply: For example, they should sample the full range of fiction and nonfiction genres (from myths and folk tales to historical and contemporary fiction, from newspapers to biographies).

Children also need to read for a variety of purposes—for pleasure and enjoyment, for information (ranging from academic to utilitarian), for intellectual growth, even for emancipatory purposes (see Walmsley, 1981).

The literacy curriculum should also include editing skills and composing. By composing we mean giving children regular opportunities to communicate their ideas in written form on a variety of topics (ranging from their own experiences and imagination to subject area topics), for a variety of purposes (ranging from expressing their own feelings to informing teachers or others what they know, exploring new topics, or persuading others to their point of view), and to a variety of audiences (ranging from the student himself to the teacher to peers).

Since one of the major purposes of learning to read is to gain access to the knowledge contained within books and other reading material, and because knowledge of the topic of a book (i.e., prior knowledge) is such an important component of the act of reading itself, we feel that the language arts curriculum should not be separated from the content areas (e.g., literature, history, science, music, art, health). These are among the most important domains from which topics for reading and writing can be drawn, and literacy activities within these areas should be considered as integral, not peripheral, components of the language arts curriculum (see Walmsley, 1994). Literacy is not just learning decoding (reading) and encoding (writing) so that children can access and communicate knowledge: It is the act of accessing and communicating knowledge itself. A literacy curriculum that prepares children for literate activities without actually engaging in them cannot properly call itself a literacy curriculum.

One of the problems teachers face is that they currently have too little time to cover the reading and writing skills required of them—what we are recommending involves fitting even more into an already overcrowded day. Walmsley (1991, 1994) has suggested some ways in which teachers might address this problem: They include eliminating the redundancy of overlapping language arts activities (e.g., combining separate instruction in spelling and other editing skills into a unified editing program; eliminating repetitive units and activities in basal readers; reducing the number of subskills taught); doing less but doing it better (e.g., doing projects that explore fewer topics but in greater depth; covering fewer skills but teaching them more thoroughly); and combining reading, writing, and content area instruction through the use of themes (so that students gain important knowledge about topics and increase their reading and writing abilities in the same activities). Rather than simply add content to the literacy curricula, teachers need to rethink their curricula so as to take advantage of the many opportunities to combine different aspects of language arts and content areas (Walmsley & Walp, 1990).

Furthermore, we need to think about the literacy curriculum in terms of the cumulative literacy experiences afforded to students across the grades. Too frequently, teachers think only in terms of what should be covered in a particular grade, and not what a student should have experienced across the elementary or secondary years as a whole. Nor are they sensitive enough to their students' prior literacy experiences—frequently, students read the same book (E. B. White's *Charlotte's Web* is a good case in point) and write on the same topics (e.g., Halloween, Abraham Lincoln) year after year. In planning the literacy experiences of a given year, teachers need to take account of not only what has gone before, but also what lies ahead.

Finally, we need to think about how the literacy curriculum is to be shared between the regular classroom and support settings. We take it for granted that the literacy experiences of children who receive instruction in both settings should be jointly planned by all the teachers concerned: The question here is, How should the curriculum be divided? We would recommend the principle that *all* children participate in the regular classroom's language arts activities. We would use the instructional support program to provide children with additional and/or more elaborated instruction (based on the same content and books wherever possible) in reading and writing skills.

Principle #5: We Need to Offer High-Quality Instruction

While instruction is not wholly independent of the curriculum materials, in this section we emphasize the need for instruction, particularly for children who find reading and writing difficult. Of all the children who attend our schools, it is these children who most need and benefit from high-quality instruction. We define high-quality instruction as that offered by teachers who have expertise in how literacy develops (and what impedes its progress), and in how to facilitate literacy development. This expertise can readily be observed in the instructional interactions between teachers and students. Expert teachers use their knowledge of literacy development and literacy processes to decide where to go next, independently of the commercial materials they use; when to intervene and when not to; when to draw children's attention to which features of text; and how to model and explain strategies in ways that children can make their own (Duffy et al., 1987). Expert teachers use their wealth of knowledge about content, and about children's books and magazines, to entice, engage, and extend children's literacy development. Regrettably, we do not always find teachers with such expertise in remedial or special education classrooms; in fact, the practice of assigning teacher aides to conduct support lessons (even though they are supervised by the classroom teacher) means that quite frequently remedial and special education students are being taught by those with the least expertise.

The professional training of remedial and special education staff has typically focused on learning to administer and interpret diagnostic tests, targeted at identifying specific subskill deficiencies, and matching students with materials of appropriate difficulty. This training commonly neglects the importance of acquiring content knowledge (i.e., literature, science, history); it also underestimates the value of understanding the relationship between the remedial and the regular curriculum, and the advantages of collaborative planning and teaching. One of the reasons for this is that most training is discipline-specific; reading teachers are educated separately and differently from special education teachers, school psychologists, and bilingual teachers, as well as regular classroom teachers. Further, most training focuses on generic teaching routines (e.g., directed reading activities, SQ3R, word attack skills) rather than on how to model specific reading or writing strategies that are appropriate in a given context. Given that much of the research and development in these areas is relatively new, it is not necessarily the case that the most experienced teachers have the most expertise.

Principle #6: We Need an Organizational Infrastructure That Supports the Teaching of Literacy

We believe that in the long term it would make much more sense to organize instructional support programs as a single entity, not as a variety of separate programs, each with its own funding sources, its state and local bureaucracies, its own teacher specialist training, and its own distinct teaching methods. Chapter I programs were originally created to alleviate the effects of poverty on children's learning. Special education programs were originally created to provide specific instruction to children with mental and emotional disorders. Some states (such as New York) have created other remedial programs to assist children who fail to pass state-mandated tests in literacy and content areas. Over the years, these programs have increasingly come to serve the same population of students—that is, students with poor academic performance.

We think it is time to merge these programs into one and call them "instructional support services." We are not opposed to separate funding sources (e.g., we see no reason why there should not be some federal money targeted at alleviating the effects of poverty, while other programs seek to alleviate the effects of mental or emotional disorders), but we believe that at-risk children would be better served within a single instructional support program. This proposal is more easily made than carried out: It will involve dismantling and reorganizing enormous federal and state bureaucracies, as well as merging teacher training programs in remedial reading and special education.

We are encouraged, however, by initiatives at both the federal and state level to begin this process (see Will, 1986); we also note, within our own university, a growing collaboration between faculty and students in the departments of reading and special education. One of the benefits of fully merging these services and training, however, will be the training of specialists who have a much broader knowledge of literacy development, of the many manifestations and causes of literacy difficulties, and of appropriate instructional support strategies.

However, creating a single, unified program of instructional support services would not negate the importance of providing children with access to high-quality classroom instruction. We would suggest that current preservice teacher training and in-service professional development opportunities for classroom teachers must be modified to include a greater emphasis on supporting at-risk children in the classroom. In addition, classroom teachers as well as specialist teachers need to develop the interpersonal skills needed to collaborate effectively on instructional planning and delivery. A single, unified instructional support program focused on enhancing the quality of core curriculum instruction will require all teachers to renegotiate their roles and responsibilities.

REFORMING INSTRUCTIONAL SUPPORT PROGRAMS

Under current federal and state regulations, school districts will find it exceedingly difficult, although not impossible (see Hyde & Moore, 1988;

Office of the Superintendent of Public Instruction, 1987), to implement our proposal to reorganize their remedial and special education programs into a single, unified instructional support program, but this may be changing as federal and state education agencies pursue deregulation and more site-based decision making. Schools can, however, use the principles laid out above to begin a process of reform that will substantially unify the various instructional support efforts. It should be noted at the outset that reforming these programs necessarily involves reforming regular programs—no amount of tinkering with Chapter I and special education programs on their own will achieve the desired results.

How might a school district go about rethinking its instructional support programs? First, a planning team needs to be established. This team should include representatives from the following groups: remedial and special education faculty, classroom teachers, school librarians, administrators (principals, directors of reading and special education, assistant superintendents), the school board, and parents. It also helps if the services of an outside consultant can be obtained, partly because it is valuable to have an objective outsider to help collect sensitive data or resolve internal debates, and partly because a consultant can help the planning team relate its work to the professional literature as a whole. We recommend that the planning team be relatively small in number so it can actually get its business done, but have frequent contacts with other faculty, administrators, and parents throughout its deliberations.

Assessing the Current Status

The planning team should first address itself to *an assessment of the current status of regular and support instruction* (e.g., the degree to which regular and support staff take responsibility for all children's education; the degree to which all children are afforded equal access to literacy materials and instruction; what the current literacy curriculum comprises in both regular and support settings—including literacy activities, instruction, and evaluation; the expertise of regular and support faculty; difficulties children have in reading and writing; and how children are selected for/graduate from instructional support services). The team needs to approach the assessment of the current status of regular and support instruction in a manner that encourages an honest appraisal of where the programs stand. We have found that questionnaires and paper-and-pencil surveys yield adequate data, but they need to be followed up with personal interviews (preferably with a trusted outsider) to get beneath the surface of current instructional practices.

Our experience has been that the more we can get participants to *describe* what they and their students do in terms of literacy activities, rather than *judge* the program's strengths and weaknesses, the better we begin to understand the current status of regular and support instruction. It is important that the team itself—not just the consultant—participate in the description of the current status, so that it is not just the consultant who has a full knowledge of what currently goes on. Not only does this help prevent the consultant's bias from permeating the description, but it also helps the team begin the process of reform from the very outset, rather than waiting until the descriptive data are gathered and analyzed. We recommend that some of the information be gathered by team members (e.g., they could "shadow" children for a day and write up the results; they could do analyses of achievement data independently of the consultant); all information on the current status of the program should be thoroughly discussed by the team and not simply accepted "as is" from a consultant.

Next, the team needs to address the following tasks: *an articulation of program philosophy* (i.e., what assumptions does it hold with respect to literacy development, to reading and writing disability, to the relationship between regular and support instruction, to instructional strategies?); *an articulation of expectations for students, and of the language arts program for regular and support programs* (i.e., what does the program aim to accomplish in terms of its students' literacy development, and with what activities, materials, and evaluation procedures?); and *organization of instructional support services* (e.g., alternatives to retention practices, entrance and exit criteria, scheduling, personnel, congruence procedures, resources).

To address these tasks, we recommend that the team draw on the following resources: teachers, administrators, and members of the immediate community (through personal interviews, presentations, discussions, written descriptions and commentaries); teachers and educators in other communities (e.g., through visits or attendance at professional meetings); and the professional literature (e.g., articles in professional journals and books). We also recommend that information on current practices be written down and shared with those who provided it, so it can be revised and reflected upon.

In each of these tasks, the team does not have to reinvent the wheel, but it does need to do its homework. For example, team members will need to examine current theories on literacy development and on the nature of literacy disabilities; they will also need to examine current thinking on the relationship between regular and support programs. This will certainly involve extensive reading of the professional literature; it might also be profitable to bring in educators or scholars for brief visits to help work through specific issues. In each of these tasks, the team will find that opinions are divided, among the team members, among faculty in the school or district, and also in the professional literature. We would urge that all sides of educational controversies be examined with equal rigor: Professional reading should not be undertaken merely to support a previously held point of view—or to find proof of the inadequacies of opposing points of view—but rather to deepen all the team members' understanding of the questions under study. Ultimately, the team will need to choose a path among competing approaches that makes the best fit between what is recommended in the professional literature and what is feasible and appropriate for the school, its students, and its faculty.

Articulating a Program Philosophy

It would seem logical that a program's philosophy should be decided first, so that all the activities and procedures could naturally flow from an established philosophical position. Our experience as program consultants leads us to the conclusion that a program's philosophy emerges as a consequence of articulating the practical routines and procedures of a program and is much easier to articulate after the program's specifics have been worked out, in much the same way that it is sometimes easier to write the outline of a paper after the paper has been written. Trying to articulate the program philosophy in advance tends to produce grand-sounding platitudes about children "reaching their full potential in the communicative arts." We recommend a brief discussion about philosophy at the beginning; then leave the issue until after all other aspects of the curriculum have been worked through.

What philosophical issues should the team discuss? We urge team members to examine their assumptions about what counts as literacy. For example, should our students have utilitarian literacy skills (i.e., the ability to read and write to survive in a complex technological society), academic literacy skills (i.e., the ability to read classical literature and write academic prose), or should we aim more toward romantic goals (i.e., reading and writing for pleasure)? Or should we be more concerned about what children know as a consequence of reading and writing? Or is the ability to think more important? We also would urge team members to examine competing views of literacy instruction, especially those that relate to the instruction of less able students. Should we adopt or adapt a particular instructional philosophy, or should we attempt to combine competing views? How do we deal with legitimately different points of view? Finally, we urge the team to consider philosophical issues surrounding congruence between the regular classroom and support programs (see Walp & Walmsley, 1989).

Articulating a Language Arts Program and Expectations for Students

In an era when curriculum was defined in terms of skills mastery, the process of articulating a language arts curriculum was relatively easy to accomplish. As the curriculum has come to be defined more broadly, it needs to include not only outcomes but also materials, instructional activities, and evaluation procedures. For example, Figure 1.1 illustrates what teachers in Adams-Cheshire Regional School District in Adams, Massachusetts, felt were the major attributes they wanted all students to have on completion of elementary school. Figure 1.2 lists one of these attributes with its corresponding instructional activities and its assessment.

FIGURE 1.1. Language arts attributes that teachers in Adams-Cheshire Regional School District expect of all children by the end of Grade 6

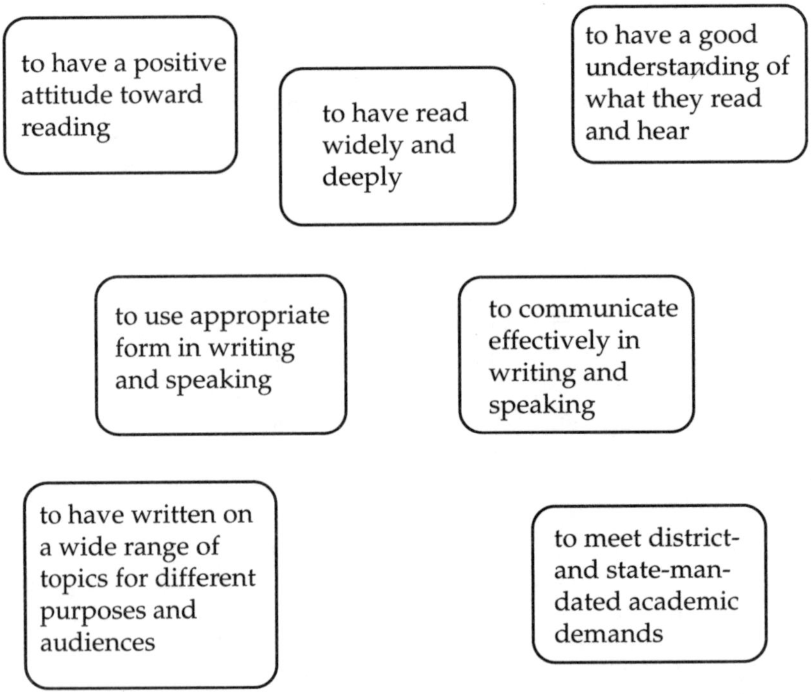

to have a positive attitude toward reading

to have read widely and deeply

to have a good understanding of what they read and hear

to use appropriate form in writing and speaking

to communicate effectively in writing and speaking

to have written on a wide range of topics for different purposes and audiences

to meet district- and state-mandated academic demands

Source: Adams-Cheshire Regional School District Language Arts Guide, 1991.

FIGURE 1.2. Language arts attribute, with its associated instructional practices and assessment procedures

---

Attribute #1: To have a positive attitude toward reading and writing
Children need to value reading and writing as pleasurable and enriching experiences. The desire to read is as important as the act of reading. Reading to relax, to satisfy curiosity, and to gain new information are important benefits. A love of books, enthusiasm for reading and writing, and a positive attitude, if established at a very early age, greatly facilitate literacy development. In their encounters with reading and writing, children's emotions are engaged and their imaginations stirred and stretched. If children are to develop lifelong reading and writing habits, they must experience the excitement and personal fulfillment that print brings to them.

Instructional Practices
- read aloud to children
- model desirable reading and writing behaviors
- provide time for personal reading and writing
- make available a wide range of reading and writing materials
- share what is read and written
- use class, school, home, and public libraries
- encourage parents to provide pleasurable experiences with literature

Assessment
Children's positive attitudes are evident when they:

- handle books
- volunteer to share what they read or write
- voluntarily bring in books, magazines, newspapers
- ask for books as gifts, spend own money on books, join book clubs
- borrow books from the school and public libraries
- read books/magazines at home and school for pleasure

Source: Adams-Cheshire Regional School District Language Arts Guide, 1991.

Recently, due to the emergence of developmental (or "process") approaches to education, in which the curriculum is adapted to the developing needs of students, this task has become considerably more difficult. We are not recommending one specific approach, but we do suggest that the curriculum be articulated in a manner that is consistent with the philosophy(ies) from which it is drawn. For example, listing a scope and sequence of reading and writing skills to be mastered at each grade level is entirely inappropriate if one's educational philosophy promotes "growth" in language ability rather than "mastery" of language skills. A curriculum based on a developmental philosophy would instead define what it meant by growth in reading and writing, and would articulate the kinds of activities it felt would best promote that growth (see Manchester Elementary School, 1990).

Organization of Instructional Support Services

The organization of instructional support services will ultimately depend on how a school district defines literacy, what assumptions it makes about instruction, and how it decides such issues as retention. What is critical is the development of a plan that represents at least a working definition of the program's philosophy, the curriculum goals, and the organization of the program. This plan also should lay out the action steps necessary for implementing the plan, including the resources needed to bring about the proposed changes. For example, if it is decided that all children need equal access to high-quality literature, the school will need not only experienced librarians to assist in book selection, but also access to the books themselves, and possibly in-service workshops on methods for teaching these books. If the school decides to adopt Reading Recovery (Clay, 1985) as an instructional support program, it will need to commit itself to the training necessary for such a program to succeed. If the school decides to abolish retention, it will need to commit itself to extensive retraining of teachers and redesign of programs so as to make the alternatives work. This might include rethinking nursery school or other preschool experiences so as to greatly increase the amount and quality of reading of children aged three to five (Adams, 1990); it will certainly involve systemic changes in the design of kindergarten and first grade programs so as to ensure that teachers meet the developmental needs of children of widely varying abilities. Such a decision might involve rethinking the school day or school year. Extended-time models—where after-school instruction is offered or where summer school provides at-risk children with additional instructional time and additional instructional support—have proven both popular and effective in addressing the needs of children who find learning to read and write difficult (Cunningham & Allington, 1994).

CONCLUSION

In this chapter, we have traced the historical origins of current support services and have shown that while two completely different kinds of programs have emerged to assist children with literacy difficulties, the majority of children they serve seem to have similar kinds of literacy problems. We also found evidence that assignment to either remedial or special education programs does not necessarily improve the quantity and quality of instruction support provided to children with literacy difficulties.

We have argued that the continued separation of remedial and special education programs is no longer justified, and that they should be reorganized under the broad title of "instructional support services." This action is necessary, but by itself it is not sufficient if we are to turn the tide against the rising numbers of children for whom remedial efforts are unsuccessful. We have to redesign both regular and instructional support programs together. We have offered several principles that we think will best guide this redesign, but ultimately reforms depend on the determination and expertise of educators to carry them out. To assist in this process, we have offered some suggestions as to how a district might actually go about rethinking its approach to regular and support programs.

School districts do not need to design new programs from scratch. There are plenty of examples of approaches that work, if only a commitment is made to implement them and follow them through. We already know how to prevent school literacy failure in the majority of cases, and we have excellent methods for dealing with literacy problems that arise during the course of the elementary years, if only teachers knew about them and applied them. Indeed, in the chapters that follow, a number of approaches are described that have been very successful in reducing the number of children who fail to develop adequate literacy abilities. This does not mean that we should abandon the search for better methods—the fact that even the most successful approaches still fail to meet the needs of 1 to 2 percent of the population makes it imperative that we continue our research in this area—but it does mean that schools whose literacy failure rates are high have little excuse for not rethinking their instructional support programs for children at risk.

REFERENCES

Adams, M. J. (1990). *Beginning to read: Thinking and learning about print.* Cambridge, MA: MIT Press.

Allington, R. L. (1983). The reading instruction provided readers of different reading abilities. *Elementary School Journal, 83,* 549–559.

Allington, R. L. (1986). Policy constraints and effective compensatory reading instruction: A review. In J. Hoffman (Ed.), *Effective teaching of reading: Research and practice* (pp. 261–289). Newark, DE: International Reading Association.

Allington, R. L. (1994). What's special about special programs for children who find learning to read difficult? *Journal of Reading Behavior, 26,* 1–21.

Allington, R. L., & Johnston, P. A. (1989). Coordination, collaboration, and consistency: The redesign of compensatory and special education interventions. In R. Slavin, N. Karweit, & N. Malden (Eds.), *Effective programs for students at risk* (pp. 320–354). Boston: Allyn-Bacon.

Allington, R. L., & McGill-Franzen, A. (1989a). Different programs, indifferent instruction. In A. Gartner & D. Lipsky (Eds.), *Beyond separate education: Quality education for all* (pp. 75–98). Baltimore: Brookes.

Allington, R. L., & McGill-Franzen, A. (1989b). School response to reading failure: Chapter I and special education students in grades 2, 4, & 8. *Elementary School Journal, 89,* 529–542.

Birman, B. F., Orland, M. E., Jung, R. K., Amon, R. J., Garcia, G. N., Moore, M. T., Funkhouser, J. E., Morrison, D. R., Turnbull, B. J., & Reisner, E. R. (1987). *The current operation of the Chapter I program: Final report from the National Assessment of Chapter I .* Washington, DC: U.S. Government Printing Office.

Carter, L. (1984). The sustaining effects study of compensatory and elementary education. *Educational Researcher, 12,* 4–13.

Clay, M. M. (1985). *The early detection of reading difficulties, 3rd edition.* Portsmouth, NH: Heinemann.

Collins, J. (1986). Differential instruction in reading groups. In J. Cook-Gumperz (Ed.), *The social construction of literacy* (pp. 117–137). New York: Cambridge University Press.

Cunningham, P. M., & Allington, R. L. (1994). *Classrooms that work: They can all read and write.* New York: HarperCollins.

Dolch, E. W. (1931). *The psychology and teaching of reading.* Boston: Ginn.

Duffy, G. G., Roehler, L. R., Sivan, E., Rackliffe, G., Book, C., Meloth, M., Vavrus, L., Wesselman, R., Putnam, J., & Bassiri, D. (1987). Effects of explaining the reasoning associated with using reading strategies. *Reading Research Quarterly, 22,* 347–377.

Fraatz, J. M. B. (1987). *The politics of reading: Power, opportunity, and prospects for change in America's public schools.* New York: Teachers College Press.

Gartner, A., & Lipsky, D. K. (1987). Beyond special education: Toward a quality system for all students. *Harvard Educational Review, 57,* 367–395.

Gelzheiser, L. M., Meyers, J., & Pruzek, R. M. (1992). Effects of pull-in and pull-out approaches to reading instruction for special education and remedial reading students. *Journal of Educational and Psychological Consultation, 3,* 133–149.

Glass, G. V. (1983). Effectiveness of special education. *Policy Studies Review, 2,* 65–78.

Haynes, M. C., & Jenkins, J. R. (1986). Reading instruction in special education resource rooms. *American Educational Research Journal, 23,* 161–190.

Hiebert, E. H. (1983). An examination of ability grouping for reading instruction. *Reading Research Quarterly, 18*, 231–255.

Hyde, A. A., & Moore, D. R. (1988). Reading services and the classification of students in two school districts. *Journal of Reading Behavior, 20*, 301–338.

Johnston, P. A., & Allington, R. L. (1991). Remediation. In R. Barr, P. Mosenthal, M. Kamil, & P. D. Pearson (Eds.), *Handbook of reading research, Volume II*. New York: Longman.

Johnston, P. A., Allington, R. L., & Afflerbach, P. (1985). The congruence of classroom and remedial reading instruction. *Elementary School Journal, 85*, 465–478.

Kavale, K. A. (1988). The long term consequences of learning disabilities. In M. C. Wang, M. C. Reynolds, & H. J. Walberg (Eds.), *Handbook of special education research and practice: Mildly handicapped conditions*. New York: Pergamon.

Kirk, S. A. (1940). *Teaching reading to slow-learning children*. Boston, MA: Houghton Mifflin.

Larrivee, B. (1985). *Effective teaching for successful mainstreaming*. New York: Longman.

Leinhardt, G., & Pallay, A. (1982). Restrictive educational settings: Exile or haven? *Review of Educational Research, 52*, 557–578.

Lyons, C. A. (1989). Reading recovery: An effective early intervention program that can prevent mislabeling children as learning disabled. *ERS Spectrum, 7*, 3–9.

Manchester Elementary School. (1990). *Final Report: K–8 Reading Curriculum*. Manchester, VT: Manchester Elementary School District.

McGill-Franzen, A. (1987). Failure to learn to read: Formulating a policy problem. *Reading Research Quarterly, 22*, 475–490.

McGill-Franzen, A., & Allington, R. L. (1990). Comprehension and coherence: Neglected elements of literacy instruction in remedial and resource room services. *Journal of Reading, Writing and Learning Disabilities, 6*, 149–180.

McGill-Franzen, A., & Allington, R. L. (1993). Flunk 'em or get them classified: The contamination of primary grade accountability data. *Educational Researcher, 22*, 19–22.

Mehan, H., Hartweck, A., & Meihls, J. L. (1986). *Handicapping the handicapped*. Stanford, CA: Stanford University Press.

National Center on Educational Outcomes. (1993). *Educational outcomes and indicators for students completing high school*. Minneapolis, MN: University of Minnesota.

Office of the Superintendent of Public Instruction. (1987). *Program linkage: Coordinating programs for students with mild learning problems*. Olympia, WA: Office of the Superintendent of Public Instruction.

Pelosi, P. L. (1977). The roots of reading diagnosis. In H. A. Robinson (Ed.), *Reading and writing instruction in the United States: Historical trends* (pp. 69–75). Newark, DE: International Reading Association.

Reschly, D. J. (1987). Learning characteristics of mildly handicapped students: Implications for classification, placement, and programming. In M. C. Wang, M. C. Reynolds, & H. J. Walberg (Eds.), *Handbook of special education: Research and practice* (pp. 35–58). New York: Pergamon.

Shepard, L. A., & Smith, M. L. (1989). Introduction and overview. In L. A. Shepard & M. L. Smith (Eds.), *Flunking grades: Research and policies on retention* (pp. 1–15). Philadelphia: Falmer.

Shepard, L. A., & Smith, M. L. (1990). Synthesis of research on grade retention. *Educational Leadership, 47*, 84–88.

Singer, J. D., & Butler, J. A. (1987). The Education for All Handicapped Children Act: Schools as agents of social reform. *Harvard Educational Review, 57*, 125–152.

Slavin, R. E. (1987). Making Chapter I make a difference. *Phi Delta Kappan, 69*, 110–119.

Slavin, R. E. (1991). Chapter I: A vision for the next quarter century. *Phi Delta Kappan, 72*, 586–589.

U.S. Department of Education. (1992). *To assure the free and appropriate public education of all children with disabilities: Fourteenth report to Congress on the implementation of IDEA.* Washington, DC: Office of Special Education and Rehabilitation Services, Division of Innovation and Development.

Vanecko, J. J., Ames, N. L., & Archambault, F. X. (1980). *Who benefits from federal education dollars?* Cambridge, MA: ABT Books.

Walmsley, S. A. (1981). On the purpose and content of secondary reading programs: An educational ideological perspective. *Curriculum Inquiry, 11*(1), 73–93.

Walmsley, S. A. (1991). Literacy in the elementary classroom. In A. C. Purves & E. M. Jennings (Eds.), *Literate systems and individual lives: Perspectives on literacy and schooling* (pp. 139–164). Albany: State University of New York Press.

Walmsley, S. A. (1994). *Children exploring their world: Theme teaching in elementary school.* Portsmouth, NH: Heinemann.

Walmsley, S. A., & Walp, T. P. (1990). Integrating literature and composing into the language arts curriculum: Philosophy and practice. *Elementary School Journal, 90*(3), 251–274.

Walp, T. P., & Walmsley, S. A. (1989). Instructional and philosophical congruence: Neglected aspects of coordination. *Reading Teacher, 42*(6), 364–368.

Will, M. (1986). *Educating students with learning problems: A shared responsibility.* Washington, DC: Office of Special Education and Rehabilitation Services, U.S. Department of Education.

Winfield, L. F. (1986). Do Chapter I programs promote educational equity? A review and some comments. *Journal of Educational Equity and Leadership, 6*, 61–71.

CHAPTER 2

Flunking: Throwing Good Money After Bad

RICHARD L. ALLINGTON
ANNE McGILL-FRANZEN
State University of New York at Albany

Schools in the United States currently throw billions of dollars of good money each year after bad practice. Using a nationally estimated 6 percent annual rate of pupil retention in grade and a $4000 per year estimated annual per pupil educational cost, Shepard and Smith (1990) calculated a $10 billion expense. But many school systems spend far more than the average Shepard and Smith reported. In New York State, for instance, the average per pupil cost is over $7000. In addition, many school systems, especially those serving large numbers of children from poor families, retain far more than 6 percent of their students. This is good money badly spent. There is probably no other single educational practice that can match retention with such a consistently demonstrated negative impact on students (National Education Association, 1959; Otto, 1932; Smith & Shepard, 1987).

Retention has a long-standing history in American education. At the turn of the century, Ayres (1909), for example, reported that one-third of American children were flunking first grade. In the 1930s, Otto reported first grade retention rates ranging from 10 to 40 percent. Today, some school districts report retaining virtually no students, while other school districts, such as Philadelphia, retain nearly a quarter of their first graders (Olson, 1990). Retention seems more popular in some schools than others. We found widely varying rates of early grade retention—from 0 to 40 percent (Allington & McGill-Franzen, 1991). Although most states do not collect information on retention, flunking seems more common in some regions than in others. In Florida, one of the states that does collect retention data, Shepard and Smith report that 41 percent of first graders are retained. In Arizona, they found that roughly half of all students are retained at least once during their school careers.

Among the industrialized nations of the world, flunking seems to be almost uniquely American. Japan, Sweden, and Great Britain report no retention in grade, while France and Germany report rates of about 1 percent. Only schools in Third World nations, such as Cuba and Kenya, respond to learning difficulties by flunking students as frequently as do American schools.

Why has such an expensive and yet ineffective response to learning difficulty been perpetuated? Is the evidence of the negative impact of retention really consistent? Do transitional-grade programs between kindergarten and first grade or between first and second grade work better than flunking? What alternatives to retention are available? In this chapter we will explore these issues and offer a method for gathering and organizing information about retention and its effects on children.

WHAT DO WE KNOW ABOUT THE EFFECTS
OF RETENTION ON CHILDREN?

Perhaps the 1959 NEA Research Memo said it most clearly: "The evidence shows that pupils of low achievement usually do not improve when they repeat a grade or subject" (p. 11). However, that document simply echoed what had been known for a quarter of a century (Otto, 1932). The NEA message was reiterated twenty years later by Abidin, Golladay, and Howerton (1971), and their analyses added another dimension, that "retention is largely a de facto discriminatory policy against the [children of the] poor" (p. 415). It was primarily poor children who were being retained in large numbers, while schools serving middle-class children more often routinely promoted all children with their peers. Twenty more years pass and we find Shepard and Smith (1990) arguing that the evidence points to increasing use of retention, with the expected results: Academic achievement and self-concept of retained students are negatively affected, and those children are far more likely to drop out of school than students who were never retained.

We have known of the negative effects of retention for over half a century, but still teachers retain children who have difficulty with literacy learning, and administrators and taxpayers support the use of retention as a response to learning difficulty. Several of the early national reports calling for educational reform recommended abolishing social promotion and establishing grade-level standards that children would have to meet to be promoted to the next grade. The general public, as assessed in a Gallup Poll, agreed with this position (Johnson, 1984).

Some states and school districts went so far as to set performance standards for promotion from one grade to the next. In New York City one such effort, the "promotional gates program," was initiated with much fanfare and was finally dropped after nearly a decade because every evaluation of the program's effects indicated no benefit to children, even though the cost to the school system was enormous (Olson, 1990). Likewise, various states initiated promotion standards, including kindergarten entrance standards. Virtually all of these efforts have been dismantled as the evidence of negative effects on children accumulated. In fact, some states have now moved in the opposite direction, banning retention and transitional-grade classes, because of the evidence on the lack of educational benefit and cost-effectiveness (Cohen, 1990).

Studies of the impact of retention on children's academic development—primarily studies of literacy development in elementary school children—illustrate unequivocally negative effects on children who are retained. Perhaps because of the continuing popularity of retention in spite of such evidence, there are a large number of reasonably well-designed studies of the effects of retention. These studies typically attempt to match pairs of low-achieving students, one of whom is retained while the other is promoted to the next grade. Over the next few years, the achievement and attitudes of both groups of students are studied systematically. In a meta-analysis of sixty-three such studies of retention, Holmes (1989) found that the students who were retained had achievement levels significantly below the levels found for promoted students ($ES = -.31$). Comparisons on a range of other measures also favored the socially promoted students.

Transitional-grade classes are offered in some school districts as an alternative to retention in the early grades. Often these are designated as "developmental kindergarten," "pre-first," or "transitional first" (T-1), and all typically create a three-year route to second grade. The original concept of the transitional class was to reduce class size while accelerating the pace of instruction across the year, with the expectation that most children would then continue through the grades on schedule, although a few would have schooling extended by a year. In other words, this plan had low-achieving children entering a transitional-grade class after first grade. It was assumed that the planned "enriched" instruction would accelerate the literacy development of most of these children so that the following year they would rejoin their classmates in a regular third grade. It was expected that a few would move from this transitional-grade class into second grade, a year behind their peer group.

Unfortunately, even early studies illustrated that transitional-grade programs tended to slow the pace of instruction, offer fewer opportunities to actually read and write, and, as a result, produce few children judged ready to be promoted to third grade. When the effects of attending a transitional-grade program were compared to social promotion of low-achieving

children, it was the socially promoted children who fared better academically and socially (Leinhardt, 1980). Later studies have documented
the lack of positive impact of transitional-grade programs on children (Kilian, 1989; Kirkwood School District, 1984; Smith & Shepard, 1987;
Southard, 1990). In effect, transitional-grade classes do not benefit children—the impact of these programs is virtually no different from that of
flunking them.

Transitional-grade classes are recognized by children as comparable to
flunking. As one high school senior noted, "Now and then I'd get teased up
until last year. They'd say, 'You flunked a class'" (Spiro, 1990, p. 1).
Participation in transitional-grade programs carries a stigma that stays with
students at least as long as retention. "Sometimes I'd try to figure out why I
went to pre-first. I guess I was a little slow, but I don't know how you could
not learn in kindergarten" (Spiro, 1990, p. 1). It seems that transitional-
grade classes do not mask the stigma of school failure from children, as
many had presumed they would.

HOW MANY CHILDREN ARE BEING RETAINED?

While rates of retention decreased from 1900 to 1950, they seem to
have been on the rise again recently. In a study of school responses to
learning difficulties between 1980 and 1990 (Allington & McGill-Franzen,
1992a), we found increases in primary grade retention (as well as even
larger increases in primary grade special education referrals). The advent of
the public accountability era and its accompanying high-stakes testing
seemed to explain the increases. In other words, as states set minimum
performance standards for children's reading proficiency, schools responded by retaining (or placing in special education) children who would
not, or were not expected to, meet the state standard (McGill-Franzen &
Allington, 1993). For instance, if a state set a third grade performance
standard and scheduled a statewide test of reading proficiency, then first
and second graders who were experiencing difficulty were often retained to
provide an extra year to meet the standard. Of course, merely deciding not
to promote the child did not make him or her a better reader, but by
removing that child from the state testing program, the results made the
school look as if its children were achieving better. Retention removed the
lowest-achieving children from the tested group for at least a year.

It is common to underestimate the impact of cumulative retention effects. Imagine a K–5 elementary school where one child in every classroom
is retained each year (with 25 children per classroom). By the time a kinder-

garten cohort moves through the grades and on to middle school, a quarter of them will have flunked once (4% × 6 years = 24%). If two children in each room are retained, or placed in transitional-grade classes, then half of the cohort will have repeated a grade.

Of course, no school produces a pattern of one child flunking from each class each year. Instead, the general pattern today seems to lean toward early retention, usually before third grade. In addition, some teachers seem to routinely retain more children than others—often significantly more—even though the composition of classes seems not to reflect enormous differences.

IF RETENTION DOESN'T WORK, IS
SOCIAL PROMOTION THE ANSWER?

At this point the answer might seem obvious, but it is not. While the evidence seems to overwhelmingly favor social promotion, the data reveal dilemmas that often go unnoticed. Very simply, when children are socially promoted they fare better than retained children, but they usually remain among the lowest-achieving members of the group (only retained children perform less well). In one sense, then, neither retention nor social promotion are options that we would select for our own children. While the evidence on the high costs and negative effects of retention would seem to preclude any consideration of retention (or transitional-grade programs) as a viable option, we would hope that educators would also seriously examine the impact of simply promoting low-achieving students and doing nothing else.

"Social promotion" is probably an inappropriate term. We would rather view regularly promoting all students alongside their peers as continuous progress and as preferred practice. As currently used, social promotion carries a stigma and seems to locate the learning difficulties in the child. It suggests that the child does not really deserve promotion, but that we will go along with it for now. However we say it, social promotion makes it seem as if we are doing something extraordinary for the child. An alternative idea is that schools should not penalize students for the failure of the educational system, in this case for the failure to design early school educational environments that accelerate the literacy development of children who begin school behind their peers. Children belong with their peers, that is, with their original kindergarten cohort. The guiding principle is for all children to remain with their peers while we work to improve access to more and better instruction for children who need acceleration of their literacy development.

WHY DO SCHOOLS VARY IN
THEIR USE OF RETENTION ?

In our research we have found schools that retained literally no children and other schools that retained 40 percent of the children in the primary grades. Generally, we found that schools with many poor children retained children more often than schools with few, and schools with many minority students retained children more often than schools with few. On this last point our sample was small, but a larger study of Chicago schools (Hess & Greer, n.d.) demonstrated the same pattern. They compared schools that were similar in students' achievement and numbers of children from poor families but differing in racial composition. Schools with a majority of African-American students retained a substantially larger proportion of students than schools with mostly white children even though the schools were comparable on other features (e.g., the schools were similar in the proportion of low-achieving children). The authors note that one can only interpret these results as indicating that nonacademic, culturally biased criteria seemed to govern decisions about who to retain.

There seems to be a pattern of schools with formal retention policies and plans retaining more children than schools without such policies and plans (Schwager & Balow, 1990). Not surprisingly, we found that schools with policies banning retention have the fewest retentions. It seems that when schools create formal retention policies, it signals that some students are supposed to be retained each year. When schools set academic promotion standards, retentions soar. Standards, if they are to mean anything, must be unobtainable by some students (or at least challenging, and high enough to impress parents). Standards are supposed to signal the imposition of some sort of renewed rigor into the educational system, and failure to meet those standards is expected so that those promoted and the school appear worthy. Other schools weigh estimates of maturity, or developmental readiness, more heavily than measures of academic development. However, school use of maturity checklists, developmental readiness assessments, and retention rating scales also seem to increase the number of students retained. While many of the commonly used instruments purport to be useful in retention decision making, they cannot be recommended because, invariably, there is not sufficient empirical evidence supporting the use of these devices for such purposes.

We have found (Allington & McGill-Franzen, 1992b) that schools with similar student populations do not necessarily respond in similar ways to children's difficulty with literacy learning in the primary grades. Two schools, for instance, with about 20 percent of their children eligible for free or reduced-price meals differed remarkably. In the first, those children experiencing difficulty were placed in pre-first transitional-grade classes or retained in kindergarten or first grade (a substantial number of such children were also referred as learning disabled). Ultimately, nearly two of every three primary-grade children were transitioned, flunked, or placed in special education. With every year of schooling, it seemed, the number of children experiencing difficulties with literacy learning increased. Over 10 percent of the regular fifth graders had been retained twice. The school employed a special education teacher for every 100 students enrolled.

In the second school, fewer than 5 percent of the children were retained in grade, with about the same number referred for special education services. Hence about one child in ten experienced retention or special education placement. In this school, every year of schooling reduced the number of low-achieving children. While 35 percent of the kindergartners had test scores below the twenty-fifth percentile, fewer than 10 percent of the fifth graders' scores fell below that point.

These two schools seemed to exhibit quite different institutionalized belief systems about children, especially children from low-income families. In the first school, where retention, transition, and special education referrals ran wild in the primary grades, teachers often told us that there seemed little they could do given what they had to work with.

> Our second grade is really a slow group. I mean they were born under that moon. Reading at home is a foreign language. . . . We talk about the gift of time.
>
> Parents, to a large extent, have given up and are not taking responsibility for their children. . . . I think that is the reason we are having these numbers [of retentions and referrals].

Several themes ran through our discussions with teachers and administrators in this school. First, virtually no one addressed the potential inadequacies of the instructional environment as contributing to the difficulties these children experienced. Second, and relatedly, we heard primarily about poor parenting and immaturity by way of explaining the high rates of retention and transitional-grade placement, although references to neurological or emotional bases for school difficulties were also frequent. While the staff at the school asserted the effectiveness of their transitional-grade programs and spoke of the positive effect of retaining some low-achieving children (those dubbed immature), the evidence from the school records contradicted this. When this information was shared with the district superintendent, the primary concern was whether reducing retentions and eliminating transitional-grade programs would negatively impact the school's performance on the statewide third grade reading test.

In this school there were de facto promotion standards in the form of trade books assigned as the reading curriculum at each grade level. Children who had been promoted but who could not read the assigned books at the next grade level were "sent back down." Lower-grade teachers reported substantial professional embarrassment when this occurred (even though they felt there were good reasons to promote the children). In our conversations we heard repeated comments about cautionary judgments to hold a child back if assigned a particular teacher the following year. Each grade-level teacher group seemed to have developed a general set of standards for entry into that grade, including kindergarten. While teachers often complained about the grade-level standards above them, they also complained that lower-grade teachers did not seem to understand their minimum standards. In kindergarten this played out as recommending to some parents that their children should be held out another year, even when age-eligible to begin school. While this practice has been banned by the state education agency, teachers reported subtle methods of communicating the message that most parents picked up on. The result, of course, was that children from poor homes often spent another year at home rather than at school engaged in literacy learning. When these children did begin school, they were overaged and became possible candidates for referral to special education.

This district employed a "developmental screen" to evaluate all entering kindergarten children. Children deemed "immature" after this screening were given the "gift of time" through an additional year at home or in a transitional-grade program. Such screening has a long history of producing school responses that do not benefit children (May & Welch, 1984; Smith & Shepard, 1987). Any sort of educational screening should be used simply to adapt the educational environment to accelerate academic development of those children who arrive with the fewest relevant preschool literacy experiences. When the notion of "developmental education" is used to deny some children access to the very educational resources they will need in order to develop, it is misguided and pernicious (McGill-Franzen, 1992). In this school, children from families living in poverty were the children most likely to be denied access to school when they reached the appropriate age and to be placed in a "gift of time" program that was designed to slow development.

In the second school, with few retentions or special education placements, we found a different tenor in our conversations with teachers and administrators. The attitude was perhaps best represented by a phrase we heard several times: "We take them wherever we get them and try to get them as far as they can go."

We heard hardly a complaint about parents, drugs, divorce, neurological problems, and the like. We heard, instead, about collaboration between classroom teachers and specialists, we heard about consultant teachers who worked with children in the classroom, we heard about before- and after-school lessons that were offered for low-achieving children, and we heard about early intervention to accelerate literacy development. In short, what we heard was strikingly different from the previous school.

The two communities were not very different, although poverty was higher in the second school. What was different was the institutional ethos in each. The teachers in the first school talked about parents and students in adversarial tones ("us versus them"). In the second school, teachers talked much more respectfully about the children and their parents. The teachers in the two schools simply had quite different perspectives on schooling, children, learning, parents, and community. Perhaps this is the notion of "school climate" that has been bandied around in the professional literature, but what we heard went deeper than climate. Teachers in both schools were generally very cordial in their interactions with children, and the hallways of both schools were bright and decorated with student work (the first school even displayed banners and plaques that had been awarded to denote its excellence). Neither school was a "hard place" where one would immediately shudder if they had to send a child to school there. In fact, because we were somewhat familiar with each school, the striking differences in the professional ethos were quite a surprise to us. The climate—the daily interactions between children and their teachers—was similar in both buildings. The differences ran deeper and were masked by the surface commonalities.

In the long run the heavy use of retention, transitional grades, and special education came back to haunt the first district. Sixth-grade statewide test results were declining, and discipline problems in the junior high school were climbing. In addition, the costs of repeating so many children in grade (and of adding so many extra teachers, aides, and portable classrooms to deal with the skyrocketing special education population) took its toll on taxpayers, who began to wonder why achievement was not better given the amount of money spent.

The teachers in the first school seemed to reflect what Shepard and Smith (1987) have dubbed "nativist" views of children and learning. In this view, cognitive development is relatively fixed and tied to physical development. Thus, it makes little sense to try to teach children who are "unready." Better, in this view, to give them "the gift of time." But this gift is actually no gift at all, especially when it is poor children who are the primary recipients. The gift of time sets children on a spiral of failure and missed opportunities. Nativists tend not to envision instructional settings to address this unreadiness, this immaturity. On the other hand, "remediation-ists," teachers like those in the second school, tend to believe that learning is substantially influenced by environment. In this view, children who enter school with few literacy experiences are prime candidates for immersion in print. This is seen as appropriate to accelerating development, which becomes the goal. Thus, instructional efforts are sharpened and redoubled, with the net effect being that at-risk children develop the knowledge necessary to successfully negotiate the academic demands of the primary grades.

EXAMINING THE EFFECTS OF LOCAL PRACTICE

In our recent work (Allington & McGill-Franzen, 1991) we heard from administrators and teachers about how well retention or transitional-grade programs worked in their schools. We heard about how their policies and procedures were not like those in the places where retention and transitional classes had negative effects. We worked with these school districts to identify just what were the effects of these responses on their students. We used a strategy we called "cohort review," which is reasonably straightforward and could be implemented by virtually any school that wanted to assess the effects of retention on literacy development.

Table 2.1 provides an example of the work sheet we used to track cohorts of children who entered kindergarten together. The example has entries for several members of a 1985–86 kindergarten cohort (all children who entered kindergarten in that school in the fall of 1985). We initiated our cohort review in the fall of 1990 and had to gather some of the data for previous years from existing school records (which was not always easy given the state of records in some schools). However, the 1990–91 school year information was easily acquired at the end of the year. The use of such a systematic procedure for tracking the effects of retention (or transitional-grade program participation) not only allows school personnel to identify the rates of retention but also allows examination of longitudinal effects of these decisions on children.

The most appropriate comparison to determine the effects of retention on literacy development is with agemates—those children in the original kindergarten cohort who were never retained. We use simple grade-equivalent scores from standardized tests for our comparisons. Percentile ranks and stanine comparisons do not work because the rankings earned by the retained students are typically rankings within a different cohort and a different grade and age group.

In the sample of ten children illustrated in Table 2.1, one can track the school progress of individual children across a six-year period. Note that only half of the original cohort completed fifth grade on schedule. One child

TABLE 2.1. Sample of partially completed cohort analysis illustrating the school careers and achievement growth of different students

School Years

Student	1985-86		1986-87		1987-88		1988-89		1989-90		1990-91	
	Grade	G.E.	Grade	G.E.	Grade	G.E.	Grade	G.E.	Grade	G.E.	Grade	G.E.
Taritha C.	K	1.1	1	2.1	2	3.0	3	4.2	4	5.1	5	6.4
Bobby B.	K	K.2	Prelst	1.3	1	1.8	2	2.3	2	2.7	3	3.3
Woods D.	K	1.0	1	2.0	2	2.8	3	3.4	3	4.0	4	4.7
Richard Z.	K	K.8	1	1.5	1	2.1	2	2.5	3	3.1	4	3.9
Heidi A.	K	1.5	1	2.5	2	3.4	3	4.5	4	5.3	5	6.1
Marcella M.	K	K.8	Prelst	1.5	1	2.1	2	3.0	3	4.1	4	5.0
Justice P.	K	1.3	1	2.2	2	3.2	3	4.3	4	5.3	5	6.2
Jonjin C.	K	1.3	1	2.1	2	3.3	3	3.8	4	4.7	5	5.6
Marcus L.	K	K.7	1	1.8	2	2.2	2	2.5	SPED	2.8	SPED	3.2
Jamie C.	K	1.5	1	2.6	2	3.8	3	4.9	4	6.2	5	6.5

Notes: Grade is the grade-level placement for the academic year indicated; *G.E.* is the end of year grade equivalent score on a group standardized reading achievement test; *SPED* indicates student was classified as disabled during that year.

enrolled in an ungraded special education program, three others completed fourth grade, and one (Bobby) completed only third grade. While this school had a policy that allowed only a single retention in the elementary grades, Bobby was two years behind his cohort because the pre-first transitional-grade program was not considered a retention. The achievement scores in Table 2.1 illustrate the academic performance of children in relation to other children in their kindergarten cohort, not their current grade-mates. Such a comparison accurately highlights the impact of retention but also portrays the achievement of the retained in a way not normally examined by teachers and principals. In fact, if we examine the achievement scores of the three children who have completed fourth grade, it seems as if Marcella is still holding her own in comparison to other fourth graders, Woods is slipping into the middle of the pack, and Richard is a year behind his younger classmates. The comparison with the children in their original cohort, however, is what most researchers view when they complete their analyses, and all five of the retained children have achievement scores well behind those peers. It may be this difference in which comparison groups are used in examining the careers of children who have been retained that accounts for the differences between researchers' and teachers' understandings of retention effects.

In addition, retention effects differ if one examines short- versus long-term achievement patterns. Often, it seems, practitioners not only compare retained children to their younger classmates, but also pay particular attention to the impact during the retention year. Researchers have tended to take a longer-term view, examining achievement trends over a three-, four-, or five-year period. When viewed in the short term, retention usually looks as if the effects are more positive than in longer-term analyses.

For instance, take a child who is nearing completion of first grade and earns a twenty-third percentile ranking on a standardized reading achievement test. Based on this test result and classroom performance, the child is retained in first grade. After a second year in first grade, the child again takes a standardized achievement test and earns a score that places him at the forty-fifth percentile. This seeming improvement in his performance is then used as evidence that retention worked.

There are two problems with this interpretation of the test results. As suggested above, the most appropriate comparison is with children in the original kindergarten cohort who were promoted. If we take that second year of first-grade achievement test scores and calculate the second-grade percentile ranking—a possibility on many standardized tests—the child's ranking drops dramatically, to below the twentieth percentile. Another way of accomplishing the appropriate comparison is through the use of grade-equivalent scores. This same child might earn a grade-equivalent score of 1.4 at the first testing and a 1.8 at the second testing, after repeating the grade. The 1.8 score, however, puts him a full year behind his original kindergarten cohort, who have now completed second grade (with a 2.8–3.0 expected achievement range) and just barely into the average for the younger group of children he now has as classmates.

A second difficulty lies in the fact that in most studies it has been noted that there does seem to be a bit of "bounce" in achievement during the retention year, but that in following years retained children's achievement slides gradually downward. Three or four years after retention many of these children are again in the bottom group, but at the bottom of the group of younger classmates they joined when retained.

Compilation of the information on the cohort review form provides the basis for examining long-term effects on academic performance and also permits several other useful analyses. For instance, are children more likely to be referred for identification as handicapped after retention? Are boys more likely to be retained than girls? Adding a notation for child eligibility for free or reduced-price lunch permits analyses of whether poor children are more often retained than children who are not. Adding an ethnicity notation permits analyses of whether minority children are overrepresented among retained students. This may be important, since some studies have found that minority students are more likely to be retained than comparable nonminority children (Hess & Greer, n.d.). These added analyses primarily address the issue of bias. Are retention decisions biased such that gender, ethnicity, or family wealth predict whether some children are more likely to be retained? Or, put another way, do current school programs work better for some kinds of children than others? Is the school program biased such that certain children can be predicted to have more or less difficulty just based on their gender, family socioeconomic status, or ethnicity?

We have some experience with compiling the information on the form. To simplify the procedure, we suggest just gathering complete information only on those children who still attend the school (indicate when students transferred out on the sheet). If many students still attend school in the same district but at another school, it will be useful to gather information on those children, but it is more time-consuming. Our experiences with gathering the information varied widely from school to school. In some schools we had to rely on kindergarten class photographs to determine the original cohort because there were no records that provided that information. Some schools had information on retention that was easily located in an office file. In other schools we had to review school records for all students to identify who had been retained or transitioned.

Nonetheless, we would provide a ballpark estimate of three to five hours to complete the form for a kindergarten cohort of fifty to one hun-

dred children who entered school three or four years earlier. The time will
be well spent. It is, we suppose, possible that someone actually has a retention practice (or a transitional-grade program) that produces large academic
benefits for children. We have located none in our work, however. If compilation of the information illustrates that general pattern of no long-term
benefit to students, then serious reconsideration would seem to be in order.
This procedure responds to Shepard and Smith's (1989) call for local evaluation of educational practices: "Ultimately ideological beliefs are not likely
to change unless educators themselves collect evidence on the consequences
of their own retention practices" (p. 12).

CONCLUSION

Retention does not benefit children. Transitional-grade programs do
not benefit children. It may be that both offer benefits to schools, administrators, and teachers, but neither benefit children. We have also argued that
retention and transitional-grade programs do not benefit taxpayers because
it is throwing good money after bad practice. Retention and transitional
grades extend schooling by a year. Thus, at minimum these responses to
literacy learning difficulties primarily cost whatever the annual per pupil
costs might be for a school. Generally such costs fall in the $4,000–$7,000
per year range. But that, in our view, is an underestimate because retaining
or transitioning children requires additional teachers and classrooms, as
some children remain in the school for an extra year. When class sizes are
reduced for transitional-grade programs, costs rise above the average range.
In addition, there are costs associated with any additional testing, meetings,
and communications that are generated by retention activities. Very simply,
retention and transitional-grade programs eat up enormous amounts of
money that could be far better spent. Retention and transitional-grade
classes would be expensive responses even if they were effective, and they
are not. We have tagged both as "pay me now and pay me later" responses
because they are expensive and ineffective. We pay $4,000–$7,000 when
we retain and then pay again and again, for remedial services, psychological
services, and special education, as it becomes clearer that the retention
experience resolved none of the achievement difficulties.

We must work to eliminate retention and to hold onto some of the
money that will be realized in savings (which, according to Dyer and Binkney in the next chapter, turn out to be considerable). It is with that money
that we can fund educational efforts that will accelerate literacy development and make it clear that all children can become literate along with their
peers. As we approach the year 2000, it is finally time to rid schools of the

century-old practice of flunking children and implement, instead, programs and practices that develop children's potential.

REFERENCES

Abidin, R. R., Golladay, W. M., & Howerton, A. L. (1971). Elementary school retention: An unjustifiable, discriminatory, and noxious educational policy. *Journal of School Psychology, 9*, 410–417.

Allington, R. L., & McGill-Franzen, A. (1991). *Educational reform and at-risk children: Exclusion, retention, transition, and special education in an era of increased accountability.* Final report to the U.S. Department of Education, Office of Educational Research and Improvement (Grant # R117E90143).

Allington, R. L., & McGill-Franzen, A. (1992a). Unintended effects of educational reform in New York State. *Educational Policy, 4*, 396–413.

Allington, R. L., & McGill-Franzen, A. (1992b). Does high-stakes testing improve school effectiveness? *ERS Spectrum, 10*, 3–12.

Ayres, L. P. (1909). *Laggards in our schools.* New York: Russell Sage Foundation.

Cohen, D. L. (1990). Texas Board votes to forbid retention before the first grade. *Education Week, 9*(August 1), 1 & 15.

Hess, G. A., & Greer, J. L. (n.d.). *Categorizing, sorting, and bending twigs: Elementary school influences on dropping out.* Chicago: Chicago Panel on Public School Policy and Finance.

Holmes, C. T. (1989). Grade level retention effects: A meta-analysis of research studies. In L. A. Shepard & M. L. Smith (Eds.), *Flunking grades: Research and policies on retention* (pp. 16–33). Philadelphia: Falmer.

Johnson, J. R. (1984). Synthesis of research on grade retention and social promotion. *Educational Leadership, 42*, 66-68.

Kilian, L. J. (1989). *Evaluation of prefirst grade programs.* White Plains, NY: Office of Research, Testing, and Evaluation, White Plains Public Schools.

Kirkwood School District. (1984). *Evaluation of transition rooms.* Kirkwood, CO: Kirkwood School District.

Leinhardt, G. (1980). Transition rooms: Promoting maturation or reducing education? *Journal of Educational Psychology, 72*, 55–61.

May, D. C., & Welch, E. (1984). Developmental placement: Does it prevent future learning difficulties? *Journal of Learning Disabilities, 17*, 338–341.

McGill-Franzen, A. (1992). Early literacy: What does "developmentally appropriate" mean? *Reading Teacher, 46*, 56–58.

McGill-Franzen, A., & Allington, R. L. (1993). Flunk 'em or get them classified: The contamination of accountability data. *Educational Researcher, 22*, 19–22.

National Education Association. (1959). *Pupil failure and nonpromotion* (NEA Research Memo No. 1959-2). Washington, DC: National Education Association.

Olson, L. (1990). Education officials reconsider policies on grade retention. *Education Week, 9*(May 16), 1 & 13.

Otto, H. J. (1932). Implications for administration and teaching growing out of pupil failures. *Elementary School Journal, 33*, 25–32.

Schwager, M., & Balow, I. H. (1990). *An analysis of retention policies and their possible effects on retention rates.* Paper presented at the annual meeting of the American Educational Research Association, Boston.

Shepard, L. A., & Smith, M. L. (1987). Effects of kindergarten retention at the end of first grade. *Psychology in the Schools, 24*, 346–357.

Shepard, L. A., & Smith, M. L. (Eds.). (1989). *Flunking grades: Research and policies on retention.* Philadelphia: Falmer.

Shepard, L. A., & Smith, M. L. (1990). Synthesis of research on grade retention. *Educational Leadership, 47*, 84–88.

Smith, M. L., & Shepard, L. A. (1987). What doesn't work: Explaining policies of retention in the early grades. *Phi Delta Kappan, 68*, 129–134.

Southard, N. A. (1990). *The effects of pre-first grade on student achievement, attitudes, and self-concept.* Unpublished doctoral dissertation, State University of New York at Albany.

Spiro, R. (1990). *The process of evaluation of a transition room program: A consideration of students' self-concepts as literate individuals.* Paper presented at the National Reading Conference, Miami.

CHAPTER 3

Estimating Cost-Effectiveness and Educational Outcomes: Retention, Remediation, Special Education, and Early Intervention

PHILIP C. DYER
West Bridgewater Public Schools, MA
RONALD BINKNEY
North Andover Public Schools, MA

Today schools are facing escalating battles to garner the financial resources necessary to educate at-risk children. Because of this, public schools need to ensure that educational moneys are well spent. It may be that we need to consider reallocating current funds rather than search for additional money to support new projects and initiatives. For instance, many districts report an interest in developing early education interventions but find it difficult to generate the funds to support such efforts. However, schools presently spend substantial money on educational programs and practices of questionable value. For instance, the long-standing practice of retention in grade has been documented to be detrimental to the progress of these children and to the school mission (see Allington and McGill-Franzen, Chapter 2). The value of traditional interventions such as remediation and special education is facing further scrutiny as well (see Walmsley and Allington, Chapter 1). While most school systems are fighting just to maintain the present operational budget, visionary superintendents, school board members, and administrators will consider both the short-term costs and

This chapter is a revision of the article "Reading Recovery: A Cost-Effectiveness and Educational-Outcomes Analysis," originally published by Educational Research Service in the Winter 1992 issue of *ERS Spectrum, 10*, 10–19.

long-term benefits of current programs and practices and more recently proposed interventions.

This chapter examines the cost-effectiveness of traditional school responses to reading and writing difficulties, such as grade retention, Chapter I, and special education programs, and the long-term cost-benefits of an early education intervention program called Reading Recovery, which provides one-to-one instruction for at-risk first graders who need extra help in beginning reading and writing (see Lyons and Beaver, this volume). Examples of the use of the cost-benefits analyses in several school districts are also included. The cost-estimation process presented here provides educators with one practical model for examining long-term costs and benefits of different educational programs and practices.

EDUCATIONAL OUTCOMES OF TRADITIONAL PROGRAMS

When evaluating educational programs, we need to look at more than just costs alone, but the expense of programs and practices has rarely received close scrutiny. Of all the possible benefits of educational programs and practices, student achievement is the one most frequently selected for evaluation. Most evaluation designs ask whether the intervention had a positive impact on student academic learning over a fairly short time period (e.g., fall-to-spring or fall-to-fall growth). Other educational outcomes are sometimes evaluated, but more often short-term annual achievement gains are the primary yardstick by which the successes or failures of interventions are measured.

Unfortunately, it seems that few schools actually conduct evaluations of the educational outcomes of programs they implement. Few schools that use transitional-grade classes, for instance, seem to have conducted any sort of evaluation of the outcomes of these programs. Few schools study the impact of their retention practices. While most schools are required to conduct an evaluation of their Chapter I programs, few schools report actually using the evaluation data once collected (David, 1988). Even when evaluations are conducted, the focus is often on short-term student outcomes. Evaluations are more likely to report on annual student achievement data than on five- or ten-year longitudinal analyses. Evaluation reports are more likely to present an array of standardized test scores or survey responses than case studies of students or cost-benefit analyses.

However, it would be preferable to have evaluations focus more frequently on long-term impacts and on other outcomes in addition to annual achievement gains. As Allington and McGill-Franzen (this volume) note, there seems to be a substantial difference in the way many practices are viewed by school educators and by university researchers. They suggest that these differences may stem from the short-term view that predominates in school-based evaluations and the longer-term view that is more prevalent in the research literature. It is unlikely that educators would continue to intervene in ways that do not benefit students if they were aware of the low likelihood of positive effects. When we examine the traditionally popular responses of schools to difficulties in literacy learning, we must conclude that the educational community remains largely unaware of the long-term ineffectiveness of their most commonly adopted programs and practices. Most educators also remain largely unaware of program costs, although short-term costs seem easier for them to estimate. Some educational interventions may prove their effectiveness only over the long term (e.g., Head Start); cost-benefit analyses almost always require long-term views to avoid "robbing Peter to pay Paul."

What follows is a brief overview of the most common responses to difficulties children experience in learning to read and write in schools, and an analysis of their long-term outcomes and relative costs.

OUTCOMES AND COSTS OF THE MOST COMMONLY USED APPROACHES

Grade Retention

The common practice of grade retention is coming under renewed examination. Almost 2.5 million students are retained annually in the United States (Shepard & Smith , 1990). A study by the California Education Research Cooperative found that the retention of pupils resulted in the need for additional teachers, facilities, and materials at a rate approximating the retention rate (Balow & Schwager, 1990). Therefore, a 3 percent or 7 percent retention rate would increase annual school expenditures by an equivalent percentage. Balow and Schwager concluded that retention showed no positive effects on student achievement or in motivating students to work harder, and noted that few benefits to children accrued from this practice. In the past few years, retention fever has added "pre-kindergarten readiness" classes and transitional-grade or "junior classes," but the available research does not support these alternatives either (Shepard & Smith, 1989). Research shows that grade retention has little or no long-term positive effect, and it may have a serious negative effect on students all the way through graduation (see Allington and McGill-Franzen, this volume).

Retention costs vary but have been estimated at $5,028 per student nationally. This estimate is derived from the average annual per pupil educational cost (National Education Association, 1991). There are wide variations in school spending (from $3,000–$9,000 annually), however, and educators can often identify the average expenditure for children in their districts. Costs for transitional-grade classes (e.g., pre-firsts, developmental kindergartens, and so forth) and other retention-related responses are often higher than simple retention because the usual practice is to reduce transitional-grade class sizes and to provide extra instructional assistance in the form of paraprofessional support. Any way one estimates the costs of retention or related responses, they remain enormously expensive compared to virtually every other option available. Consequently, it seems incredible that educators are willing to allocate substantial money to support this practice with few, if any, positive outcomes for students!

Chapter I Programs

The U.S. Department of Education reports that Chapter I serves one out of every nine children enrolled in American elementary and secondary schools (Birman et al., 1987). Federal contributions to the program account for 21 percent of the U.S. Department of Education's 1992 budget, or about $6 billion (Final Education Department Budget, 1991). According to a recent federal report, children in typical Chapter I programs receive remedial reading instruction in pullout groups of five children three to five days a week at an average annual expenditure of about $950 per child (Birman et al., 1987). Chapter I interventions generally do not seem to have an impact on achievement after third grade and have minimal impact on achievement even in the earlier grades (Pogrow, 1992).

An evaluation study by the U.S. Department of Education (Kennedy, Birman, & Demaline, 1986) found that students receiving Chapter I services experience larger increases in their standardized achievement scores than comparable students who do not participate. However, the achieved gains do not move them substantially toward the achievement levels of more advantaged students. The average gains reported are in the three to five percentile rank increase range. A child at the twenty-fifth percentile when entering the program might achieve a twenty-eighth to thirtieth percentile rank after a year of program participation. This small improvement has no practical effect—these children remain among the lowest-achieving children in a school.

A more recent evaluation of Chapter I programs (Allington & McGill-Franzen, 1990) found that participation in most programs results in actual loss of total reading instruction time for students. This is often coupled with low expectations for academic progress for these students (Rowan et al., 1990). There is only a 2 percent difference (12%–10%) between the proportion of children eligible for services in first grade and in sixth grade, suggesting that Chapter I programs generally have a minimal impact on the achievement of at-risk children (Kennedy et al., 1986). Because Chapter I participation produces only small achievement gains, children typically remain enrolled in the Chapter I program for an average of five years or until the program is no longer available at their grade level. Chapter I programs are typically neither particularly intensive nor offered early in children's school careers. As a result, multiyear participation in Chapter I is typical. We might consider alternative Chapter I interventions that substantially increase the intensity of instructional services offered and thereby accelerate achievement. While increasing intensity may increase short-term educational costs, it may be possible to substantially reduce program participation time. This would then have the potential for long-term cost savings.

Special Education Programs for the Mildly Handicapped

In response to difficulties they experience learning to read and write, some children may be classified as "learning disabled" and receive special education services. Recent reports by the U.S. Department of Education note that the number of children classified as learning disabled has more than doubled during the last ten years. Today almost two million children are so classified, or about half of all children receiving special education services (U.S. Department of Education, 1990).

Like Chapter I instructional programs, special education programs for children who are classified as learning disabled have come under increased scrutiny. Clay (1990) described the difficulty of trying to separate those very few children who have true organic learning disabilities from those whose reading difficulties stem from "external influences," such as ineffective instruction or low-literacy-use home environments. Although educators have no reliable way to distinguish between children with organic learning problems and those who need more and better instruction, the federal and state funding requirements for special education make it necessary for schools to expend extensive resources attempting to identify and label children as learning disabled. This is required before students can be given special assistance, and almost a decade ago the cost of this assessment was estimated at around $1,300 per student (Moore et al., 1988).

Once children are classified as learning disabled, few ever attain academic achievement comparable to their peers. Few schools have developed special education interventions that accelerate the literacy development of children classified as learning disabled. Few school districts evaluate special education programs in terms of accelerated student achievement. What little evidence is available suggests that most children classified as learning

disabled fall further behind their peers even after participating in special
education programs (see Walmsley and Allington, this volume).

However, a recent study by Lyons (1989) found that many children
diagnosed as learning disabled were not really organically disabled at all,
but were only having difficulty learning to read. When these students were
placed in an intensive tutorial program, Lyons found that a high proportion
(73.3%) developed balanced reading strategies and were reading at the
average levels of their classmates after an average of thirteen weeks of
assistance. In teaching "learning disabled" students, Lyons and other researchers found that these children are often placed in programs that present children with a limited set of reading strategies, with progress targeted
to move at a slower pace. In a similar vein, Allington and McGill-Franzen
(1990) concluded from their research that "too often these interventions
provide no educational advantage to the children who participate in them,
even though the added costs are often substantial" (p. 8).

External Funding Patterns. The current categorical method used to
fund instructional support programs complicates the issue. Classifying a
child as learning disabled or otherwise in need of special education services
enables the school district to receive additional funds from state and federal
sources. When a school district provides effective early intervention and
reduces the numbers of students classified as learning disabled, it stands to
forfeit a certain amount of outside funding.

A somewhat similar situation often exists in the distribution of funds
for remedial and compensatory education programs. When funding is
linked to the number of low-achieving students, the funding formula creates
a disincentive for developing programs and adopting practices that reduce
the numbers of low-achieving students. Likewise, funding patterns for instructional support programs can create a disincentive for developing effective early intervention programs if the funds only become available after
children have completed some schooling and are at that point exhibiting
low achievement. Nonetheless, effective early intervention seems justified
on a cost-benefit basis even with the current structure of funding patterns
for special and remedial education interventions. At the same time, we
would suggest that it is time that funding patterns be restructured to reward
schools for designing effective educational programs and practices, especially early intervention efforts.

It is clear that by avoiding unnecessary special education placements
and special treatments, not only do children benefit but money is also
saved, whether at the national, state, or local level. Substantial savings
in educational dollars can be achieved when early, intensive intervention
programs reduce the number of children who are incorrectly and unneces-

sarily diagnosed as handicapped. Early intervention programs that decrease the numbers of children retained in grade or placed in transitional-grade programs produce real dollar savings, as do programs that reduce the number of children who qualify for Chapter I and other remedial programs.

ESTIMATING COST FACTORS

Since the cost of educational interventions should be an important concern, information about the costs and learning outcomes for students in both traditional and alternative instructional programs can be a valuable resource to school district officials who are considering implementing new approaches.

A comparative program cost-benefit analysis can be made using national educational program cost averages. Such an analysis focuses on both student benefits (e.g., accelerated academic development) and fiscal benefits and takes into account the potential reductions in student retention and special program placements that could result from the implementation of more effective alternative programs and practices. Such an analysis should include the time allocations versus the time costs in a comparative evaluation of first grade retention, typical Chapter I remedial instruction, special education services, and alternative interventions. Both the annual and the cumulative amounts of time that a child would spend in each intervention design must be examined. An analysis of the costs and time commitments per child in each of the traditional responses to reading difficulties shows dramatic variation.

Retention Costs

Retaining a student in grade means adding another full year of schooling for that child, or a total of 1080 hours (6 hours per day × 180 days) at the annual per-pupil expenditure in the school district ($5,208, using the national average per-pupil expenditure). In most school districts, this means a repeat of the school experiences that didn't work the first time, but with a different teacher.

Chapter I Costs

If a child participates in a Chapter I program, then the remedial reading instruction pullout time typically allocated is 105 hours per year (35 minutes a day × 180 days). Currently, a child who is placed in Chapter I typically receives help for five years. Therefore, the total time allocation for this intervention is 525 hours. Chapter I teachers typically teach remedial reading to thirty-five students for the school year (Birman et al., 1987). The major financial cost is the salaries of the Chapter I teachers who provide that instruction ($943 per student annually, using the national average teacher salary).

Special Education Costs

A child who is placed in a special education resource pullout program for learning disabilities spends an average of 1.4 hours per day, or 252 hours each year, in this program (Moore et al., 1988). The child typically receives services in the program for six years in the elementary grades, or a total of 1512 hours, with many students remaining in the program throughout their school careers (Moore et al., 1988; Ribadeneira, 1990). Special education teachers who serve mildly handicapped children teach approximately twenty students each day. The major financial cost of this intervention can be estimated conservatively from the salaries of the teachers who provide that instruction for that child ($1,651 annually, using national average salary figures). However, with special education there are other substantial costs for assessment and administration which have been estimated to amount to about two-thirds of the teacher salary ($1,100 per student).

Costs of One Early Intervention

Reading Recovery is one early intervention that has demonstrated effectiveness (Clay, 1991; Chapter 6, this volume). In New Zealand, for instance, 99 percent of the children in ten educational districts where Reading Recovery was fully implemented were reading at or above grade level. In the U.S., about 85 percent of the low-achieving children participating in Reading Recovery sessions in first grade had their literacy development accelerated and were discontinued from the program when their reading achievement was on par with their classmates and when they had demonstrated independent reading strategies for making continued progress. In addition, in a longitudinal study Reading Recovery graduates maintained reading development in the average achievement band through third grade without additional extra-instructional support (Pinnell, DeFord, & Lyons, 1988). Reading Recovery has been identified as an educationally effective early intervention program by the National Diffusion Network (NDN) of the U.S. Department of Education (Groom et al., 1992).

In spite of the impressive educational results of Reading Recovery programs, some school districts hesitate to initiate the program because of its obvious financial costs. Allocating one-half of a teacher's workday and adding up to $7,000 for training costs per teacher to work with eight to ten students per year seems very expensive. Even more expensive is the cost of sending a teacher leader to graduate training at a regional training site, which can cost as much as $17,500 plus salary expenses. Implementation of this program does require time, money, and commitment, but examining potential long-term cost-benefits may shed new light on this intervention.

A major startup cost of initiating the Reading Recovery program in a school district is initial staff training. Reading Recovery training is offered on three levels: (1) Reading Recovery teacher instruction prepares experienced teachers to provide instruction to children; (2) Reading Recovery teacher leader instruction prepares qualified individuals to train teachers, instruct students, and operate a Reading Recovery site; (3) Reading Recovery teacher leader trainer instruction prepares individuals to operate a regional training site for the instruction of teacher leaders; the site is usually associated with a college or university. All Reading Recovery training includes a full year of instruction followed by extensive contact and participation in national research efforts. The program requires continuing teaching of students as long as the teacher, teacher leader, or teacher leader trainer works in the program. For larger districts that need their own teacher leader, the training requires that at least one teacher leader, selected by the school district (or a group of neighboring school districts), attend a Reading Recovery training center (now located at twelve American universities) for one academic year. The teacher leader returns to the school district after this year to conduct training for the district or a group of districts, and to train and assist teachers-in-training throughout the initial school year and future years. It is important to note that during the yearlong teacher training period, each teacher is teaching Reading Recovery children.

A teacher leader can train up to sixteen teachers per year, so smaller districts can share the cost of the initial training of one teacher leader. For example, over a two-year period, the Wareham School District (MA), with two trained teacher leaders, trained six of its own teachers as well as forty-eight teachers from neighboring school districts on a fee basis.

The largest ongoing cost of Reading Recovery is the salary to provide the one-to-one instruction for the children in the program. Children receive daily thirty-minute lessons, so that the teacher spending a half day in Reading Recovery can work with only four or five first grade children each day. However, since most children are successfully discontinued from the program in twelve to sixteen weeks, the one-to-one instruction is short-term, allowing the teacher to work with eight to twelve children over the course of the year. The other half of the teacher's day is determined by the instructional needs of the school. The teachers' responsibilities for the remainder of the day have included working as a classroom teacher, resource or special needs teacher, bilingual teacher, and reading or Chapter I teacher.

Reading Recovery has a substantially smaller time commitment for students than traditional programs and practices. Students participating in Reading Recovery are involved for only forty hours total if the child spends thirty minutes per day in the program for an average sixteen-week period. After the initial training costs of the program have been met, the basic financial cost of the program is the salary of the Reading Recovery teacher who provides this relatively short-term individual instruction.

ESTIMATING COST SAVINGS OF AN EARLY INTERVENTION

Viewed from the short-term perspective of annual costs, Reading Recovery is less expensive than retention, but more expensive than typical Chapter I or special education services. However, the short-term investment in Reading Recovery seems to have significant long-term payoffs.

For example, since Chapter I remedial reading instruction continues for an average of five years, the long-term cost is $4,715 per student served (this expense provides no assurance that the child will be reading at average levels for their class), compared with $2,063 per student served in Reading Recovery teacher's salaries. Long-term teacher salary costs associated with serving a child classified as learning disabled in special education (participation across six years in the elementary school) will be $9,906 per student (this estimate is conservative in that it does not consider the annual special education assessment costs of $1,100 or that many of these students continue to receive services beyond the elementary grades), as compared to the one-time cost of $2,063 to provide Reading Recovery services for that child.

Table 3.1 contrasts estimates of costs and implementation of Reading Recovery with three traditional responses by comparing the instructional time and teacher salary costs on a per-pupil basis using national averages. This estimation process is, perhaps, rudimentary, but it does provide educators with one method of developing cost-benefit analyses of programs and practices. It may be relatively easy in some districts to gather fairly accurate estimates of local costs, and in these cases actual local expenditures can be substituted for the national averages used here. For instance, if a district's per-pupil expenditure is above the national average (say in the $7,000 range) then retention becomes an even more expensive option.

TABLE 3.1. Reading Recovery savings: Comparison with grade retention, Chapter I, and Special Education in the elementary grades

Intervention	Annual Cost*	Average Years in Program	Total Program Time	Total Cost Per Student*
Retention (1st grade)	$5,208 (all costs)	1	1,080 hrs	$5,208 (all costs)
Chapter I	$943	5	525 hrs	$4,715
Special Education (LD)	$1,651	6	1,512 hrs	$9,906
Reading Recovery	$2,063	1/2	40 hrs	$2,063

*Costs in 1990-91 dollars; inflation and salary increases are not included.

EXPERIENCES OF SCHOOL DISTRICTS USING READING RECOVERY

Results from school districts that have implemented Reading Recovery have shown that they can expect to substantially reduce the number of children retained, qualifying for remediation, or classified as learning disabled. Thus, this early intervention program not only benefits children academically, but also produces long-term savings for schools. A few examples illustrate the typical results of implementing Reading Recovery.

Prior to the introduction of Reading Recovery, the Upper Arlington School District in Ohio retained an average of ten first-grade students each year. In the five years since Reading Recovery began, the district has retained an average of only three students per year, resulting in a reduction of 35 retentions during the five-year period (Lyons and Beaver, this volume). A San Antonio, Texas, school administrator reported that first grade retentions had been reduced from twenty-seven to six after implementing Reading Recovery (Groom et al., 1992). Gerry Haggard, Reading Recovery teacher leader in Plano, Texas, reported that first grade retention over three years had dropped from twenty-two to three to one. Other school districts have had similar reductions in first grade retentions after implementing Reading Recovery. For example, in the first year of implementing Reading Recovery, the Wareham School District reduced first grade retentions from fourteen children to none. During the previous five years the district had averaged twelve first grade retentions per year (Cogswell & Dyer, 1991).

In the year prior to implementing the Reading Recovery program in the Western Reserve School District in Wakeman, Ohio, the district retained twenty-four students in first grade. In the Reading Recovery staff training year, nineteen students were retained. During the first year of full implementation, nine students were retained. In the second year, the retentions dropped to one student, a remarkable change in three years (Yukish, 1989).

Using current national averages and disregarding inflation, we can estimate the possible cost savings implied in the Western Reserve School District's experience. The district avoided forty-three potential student retentions in the program's first three years of operation. Using the national average per-pupil expenditure of $5,208, such a change yields a cost savings of $223,944. The cost of the three Reading Recovery teachers for the three years, each spending a half of their day in the program and paid at the national average salary of $33,015 (National Education Association, 1991), would be $148,568. Thus, just reducing first grade retentions alone would achieve a net savings of roughly $75,000, but retained children are also more likely to be placed in remedial or special education programs at some later date than their achieving peers (see Table 3.2).

TABLE 3.2. Estimates of savings in the Western Reserve School District

Savings from avoiding 43 retentions x $5,208 per student	$223,944
Cost of 3 Reading Recovery teachers (working half the day in Reading Recovery) for 3 years	($148,568)
NET SAVINGS	$75,376

School districts implementing Reading Recovery can also expect to reduce the number of children placed in Chapter I remedial reading programs or special education programs. For example, the Wareham School District cut first grade referrals to special education in half, from an average of twenty-two to eleven (Cogswell & Dyer, 1991). This enabled the school district to reassign a special education teacher to the secondary level rather than hiring an additional special education teacher. Lyons and Beaver (this volume) report that primary-grade learning disabilities placements were substantially reduced — more than halved — in the Lancaster, Ohio, schools after Reading Recovery was fully implemented there. The earlier Ohio study by Carol Lyons (1989), in which nearly 75 percent of students previously classified as learning disabled were successfully discontinued at average reading levels, provides further evidence of the possibilities for reducing special education enrollments.

Reading Recovery also reduces the number of children who need and are eligible for Chapter I remedial services. David Curry, Chapter I Director in Danville, Illinois, reported that only 23 percent of former Reading Recovery students actually received services from Chapter I in second grade, even though one would expect that virtually all would have qualified were it not for their participation in Reading Recovery. According to Joetta Beaver, Reading Recovery teacher leader in Upper Arlington, Ohio, in the five-year period since the introduction of Reading Recovery, fewer children have required more than two years of Chapter I services, and only five out of four hundred children are now eligible for Chapter I reading services in fifth grade.

The potential savings that might be realized by implementing an effective early intervention can be substantial even in a small school district. While initial costs for implementation seem high, Table 3.3 provides an illustration of the potential long-term savings that might accrue.

These cost-benefits could be expected to occur over time as students who would otherwise be retained in grade or placed in remedial or special education programs remain in regular classrooms with their classmates. For this example, we have drawn from our own experience with the implementation of Reading Recovery and the experiences of other districts as noted above. Our estimates for potential long-term savings are based on the assumptions that a single Reading Recovery teacher working a half-day in the Reading Recovery program would work with eight students across the school year (this is a minimum). We assume that two of these children will avoid retention in grade, two will avoid Chapter I participation, and one child will avoid classification as learning disabled. The estimates of the cost savings use national average teacher salaries. This simple, straightforward estimation method makes no attempt to adjust estimates for future inflation

TABLE 3.3. Potential long-term Reading Recovery cost-benefit for one
Reading Recovery teacher working with eight students during one year

---

Expected benefits from 1 Reading Recovery teacher
working one year:

Avoid 2 grade 1 retentions @ $5,208 each	$10,416
Avoid need to serve 2 students in Chapter I programs (each child served for 5 years) @ $4,715 each	$9,430
Avoid misclassification of 1 special education student in LD resource program (child served for 6 years in elementary school)	$9,906
Total cost savings	$29,752
Less cost of 1 Reading Recovery teacher (half-year's full-time salary)	($16,508)
Net savings per Reading Recovery teacher	$13,244

---

or other related factors. In Table 3.3, the salary cost of one teacher devoting one-half day to Reading Recovery instruction for a year equals $16,508, which is one-half of the current average classroom teacher's salary. The long-term cost benefits that could be derived from this investment in early intervention would be $29,752, for a net savings of $13,244.

In establishing the potential savings from training a Reading Recovery teacher leader, one could consider the full $13,244 savings for their work in the first and second year. In the third year, the ongoing contact requirements require them to reduce their student count to four children per year, or a $6,622 savings. A Reading Recovery teacher leader typically trains fourteen teachers. Each teacher saves the school district $13,244, so the first training year nets a $185,416 from teaching plus $13,244 for two years from leaders' students gives a total of $211,904 in savings. One could argue that this represents a duplicated count, but the annual savings ($13,244) are not possible without a trained Reading Recovery teacher leader. Using the highest training costs in the country of $17,500 (training cost varies from 0 to $17,500), plus the teacher leader's full salary of

$66,030 for two years (the training year and the first year training others) and subtracting all from the savings, the net result is a positive cash flow of $128,374 in the first year of implementation. In the second year, a school district would save $185,416 (14 trained teachers) and an additional $185,416 (14 teachers in training); add to this $6,622 savings from the teacher leader's students, for a total of $377,454. Second-year savings of $377,454, minus the teacher leader salary of $33,015, would net the district $344,439.

This cost estimation model does not consider the potential positive impact that occurs when the Reading Recovery teacher applies modified Reading Recovery strategies in her classroom during the other half of the school day, or the potential benefits that might accrue from sharing the newly acquired expertise with colleagues.

CONCLUSION

All educators, but school administrators in particular, have an obligation to become knowledgeable about the effects of various alternative approaches to responding to children who find learning to read difficult. Likewise, it is incumbent upon school district administrators to keep the school board informed of the progress being made with any program initiated. Indeed, school board members need to be apprised of the benefits at-risk children derive from their long-range planning. Additionally, it is incumbent on all educators, but especially school administrators, to ensure that limited educational funds are well spent. Thus, monitoring the costs as well as the effects of any and all school programs needs to become far more commonplace. We hope that the estimation procedures we have described here will be useful in assisting others in such an effort. For too long we have taken a very limited view of program evaluation, focusing too much on compliance with regulations and short-term achievement gains and too little on the long-term impacts and overall program costs (King, 1994).

Schools today face difficult decisions about the most effective way to allocate scarce resources for the good of all children. Research indicates that early intervention programs have the greatest promise for helping children at risk of early reading and writing failure. Reading Recovery is an example of an early intervention that seems quite expensive on first glance (Viadero, 1990) but actually has enormous potential for reducing educational expenditures, while benefiting children far more than the most common and more expensive traditional responses to difficulties in learning to read.

REFERENCES

Allington, R. L., & McGill-Franzen, A. (1990). Children with reading problems: How we wrongfully classify them and fail to teach many to read. *ERS Spectrum*, *8*, 3–9.

Balow, I., & Schwager, M. (1990). *Retention in grade: A failed procedure.* California Educational Research Cooperative. Riverside: University of California.

Birman, B. F., Orland, M., Jung, R., Anson, R., Garcia, G., Moore, M., Frankhouser, J., Morrison, D., & Reisner, E. (1987). *The current operation of the Chapter One program.* Washington, DC: U.S. Department of Education, Office of Educational Research and Improvement.

Clay, M. M. (1990). Learning to be learning disabled. *ERS Spectrum*, *8*, 3–8.

Clay, M. M. (1991). Reading Recovery surprises. In D. DeFord, C. Lyons, & G. Pinnell (Eds.), *Bridges to literacy: Learning from Reading Recovery*. Portsmouth, NH: Heineman.

Cogswell, C., & Dyer, P. (1991). *Reading Recovery: A cost benefit analysis.* Address to the New England Reading Recovery Conference, Nashua, New Hampshire.

David, J. L. (1988). The use of indicators by school districts: Aid or threat to improvement? *Phi Delta Kappan*, *69*, 449–502.

Final Education Department budget for fiscal 1992. *Education Week*, *XI*(15) (December 11, 1991), 24–25.

Groom, J., Herrick, S., McCarrier, A., & Nigles, W. (1992). *National Diffusion Network executive summary 1984–91.* Columbus, OH: The Ohio State University.

Kennedy, M. M., Birman, B. F., & Demaline, R. E. (1986). *The effectiveness of Chapter I services.* Washington, DC: U.S. Department of Education, Office of Educational Research and Improvement.

King, J. A. (1994). Meeting the educational needs of at-risk students: A cost analysis of three models. *Educational Evaluation and Policy Analysis*, *16*, 1–20.

Lyons, C. A. (1989). Reading Recovery: An effective program that can prevent mislabeling of children as learning disabled. *ERS Spectrum*, *7*, 3–9.

Moore, M., Schwartz, M., Braddock, M., & Strong, E. (Decision Resources Corporation). (1988). *Patterns in special education services delivery and cost.* Washington, DC: U.S. Department of Education, Office of Special Education and Rehabilitative Services. (ERIC Doc. No. ED 303 027)

National Education Association. (1991). *Estimates of school statistics: 1990–91.* Washington, DC: Author.

Pinnell, G. S., DeFord, D. E., & Lyons, C. A. (1988). *Reading Recovery: Early intervention for at-risk first graders.* Arlington, VA: Educational Research Service.

Pogrow, S. (1992). What to do about Chapter One: An alternate view from the street. *Phi Delta Kappan*, *72*, 624–630.

Ribadeneira, D. (1990, July 3). Teachers say U.S. education investment falls short. *Boston Globe*, p. 7.

Rowan, B., Guthrie, L. F., Lee, G. V., & Guthrie, G. P. (1990). *The design and implementation of Chapter One instructional services: A study of 24 schools.* San Francisco: Far West Laboratory of Educational Research and Development.

Shepard, L. A., & Smith, M. L. (Eds.). (1989). *Flunking grades: Research and policies on retention.* Philadelphia: Falmer.

Shepard, L. A., & Smith, M. L. (1990). Synthesis of research on grade retention. *Educational Leadership, 47,* 84–88.

U.S. Department of Education, U.S. Office of Special Education and Rehabilitative Services. (1990). *Twelfth annual report to Congress on the implementation of Education of the Handicapped Act,* Table AA20, A33–34. Washington, DC: U.S. Government Printing Office.

Viadero, D. (1990, November 7). New Zealand import: A costly but effective way to teach reading. *Education Week, 10,* 1.

Yukish, J. (1989). *Site Reports 1986–87,1987–87,1988–89.* Wakeman, OH: Western Reserve School District.

CHAPTER 4

Portfolios in the Classroom: What Happens When Teachers and Students Negotiate Assessment?

LAURA P. STOWELL
California State University, San Marcos
ROBERT J. TIERNEY
Ohio State University

One undeniable feature of the current wave of educational reform, especially at the elementary school level, is substantial criticism of traditional forms of assessment of student literacy learning. Our views of the nature of literacy have evolved faster, it seems, than our assessment practices. As a result, many schools have been experimenting with alternative evaluation strategies for examining literacy learning. If our schools are to sustain literacy curricula that focus on fostering lifelong readers and writers, on integrating the language arts, and on developing more thoughtful readers and writers, then current experimentation with more "authentic" approaches to assessment will necessarily have to expand.

The traditional assessment of literacy learning has been a group-administered standardized reading achievement test. While writing and literature assessment have more recently been included in some locales, it is still the reading test that is the most common measure of literacy learning. These tests have been overwhelmingly structured around multiple choice items that purport to measure one or another reading skill. The test results are reported in percentiles, grade equivalents, and national curve equivalents, with scores aggregated by grade and school to allow for comparisons of children, classrooms, schools, and, more recently, statewide reading achievement. The crux of standardized testing has been to rank-order children's reading test performances and to compare children, classrooms, and schools.

The limitations of these standardized reading achievement tests are well documented (Darling-Hammond, 1991; Stallman & Pearson, 1990). Briefly, it has been proven that traditional tests are largely unreliable bases for making any judgments about an individual's reading development; they rarely have much demonstrated validity, simply because they assess such a narrow range of literacy activity; they are given too infrequently and at too odd times of the year for the results, even if reliable and valid, to be of much use in planning instruction; and use of standardized tests narrows the curriculum by forcing teachers to "teach the test" and works to discourage teacher–learner collaborative evaluation of literacy learning. However, less often discussed is another insidious feature of standardized tests — the role such tests can play in discouraging those children whose performance on the tests suggests that their reading development lags behind that of their peers.

It is not just that learning that a test score is below the anticipated level is discouraging (though we very much expect it is), but that even steady improvement, when reliably depicted on tests, often still leaves a child looking like a loser. For instance, a child with a twenty-third-percentile score on a standardized reading test works hard and makes more than a full year's growth (in test terminology) the following year. However, he still earns a thirty-first-percentile score at the end of that year! Even his teachers may still view him more as a "remedial reader" than as a learner who has exhibited enormous development in literacy.

There is much discussion about changing assessment practices in elementary schools, but little of that discussion has focused on how redesigned evaluation and assessment practices might benefit both teachers and learners. Evaluation of literacy learning must be renegotiated so that the focus is shifted to learner-based assessments. However, renegotiating assessment in the classroom means pursuing a new kind of partnership between teachers and students (Tierney, 1994). This partnership can expand to include parents and caregivers, administrators and testing personnel. Portfolios offer an effective way for everyone involved in a child's education to collaborate on assessment. But what does it mean to implement portfolios? What kinds of issues arise when this is done? What are the problems and benefits of using portfolios in the classroom?

We have been involved with portfolio development and implementation in a number of elementary schools for nearly a decade. We have worked side by side with elementary school teachers as they have explored the use of portfolios with their students. In this capacity, we have guided, prompted, observed, and talked with the teachers, students, parents, and testing personnel in schools who are struggling to develop portfolio assessment. We have wrestled with issues of designing a district-wide means of evaluating portfolios. Finally, we have worked on portfolio projects funded by the United States Department of Education that pursued systematic assessment of teacher change with portfolios, as well as program evaluations. Our orientation in these efforts has been tied to the view that what we were doing was a form of continuous experimentation or ongoing research and development. In other words, we were intent on gathering information on the process and effects of implementation of portfolios as student-centered assessment tools at the same time as we refined our approaches to portfolio development. Our goal has not been solely to accumulate evidence on the effectiveness of portfolios; instead, our work with portfolios has been tied to our attempts to assess assessment against tenets of constructivist views of teaching and learning. We feel that the effort has been rewarded, for it has refined our view of the nature of role of assessment in significant ways.

Our goal in this chapter is to focus on some of the issues surrounding the implementation of portfolios. While we may draw from the countless lessons that we have learned and are still learning from our various projects, we will focus our discussion on how the process of implementing a portfolio approach to evaluating children's literacy learning leads to a substantial rethinking of the roles of virtually all members of an educational community. We summarize some of the most important shifts in thinking about learning and of how learning might be evaluated that typically occurred in the schools we worked in. As a caveat, however, we would note that we suspect that some of our findings may well be idiosyncratic to ourselves and the teachers and students with whom we shared in these investigations as partners.

PORTFOLIOS AS ASSESSMENT TOOLS

One key asset of portfolios is that they provide a vehicle for student and teacher collaboration on assessment. Portfolios represent a shift toward: (1) assessment practices grounded in the classroom, and (2) responsive evaluation procedures that aspire to be collaborative. The concept of portfolios is driven by attempts to approach the issue of assessment in a manner that is responsive to what students are doing; represents the range of activities in which they are involved; documents the processes they have enlisted, their growth, and their effort; and represents the range of proficiencies that students demonstrate (Tierney, Carter, & Desai, 1991).

Our earlier work examined the shifts in teachers' beliefs and practices over time as they explored and experimented with portfolio-based assessment. We looked at teachers before portfolios were used in their classrooms, as they were being implemented, and after they had been used for a while. One set of outcomes of these studies was tied to our attempt to register and compare the influence of portfolios on classroom practice, teachers' views of students, and students' views of themselves. Such outcomes were readily apparent in these early studies. However, just as visible were the shifts that were occurring in views of the nature and role of portfolios—especially the changing roles of teachers and students and their relationships with one another.

Again, we emphasize that our portfolio efforts have involved continuous development as teachers have experimented with their use in classrooms. Our goal has always been to follow the lead of the teacher as she or he pursues portfolio implementation with some broad goals in mind. In other words, we have stressed a view of assessment emerging from the classroom rather than being externally imposed. Typically, standardized testing practices and assessment procedures (informal or formal) tied to a priori criteria represent the kind of top-down, externally driven assessment procedures that we try to avoid. Prepackaging a set of procedures (portfolio or non-portfolio) has always been the antithesis of our approach.

In broad terms, our goal has been to pursue an approach that is bottom-up (i.e., emanating from the classroom) and inside-out (client-centered, with the student at the center) compared to traditional assessment approaches. At one of our very first meetings with teacher volunteers some years ago, one member of the group made the statement, "You really do not know what you want," when confronted with our open-ended stance. In terms of the general goals of the assessment process, we do know what we want; in terms of the specific practices and procedures, we do not know what we want. However, we do know that we do not want to become prescriptive.

In broad terms, our approach has been tied to notions of assessment that reflect the following:

- A constructivist view of learning, teaching, and knowing.
- Assessment practices aligned with teaching and learning practices.
- Assessment practices that reflect what teachers value.
- Assessment practices that engage students in ongoing learning (review, reflection, evaluation, and goal-setting).
- Assessment practices that engage teachers and students in a partnership.
- Assessment practices that are grounded in real work rather than artificial measures.
- Assessment practices that are developmental and individualized rather than categorical and standardized.

Our approach to assessment involves teachers and students being willing to explore the possibility of data collection, reflection, analysis, and sharing in an ongoing fashion. Moreover, it requires that teachers begin to do some things that they did not do in the past, to change their reliance on existing testing practices, and to establish a very different relationship with the students in the context of assessment. These are not minor changes — indeed, these notions of assessment represent massive shifts in classroom practice for most teachers. We suspect that the types of shifts that we observed were perhaps more dramatic than any other shift that teachers had experienced in their careers.

However, it has been our experience that portfolio implementation may not always represent the kinds of shifts to which we have aspired. For example, in Table 4.1 we have tried to contrast some of the expanded views of and practices with portfolios to which we aspire with more restrictive views.

One of the implications that one can draw from contrasting key dimensions of portfolio processes is that we should not lump all ways of doing portfolios together, nor should we assume that one approach to doing portfolios is equivalent to another. So when someone mentions to us that they are doing portfolios, we ask them to provide more detail in order to examine how what they are doing compares with our own views of the possibilities portfolios offer.

We also hope that Table 4.1 highlights the kinds of shifts in assessment practices that we feel are necessary and portrays the emphasis on major staff development efforts that will be needed to foster significant changes for teachers. Interestingly, Lamme and Hysmith (1991) surveyed and interviewed teachers who implemented portfolios and struggled with many of the same dimensions outlined above. They found that when teachers implemented portfolio assessment practices, the ease of the portfolio accommodation into the classroom was directly related to the level of the teachers' involvement with the whole language philosophy and adherence to the principles of authentic assessment, and to their roles on the school staff. Teachers who embraced authentic assessment and whole language philosophy focused on individual children and used the assessment to inform instruction. For these teachers, portfolio assessment eliminated the need for testing and retesting children.

Teachers at low levels of portfolio implementation tended not to be enthusiastic about either whole language or authentic assessment. These teachers had difficulty understanding why they should do portfolio assessment and felt that it added extra work to the recordkeeping they were already doing. One teacher wrote, "It's not a transition, it's an addition to what I already do."

TABLE 4.1. Some key dimensions of portfolios across expanded and restricted views

	Expanded	*Restricted*
Purpose	**Primary and Central** Portfolios serve as the major source for assessment data.	**Peripheral and Supplemental** Portfolios are used to complement other sources of data.
Decision Makers	**Collaborative Negotiation** Evaluation is collaborative between students, teachers, and parents.	**Singular and Rigid** Evaluation purposes, selection, criteria, and summaries are developed without ongoing negotiation between involved partners.
Criteria/ Grade	**Multiple** Multiple criteria are developed while examining various aspects of portfolios. Criteria yield a wide variety of descriptive terms and are not viewed as the sole standards.	**Singular** A single criterion is imposed upon the portfolio or part(s) of the portfolio.
Contents	**Multiple** The portfolio can be used to display a repertoire of abilities, range of literacies, improvement, interests, and attitudes.	**Singular** Single samples such as representative writing samples are selected as a basis for evaluation.
Audience	**Multiple and Flexible** Portfolio contents assume a variety of audiences for a variety of purposes. The primary client is the student.	**Singular and Fixed** Audience tends to be restricted to one, usually the teacher.
Final Process / Product Form	**Variable and Flexible** The portfolio process varies somewhat and the final portfolio varies with the individual, the purpose, and the contents.	**Singular and Fixed** The portfolio adopts the same form for all individuals in all situations.
Summary and Report	**Differential and Flexible** Portfolio provides differential and descriptive detail of a variety of aspects of the portfolio and varies across students.	**Singular and Restricted** Portfolio summary tends to be restricted to single summary-like scale that assumes comparability and standardization across portfolios.

We have encountered similar shifts to those described by Lamme and Hysmith (1991) while working in elementary schools; some teachers embrace the portfolio concept while others do not. Some teachers may find that they want to apply traditional grading notions to the portfolio or other wholistic assessment procedures. They may want to prescribe what goes into the portfolio and restrict the students' involvement in the portfolio process. Other teachers may use the portfolio as an alternative to traditional assessment procedures. Indeed, we are aware of some situations where the portfolio was used, for instance, as the basis for reversing a decision to retain a student. We have found that in many ways teachers' initial involvement with portfolio evaluation has often mushroomed into major reforms in assessment in their classrooms and their schools.

Perhaps two continuums capture the variations that occur in how teachers appropriate portfolios. One continuum might be termed student-centered or inside-out versus teacher-directed or outside-in; the other might be termed bottom-up versus top-down. The first continuum (inside-out versus outside-in) represents the range of differences that may exist in terms of the basic goals of portfolios, their management, and perceived outcomes. In some classrooms (inside-out), portfolios are used primarily to help students assess themselves and, therefore, students are integrally involved in the entire portfolio process. In other classrooms (outside-in), portfolios may primarily be a tool for the teachers. In such classrooms the student involvement with portfolios tends to be secondary—students are required to meet standards set by the teacher or some other outsider.

The second continuum (bottom-up versus top-down) represents the range of differences that may exist in how portfolios are mandated, derived, analyzed, and used. In most bottom-up situations, the teachers negotiate with their students the purposes that portfolios might serve, as well as the contents and how the portfolio is used and evaluated. In these situations, portfolios are apt to show more variation from one student to the next and one classroom to the next. In top-down situations, there is a tendency to pursue the opposite—that is, teachers, districts, or others impose a form of standardization upon portfolios. In other words, they impose from the top down a set of guidelines that define, in an a priori fashion, the purpose, nature, and use of the portfolios. In Table 4.2, we have tried to represent the range of portfolios. It should be noted that our depiction is for purposes of gross characterization; we would not expect any particular portfolio approach to fit neatly within or pass from one level to the next.

We understand that a bottom-up and inside-out view of assessment reflects a substantial variation from traditionally held views and that a shift toward adopting such a set of beliefs will require a dramatic rethinking of assessment roles and practices in most schools and communities. Indeed, we have found some teachers who have made such major shifts and others who seemingly cannot. We believe that at the root of such shifts are some basic beliefs about assessment.

1. Teachers are capable professionals who have the capacity to facilitate intellectual and emotional growth in students.
2. Students are learning how to think for themselves and how to educate themselves over the course of their lives.
3. Diversity is not only inevitable, it is also desirable. The process of education should reflect the diversity of human experience and creativity. Only through respect for diversity can excellence be achieved, since excellence involves people working to their ultimate capacity.
4. The relationship between teachers and students involves mutual respect and is client-centered (student-centered).

It has been our experience that those teachers who are less inclined to implement portfolio assessment are those who are merely responding to state mandates or perceive doing portfolios as a faddish trend.

Students and student views are also critical to the portfolio process. It has been our experience that most students embrace the opportunity to become partners in the assessment process and relish the opportunity to examine their achievements and progress. Our studies examining shifts in students' perceptions of their learning over time suggest that with portfolio assessment students grow in their impressions of themselves and in their ability to set goals. For those students who might be deemed at-risk, the experience of developing a portfolio over time and analyzing one's progress has contributed in a very positive fashion to shifts both in students' views of themselves and in their teachers' appreciation of their progress. In addition, in schools employing pullout approaches to remediation and special education, portfolios have linked teachers with students, classroom teachers with specialist teachers, and teachers with parents. Indeed, the portfolio has become a resource in helping teachers, parents, and students to collaborate better in meeting a diverse array of instructional needs. Furthermore, portfolios often bring to the foreground the sorts of learning and the nature of the progress that have often gone unnoticed—or were substantially over-shadowed—in assessments that focused primarily on comparing students to one another rather than examining academic growth over time.

However, in our experience, not all students embrace the portfolio

TABLE 4.2. Types of teacher involvement in portfolio assessment

General Characteristic	Purposes	Content	Process	Attitudes
Not Used	• No systematic collection of anecdotal records or samples of writing in portfolio.	• Reliance on formal testing procedures.	• Periodical testing that may or may not inform practice or students.	• Dependent upon traditional forms of assessment.
Portfolios Within a Traditional Framework (*Top-Down and Outside-In*)	• To indicate a child's level of progress. • To show accumulating prerequisite knowledge and skills. • To tell what a child doesn't know. • To see what skill to reteach.	• A collection of the child's tests and writing on assigned topics. • The district exit skills checklist.	• Teacher collects with no child input. • Teacher grades and sets goals for students. • Teacher-controlled process.	• Teacher likes more structured assessment. • Teacher wants to know what must be included. • Teacher feels need for documentation of exit skills.
Portfolios and Traditional Assessment	• To collect and keep more in-depth records of what child is doing. • To tell teacher what skills to teach. • To make decisions about promotion and retention.	• Collections of children's work. • District skills checklists. • School forms used with no alterations or personal innovations. • Observations of group responses to aspects of the curriculum such as Sustained Silent Reading.	• Teacher keeps anecdotal records in head. • Teacher selects portfolio content. • Teacher integrates exit skills with curriculum. • Students may select some elements. • Classroom assessment adds other kinds of information.	• Teacher claims no time for mandated forms and portfolio assessment. • Teacher tries various ways to record information. • Teacher sees need for consistency by grade level. • Teacher needs more experience to learn purpose of anecdotal records.

General Characteristic	Purposes	Content	Process	Attitudes
Teacher-Directed Portfolio Use	• Teacher understands reasons for portfolio: determining how children actually use skills. • Information used to inform teaching. • Authentic reasons for the showcase portfolio—teacher provides an audience for children to share their best work with.	• Teacher uses a variety of strategies for collecting data: observations, checklists, scales, anecdotes, and artifacts. • Teacher keeps a log or record of what has been taught.	• Children select work for their portfolios. • Teacher observes systematically (e.g., 5 children a day, each curricular area, and so forth). • Students do some analyses of their work. • Teachers directs students to criteria.	• Teacher is concerned about time and management system. • Teacher says, "I can now see the progress of each child more clearly." • Parents are audience for portfolios. • Students are partial partners.
Student-Centered Portfolio Use	• To inform instruction. • To display and celebrate process and achievements. • For students to assess their growth. • To establish ongoing goals.	• Students (with teacher support) analyze artifacts and student logs, reading journals, and so forth. Portfolio is not a collection of things, but has interpretive data as well. • Teacher utilizes records to reflect on instruction • Students use portfolio to consider progress and establish ongoing goals.	• Children reflect on why works are included in portfolios and can explain progress, learning, and goals • Teacher and students record information as it occurs. • Students keep logs on learning. • Innovations occur in assessment systems. • Criteria emerge from the data, not set a priori.	• Enthusiastic sampling of new ideas. • Teachers and students deal with idio-syncratic and complex nature of development. • Teacher and students value different perspectives on growth and value revisiting portfolios. • Parents as partners in the activity. • Student clearly a partner.

TABLE 4.3. Types of student involvement in portfolio assessment

General Characteristic	Purposes	Content	Process	Attitudes
Non-Use	•No systematic collection of samples of students' work.	•Students' efforts are directed at a restricted range of tasks to be tested.	•Students' task is to do well on tests.	•Comparative grading and non individualized assessment.
Portfolios Embedded in Traditional Assessment Procedures (*Top-Down and Outside-In*)	•To display knowledge transmitted by teacher or acquired by student to teacher and parents.	•Students collect tests and assignments in a folder/ notebook. •Students collect district- and/or state-mandated work.	•Students collect work that has been teacher- and/or district- assigned.	•Students told what to collect. •Little or no student ownership in collecting or analyzing. •Little student understanding or investment in portfolio.
Portfolios Alongside Traditional Assessment Procedures	•To display knowledge to teacher, parents, and self.	•Teacher-assigned work. •District and/or state requirements. •Work representing in-class and out-of-class tasks. •Most collections standardized forms.	•Students begin to become selective about work they place in the folder and attempt to negotiate with teacher about work to be included in the portfolio.	•Students begin to resent teacher-mandated assignments and assessments.

General Characteristic	Purposes	Content	Process	Attitudes
Teacher-Directed and Outside-In	•Students understand purpose of portfolio and the importance of their selections and reflections.	•Teacher observational and anecdotal records. •Student reflective journals. •Conference notes. •Showcase pieces. •Work in process. •Samples from outside of class. •Samples that capture the total person. •Reflections on their choices in the portfolio. •Self-evaluations.	•Students involved in negotiating the selection process. •Students reflect on work and growth and share reflections in a conference or narrative. •While students may want to be full partners, they may not be viewed as fully equipped to articulate their own assessment.	•Students understand reasons for the portfolio and are enthusiastic. •Students become more assertive about their work and their role in its assessment.
Student-Centered Approach (*Bottom-Up and Inside-Out*)	•To inform own learning. •Students are independently assessing own work and growth.	•Teacher observa-tional and anec-dotal records. •Students' reflective journals, self-evaluations. •Conference notes. •Showcase pieces. •Work in process. •Samples from outside of class. •Samples that capture the total person. •Reflections on their choices in the portfolio. •Parent evaluation.	•Students and teachers (and possibly parents) are full partners in the portfolio process. •Students give input regarding the selection, reflection, and analysis of the portfolio.	•Students are enthusiastic, empowered, and feel ownership of their own learning and its assessment.

assessment process. Some students prefer other modes of assessment. For example, some students seem to prefer traditional tests—where they fare better when compared to other students rather than with themselves. It is important to realize that students represent a range of beliefs similar to those of teachers involved with the implementation of portfolios. Indeed, in Table 4.3 we detail some of the differences that we have encountered. Sometimes students' perceptions of portfolios come as a result of a well established history with traditional assessment procedures. In other cases, students' perceptions may be tied to cynicism. For example, students may need to learn to trust teachers when they suggest that students will be involved in the decision making. It is as if these students expect teachers to impose rather than to support, to judge rather than nurture.

As our descriptions suggest, there are a variety of issues teachers must consider during the process of portfolio assessment, including who decides what goes into the portfolio, how that material will be analyzed, when it will be analyzed, and how information will be shared. There are many stakeholders in portfolio assessment: students, teachers, caregivers, principals, school board members, and community members, as well as district and state education personnel. In a recent national survey of portfolio use (Kolanowski, 1993), it was found that rarely was the teacher the sole decision maker in developing portfolios. In many cases students were involved in selecting work to be included and evaluated. But involving students in evaluations of their own learning has not been widely practiced in elementary schools. Initiating and sustaining such involvement requires substantial learning on the part of both students and teachers.

NEGOTIATING PORTFOLIOS: THE TUG OF WAR BETWEEN TEACHERS AND STUDENTS, OR LEARNING TO DANCE

As we have suggested, at the center of our approach to assessment is a reorientation toward learner-based assessment—a form of assessment that is client-centered, collaborative, and judicious. On first glance, this might seem a natural extension of student-centered learning; on closer inspection, it represents a major shift in the relationships that exist between students and teachers even in those classrooms where teachers espouse a student-centered orientation to teaching and learning. We all carry a history of assessment practices that may work against the kind of change in teacher–student relationships that we desire. For example, in many classrooms, assessment appears to be used as a means for disciplining students—that is, ensuring that they will complete their work lest the teacher grade them poorly. Historically, assessment is something done *to* the student, rather than done *with* the student.

In a host of ways, we have found ourselves dealing with teachers who were reluctant, nervous, and with past histories that interfered with pursuing an assessment partnership with their students. In particular, we found teachers willing to entertain the notion of involving students in the portfolio development process, but then reluctant to incorporate student involvement into actual practice. Teachers have a view of portfolios they would like to implement, but the reality of this implementation can be difficult (Stowell & Tierney, 1991).

Nonetheless, many elementary teachers seem willing to explore a different kind of relationship with their students in the context of assessment. Indeed, we have been in a number of elementary classrooms where the teachers have pursued a form of leading from behind. In other words, they have pursued a relationship with the student that is more akin to a sponsorship. For example, in Mark Carter's fifth grade classroom in Upper Arlington, Ohio, students establish their own guidelines for the portfolio and pursue their own analyses of these portfolios en route to sharing them with their peers, their parents, and Mark himself.

One of the dimensions of the portfolio process in this classroom is the ongoing setting of goals based on the students' reflections of their past efforts. This is done both informally through conferencing and sharing as well as through a written narrative developed by the student. Specifically, at the end of each quarter, Mark discusses with each student elements that might be included in the portfolio (this discussion might address concerns such as the types of materials that might be placed in their portfolios, including pieces that suggest improvement, breakthroughs, new learning, and so forth), as well as such basics as number of items, ways of describing, and profiling the portfolios. During this discussion, Mark establishes the frame within which the students make decisions for themselves and, within this frame, offers support and advice while avoiding giving too much input or erring on the side of making decisions for students.

We have found, surprisingly, that primary grade teachers are apt to involve students more rather than less. The primary teachers we have worked with engaged students in a range of activities that involved students in reflecting on their improvement and development. These teachers did not shy away from giving the students an opportunity to set their own goals and savor their own development. In a small Ohio city school district, for example, the first and second grade teachers struggled with ways to engage students in such reflection. At our suggestion, they initially had their first and second graders write down reasons for the selection of each portfolio piece. Since the first and second graders were doing lots of peer conferencing and since their parents were also involved in the program, it seemed reasonable to have their friends and their parents add comments to each card. It was quickly discovered that the return was not worth the investment. Having students complete a card for each item was tedious for the students and cumbersome to manage. It seemed that students were engaged in much more meaningful self-reflection when they were interacting informally with one another and when the teacher had students pursue more overall assessments of their progress. For instance, periodically the teachers would have students look through their portfolios and simply make two lists: (1) what they could do/what they learned, and (2) what they wanted to do next/future goals.

We usually stress the following points in our discussions of portfolio development with elementary teachers:

- The process of engaging students in their own self-assessment is more important than producing a formal analysis.
- Students will become more and more astute at assessing their needs and setting future goals, but this takes time.
- Students should be allowed to develop personal criteria for looking at their progress.

As teachers begin implementing portfolios, they may feel the urge to develop charts and checklists (e.g., signs of good reading and writing) in an attempt to guide student evaluation. In too many elementary school classrooms, we found that portfolio implementation prompted teachers to list features such as spelling, punctuation, neatness, complete sentences, accurate answers, and so on. But students often turned too quickly to these listings and relied heavily upon the items as *the* criteria to which they should aspire. Unfortunately, the features most commonly included on such charts and checklists focus students' attention on the mechanical aspects of writing, rather than on what makes writing or reading involvements interesting, thought-provoking, challenging, interactive, compelling, useful, and distinctive for a child.

We prefer to encourage students to focus on why they read or wrote something; what made what they did special; what they enjoyed, discovered, or learned; what they might do differently; and where they plan to go next. Rather than pursue a generic checklist or general descriptors, we encourage students to be specific and try to be what has come to be termed "real."

Our experiences in a variety of settings suggest to us that it is how you do the portfolio and not just the portfolio itself that needs to be judged. Earlier we stressed that our orientation to portfolios is upside-down and inside-out. It is learning how to pursue the portfolio in conjunction with a call for a new professionalism by teachers and a new relationship with students that is perhaps the most demanding change that is called for, as well as what makes such changes so dramatic.

CONCLUSION

Throughout this chapter we have tried to stress the point that implementing a portfolio approach will involve more than simply the introduction of another assessment tool. With the introduction of portfolios come some major shifts in teacher professionalism, the role of classroom-grounded assessment data, and student empowerment. We have attempted to describe the issues teachers and students struggle with as they implement portfolios. Implementation requires negotiation along several dimensions, including purposes, decision making, grading, contents, audience, form of the portfolio, and reporting. Moreover, it requires recognition of the importance and power of a shift from top-down to bottom-up and from outside-in to inside-out. It requires accepting diversity and individuality, and striving for a student-centered approach to assessment.

It is not surprising that implementing authentic assessment affects the classroom and school in a variety of ways. It challenges testing practices that have been in place for a hundred years. For these reasons, portfolio implementation is not an easy and seamless transition. It may occur in bits at a time, and regressions may occur as teachers and students attempt to negotiate the many dimensions of portfolio assessment. Our experiences working in elementary schools indicate that it takes time to achieve the level of negotiation consonant with achieving a vision of authentic assessment that effectively captures the student-centered, dynamic, and multifaceted nature of student learning—several years of work, experimentation, and learning, in fact. It also requires support for such changes, understanding of what is entailed, resources for making shifts, and the recognition that it may be a turbulent journey that one travels to achieve the full potential that portfolio approaches have to offer.

REFERENCES

Darling-Hammond, L. (1991). The implications of testing policy for quality and equality. *Phi Delta Kappan, 73,* 220–225.
Kolanowski, K. (1993). *Use of portfolios in assessment of literature learning.* Al-

bany: National Research Center for Literature Teaching and Learning, State University of New York at Albany.

Lamme, L., & Hysmith, C. (1991). One school's adventure into portfolio assessment. *Language Arts*, *68*, 620–629.

Stallman, A. C., & Pearson, P. D. (1990). Formal measures of early literacy. In L. M. Morrow & J. K. Smith (Eds.), *Assessment for instruction in early literacy* (pp. 7–44). Englewood Cliffs, NJ: Prentice-Hall.

Stowell, L., & Tierney, R. J. (1991). *An ongoing examination of teacher shifts in thinking and practices in assessment: Portfolios across the disciplines in high school classrooms.* Columbus: The Ohio State University, Technical Report for Apple, Inc.

Tierney, R. J. (1994). Learner-based assessment: Making evaluation fit with teaching and learning. In L. M. Morrow, J. K. Smith, & L. C. Wilkinson (Eds.), *Integrated language arts: Controversy to consensus* (pp. 231–240). Boston: Allyn & Bacon.

Tierney, R. J., Carter, M., & Desai, L. E. (1991). *Portfolio assessment in the reading-writing classroom.* Norwood, MA: Christopher Gordon.

Part II

CASE STUDIES
OF SCHOOL CHANGE

CHAPTER 5

Literacy Partnerships for Change with "At-Risk" Kindergartners

LESLEY MANDEL MORROW
Rutgers University
ELLEN M. O'CONNOR
Bayonne, NJ Public Schools

When I* walked into the kindergarten classroom full of Title I students, the teacher was sitting across a table from the children. There was no interactive conversation between them. Rather, the teacher held a stack of cards labeled "auditory discrimination." She tested each child on the identification of the various consonant sounds that matched the respective pictures, recorded the number of correct responses, then repeated the exercise until every child in the room was able to identify the pictures correctly and to discriminate among the appropriate initial consonants.

The class was required to produce three consecutive days of 100% correct responses before they would be allowed to proceed to another activity. If after two days any of them missed a card, they went back to square one. Thus, some youngsters spent months reviewing the same auditory discrimination cards. The purpose of the procedure was to make sure that all the children knew the sounds so well that they would make no errors. The result was total boredom — for students, teacher, and observer.

That was my introduction in 1977 to my first classroom observation as the school district's Title I supervisor. The exercise was just one example of the skill-and-drill activities that I was to observe in this and other kindergarten classrooms over time. Another activity I would observe too frequently had children working on page after page of ditto sheets, one sheet for each letter of the alphabet. They first traced each letter, then wrote it on their own.

---

*In this chapter, "I" refers to Ellen O'Connor and "we" refers to both chapter authors.

As time went by, I became more and more aware of, and increasingly uncomfortable with, these activities and others like them. I saw student frustration and listened to teachers concerned about the program's rigidity. I dutifully reminded each teacher that skill mastery was (at that time) the current trend in education, but my innate feelings about children and learning were giving way to serious doubts.

Recently, I walked into Mrs. Brennan's Chapter I kindergarten class on my regular visit to observe their read-aloud program. The classroom included a literacy center filled with a vast assortment of materials for reading and writing. Sitting on carpet squares or bean bag or rocking chairs, the children were engaged in independent reading. One child held a stuffed animal snuggled under his arm. Two others listened to a taped story with headsets as they followed along in their books. Although they read silently, they could not restrain themselves from saying out loud in unison, "Are you my mother?" (Eastman, 1960) each time they found that phrase repeated throughout the story, clearly showing how much they understood and enjoyed what they were hearing. Another child quietly read a big book that stood on an easel with two others. He used a pointer to track the print from left to right across the page as he read. Still another child had used markers and paper to make his own book and ran to the teacher to have it stapled as a sign that it was now a finished product.

At the beginning of the independent reading period, Mrs. Brennan had made sure that all children were involved in one productive activity or another. She stressed the classroom rule that once each child had selected an activity, he or she was expected to stay with it through completion. She was then able to begin reading her own magazine as she modeled her interest in reading. The children knew they were to respect her reading time and they did not interrupt her.

The room was generally quiet, the only noise that of productive activity. In design and planning, the activities in which the children participated emphasized enjoyment of the learning experience. They were self-directed, largely social, and many of them collaborative. I could not help but smile as I contrasted this remedial classroom with the skill-and-drill setting I remembered having observed fifteen years earlier.

With particular emphasis on "at-risk" kindergarten children, this chapter traces the history of how the reading program in one school district changed over a fifteen-year period. It describes what originally existed and how change occurred through a district–university partnership which resulted in the implementation of a storybook reading program. But in order to follow that history, it is important to understand the kind of community in which the change occurred and its general attitude toward change. It is also necessary to describe both the district's overall reading program and its supplemental, remedial Title I/Chapter I program, and how both have developed over the years.

THE DISTRICT

Description

The district is situated about twenty minutes outside New York City. It is densely populated; approximately 65,000 people live in an area three miles square. Socioeconomically, it is predominately blue-collar working class, with a racial composition of 71 percent white, 21 percent Hispanic, and 8 percent African-American. The community has not changed much in thirty years. Young couples who marry and have children tend to remain in two-family homes in which the grandparents occupy one floor. There is limited transience. By any account, change does not come easily.

The Reading Program—A Historical Perspective

During the course of the last thirty years, the district has, however, experienced several changes in its programs of reading instruction, a program that has throughout been organized predominantly around the use of basal readers. A Scott Foresman series was used prior to and through the mid-1960s.

In the late 1960s, a rather dramatic change occurred. The district adopted the Sullivan Programmed Reading Series (McGraw-Hill), a highly structured program in which children worked their way through approximately seven workbooks each year from first through third grades. At the completion of each workbook, the children read a short storybook, then took a test of their readiness to proceed to the next workbook. Because students progressed at their own individual rates, the Sullivan series in effect introduced the district to a form of individualization. During the late 1970s, a district committee successfully recommended replacing programmed reading with a Houghton Mifflin basal series. At the present time, the district is examining for possible adoption several different basals that emphasize literature-based instruction.

The Supplemental Remedial Reading Program

The remedial program began during the 1970s, with remedial and regular classroom teachers teamed to administer the Sullivan programmed reading series. By the late 1970s Title I funds supported the remedial program.

I joined the district at that time as supervisor of the remedial programs and initiated a pullout program with different materials and methods of instruction from those used in the regular classroom. I introduced a diagnostic-prescriptive pattern of reading instruction in which teachers regularly pretested students, instructed them, then post-tested them, and in which all students worked individually to attain skill mastery. A prescribed skills array dictated the order in which skills were introduced and mastered.

After I began my doctoral studies, I became aware of major changes taking place in the field of reading instruction. I read about emergent literacy, shared reading experiences, process writing, and literature-based instruction. I regularly met with teachers in the district's remedial program and shared the information I was discovering. Together, the teachers and I discussed the pros and cons of these new ideas and how these might or might not fit into their school setting. A library of professional books was created, books that the teachers readily shared. They devoted some of their meetings to discussions of what had been read and recommendations as to whether or not a particular book should be read by all. At some meetings, they also read and discussed specific materials as a group.

My colleagues and I methodically set about changing the district's Chapter I remedial program from a skill-and-drill approach to one derived from an emergent literacy perspective and implemented concurrently with a commercial program that emphasizes the letters of the alphabet. Although most of the teachers were generally enthusiastic about the new ideas and eager to try emergent literacy strategies, many were reluctant to give up the organizational structure provided by the commercial program they had been using.

The district's regular kindergartens, by contrast, had been using a very traditional reading readiness approach dominated by a basal program. The overall situation was quite the opposite of that found in most school systems, in which regular classroom instruction typically embraced more current perspectives on literacy development while remedial programs used older skill-and-drill techniques.

DISTRICT—UNIVERSITY PARTNERSHIP
AS CHANGE AGENTS

I found myself in a professional dilemma when I began my doctoral studies. As the district's Chapter I supervisor I had introduced and endorsed a skills-mastery approach for eight years, although I had many concerns about it. However, my graduate studies had made me aware of newer theories and practices in reading instruction, practices diametrically op-posed to the methods I had initiated. In addition, as I continued to observe Chapter I instruction, I could see how bored both students and teachers were.

I realized that change was needed in the district's Chapter I program, but what changes should take place, and how were they to be implemented? None of the teachers I supervised was enrolled in graduate studies. They were generally unaware of current research and the newer practices. Given the district reading program's traditional approach, the Chapter I program's skill-and-drill orientation, and my own previous endorsement of that orien-tation, the task would not be easy. Not only would I have to convince the teachers of the need for change, but also the district administration. Fur-ther, I needed both a strong theoretical base and a corpus of empirical research to support the change.

That was when I began working closely with my university advisor, Leslie Morrow, who shared a strong interest in my goals. Together we studied the newer research on emergent literacy strategies and at-risk chil-dren, as well as research on school change. Together we formed a partner-ship between school district and university, helping to initiate change in both Chapter I and kindergarten programs while working together to achieve a common goal.

Research Supporting the Implementation of a Storybook Reading Program

We sought to substantiate the value of storybook reading as an instruc-tional strategy to help promote literacy development and found that as far back as 1908, E. B. Huey (1908) suggested that children's learning in school begin with parents reading to them at home. Our literature search led us even further back—to the eighteenth century, when Rousseau (Boyd, 1962) suggested that early childhood education include a natural approach to learning that would encourage the child's spontaneous curiosity. To Rousseau's approach, Pestalozzi (Fletcher, 1912) added an element of infor-mal instruction and emphasized the importance of a positive, supportive climate for learning. Dewey (1913) encouraged learning through active involvement, a point emphasized by Piaget (Piaget & Inhelder, 1969), who felt that as children interact with their world, they constantly alter and reorganize their own knowledge. Vygotsky (1981) stressed the importance of children's social interaction with peers and adults when learning new ideas.

Each of these theorists—from Rousseau to Vygotsky—has had an im-pact on early childhood education and theories of literacy development. It is evident that constructs related to emergent literacy are rooted in their theories. Those constructs include:

- A focus on the development of the "whole child."
- An emphasis on providing an optimal learning environment.
- An emphasis on learning rather than teaching.
- The importance of adult–child social interaction.
- Emphasis on meaningful, natural learning experiences.
- Concern for children's active participation in learning.

We agreed that these concepts would be important in the program we wanted to develop, but we recognized, too, that educators want not only theory, but also examples of successful practice documented with research findings from classroom studies. Numerous studies document the relationship between reading stories to children and their subsequent success on readiness tasks and reading achievement in school (e.g., Burroughs, 1972; Chomsky, 1972; Durkin, 1974–1975; Fodor, 1966; Irwin, 1960; Moon & Wells, 1979). In general, they have found that being read to at home correlates positively with levels of language and vocabulary development of pre-readers. Wells's (1982, 1985) research with the Bristol Language Development Project examined the effect of several different literacy activities on reading achievement. He found that listening to stories correlated positively with reading achievement in school.

Children who participate in story-reading activities realize that print differs from speech and that it carries messages. They approach reading with the expectation that it will be meaningful (Clay, 1979; Smith, 1978). Teale (1984) suggested that reading to children helps to foster four areas of early literacy development crucial in the initial phases of learning to read: (1) their awareness of the functions and uses of written language—what reading is all about and what it feels like; (2) concepts about print, books, reading, and the form and structure of written language; (3) positive attitudes toward reading; and (4) children's self-monitoring and predictive strategies.

We wanted clarification on specific aspects of reading aloud that actually enhanced literacy development. Bloome's (1985) research was helpful in that respect. He noted that reading aloud to a child is a social process as well as a process of communication. A read-aloud event involves social relationships among people—teachers and students, parents and children, authors and readers. Social integration surrounds and influences interaction with printed text. During story reading, meaning is negotiated through the interaction of adult and child; it is constructed and reconstructed throughout the event (Piaget & Inhelder, 1969).

Teale and Sulzby (1987) felt that what the adult and child talk about in the interaction holds a key to the effects of storybook reading. A number of studies of shared book experiences, both in home and school environments, illustrate the interactive nature of story reading and point to implications for developing the use of story reading as an instructional strategy in the classroom (Flood, 1977; Heath, 1980; Morrow, 1987, 1988; Ninio & Brunner, 1978; Roser & Martinez, 1985; Yaden & McGee, 1983). Overall, the results of these studies indicate that reading a book to a child may not in itself be sufficient for maximum literacy growth. Rather, the talk and activity that surround the reading of text may be equally valuable.

Materials and Strategies That Enhance Storybook Reading

The literature review convinced us that storybook reading helps young children develop literacy skills. Our next task was to decide which elements of storybook reading to include in the program, and how to effect change that included teachers as partners in the endeavor.

Many strategies of storybook reading appear in the research literature. We selected strategies that had been demonstrated to increase literacy skills in young children—specifically, directed listening and thinking activities, story retellings, repeated readings of specific storybooks, constructing story meaning through interactive reading, and activities that encouraged the development of concepts about books and print and increased children's access to books.

Directed Listening and Thinking Activity (DLTA). A DLTA consists of (1) setting a purpose for listening to a story through prereading, questions, and discussion; (2) reading the story; and (3) carrying out a postreading discussion that reflects the purpose set before the story was read. This procedure has been found to improve students' comprehension, apparently because it focuses the child's attention on a specific goal (Morrow, 1984). The structure of each DLTA remains the same, even though purposes and stories vary from one occasion to the next.

Story Retelling. Story retelling offers not only an instructional technique, but also an evaluative one. It actively involves the child in the reconstruction of a story and helps develop comprehension, oral language, and sense of story structure (Gambrell, Pfeiffer, & Wilson, 1985; Morrow, 1985, 1989). Sense of story structure includes an awareness that stories have a *setting, time, place*, and *characters*; a *theme* (a beginning event that causes the main character to react and formulate a goal or face a problem);

plot episodes (events in which the main character attempts to attain the goal or solve the problem); a *resolution* (attainment of the goal or solution of the problem); and the *ending*, which may have long-term consequences (Mandler & Johnson, 1977; Stein & Glenn, 1979). Research on the development of a sense of story structure as a means for enhancing comprehension indicates that practice in retelling can significantly improve children's awareness of story schema and understanding of narratives (Bowman, 1981; Gordon & Braun, 1982; Morrow, 1985; Spiegel & Whaley, 1980). Because it is a holistic procedure, retelling is strikingly different from the traditional piecemeal questioning approach to developing and assessing comprehension.

Repeated Readings and Attempted Readings of Storybooks. Several researchers have explored and encouraged rereading of stories. Martinez (1983) found that rereading apparently leads to a progression from strictly literal retellings of stories to more interpretive presentations. Morrow (1987, 1988) found that repeated readings led children of lower socioeconomic backgrounds to develop more inferential responses, including prediction of outcomes and greater association, evaluation, and elaboration of comments. Hiebert (1981) reported that rereading favorite stories enabled children to predict storylines and participate in the process of reading. Sulzby (1985), who studied children's attempts to read storybooks that had already been read to them many times, suggested that such attempts offer a classification scheme for examining emergent reading behavior. Naturalistic observations revealed that repeated experiences with familiar books enabled children to progress from approaching pages as individual units to treating books as total entities.

Constructing Story Meaning Through Interactive Reading. One of the primary purposes of the story-reading event is the construction of meaning through the interaction of adult and child. Some particularly useful behaviors include prompting children to respond, scaffolding or supporting responses for children to model when they are unable to respond themselves, relating responses to real-life experiences, answering questions, and offering positive reinforcement of children's responses. Many of these activities are similar to those that occur in storybook reading activities at home. However, not all Chapter I children enjoy the advantage of storybook reading activities at home.

Interactive reading of predictable books—for example, books in which certain phrases, sequences, or rhymes are repeated throughout a story for their aggregate effect—encourages children to progress from listening to participating to focusing on print. With a sufficient number of interactive experiences, children begin to develop concepts about books and print in general.

Developing Concepts About Books and Print. Children who experience read-aloud activities begin to demonstrate more sophisticated thinking about printed material. With children's frequent exposure to quality storybook readings, their remarks about story content reflect an interest in interpreting information and elaborating on it. They begin to focus on concepts about books, such as titles, authors, and illustrators (Morrow, 1988; Roser & Martinez, 1985). They also begin to demonstrate an interest in such print characteristics as names of letters, words, and sounds.

Providing Rich Literacy Environments. Allotting a designated portion of a classroom to a library corner has been found to increase children's use of literature, especially during free-choice periods (Morrow & Weinstein, 1982, 1986). A library corner provides immediate access to a wide variety of literacy materials (Beckman, 1972; Teale & Sulzby, 1987). Accessibility plus good design, supply, and appropriate use have been found to increase children's interest in looking at and reading books when compared with children who do not have access to such an area (Bissett, 1969; Coody, 1973; Huck, 1976).

Morrow (1982) identified specific design characteristics that correlated with children's use of library corners during free-choice periods. They included physical accessibility; elements of comfort such as pillows, stuffed animals, carpet, and a rocking chair; taped stories and headsets; felt boards with story character cutouts; an inventory at any one time of five to eight books per child representing varied genres of children's literature; regular turnover of books displayed and available; and a wide variety of writing paper and writing utensils.

Description of a Storybook Reading Program

Once we had thoroughly reviewed the literature, we began to prepare a tentative storybook reading program for teachers to review. First, with our help and the help of their own students, each teacher would create a classroom library corner based on the parameters suggested above. The program called for teachers to spend approximately one hour a day to include: (1) time for quiet book reading, (2) a teacher-directed literature activity, (3) an independent reading period, and (4) time to discuss a summary of the day's literacy activities. Each of those four components would be introduced one at a time to students over a period of approximately a month. By the end of that month, all four would be fully operational.

Quiet Book Reading. During quiet book reading, teachers and students alike would select one or two books each to look at or read for a short time.

Teacher-Directed Literature Activities. The format of each day's teacher-directed literature activity would follow that of a DLTA, which provides a framework for questions, prediction, and discussion both before and after a story reading. Beyond that, teachers would be encouraged to use a variety of other activities for sharing books with children, including students' retelling of stories, repeated readings of favorite stories, constructing meaning through interactive story readings, activities geared to developing concepts about books and print, reading for pleasure, role-playing, shared book experiences using literature related to content area subjects, and various other activities of their own creation. Related activities would include such events as preparing and eating bread and jam after listening to the story *Bread and Jam for Frances* (Hoban, 1960). Stories would be told using puppets, felt board characters, and props. Children would be encouraged to model storytelling techniques used by the teacher during the recreational reading periods.

Independent Reading Period. Children would be given time to select materials from the library corner during recreational reading. They would also be allowed to work either individually or with others. The area would contain books, magazines, and manipulatives such as story cassettes, felt board characters, and puppets. Paper and writing utensils would be available for children who wanted to create books of their own. The purpose of this independent reading period would be pleasurable and purposeful involvement with literature and literature-related materials.

Summary of the Day. Each class would convene for about five to ten minutes for a summary of the day, a general discussion of the story-reading events that had taken place that day. The summary would reinforce and allow children to share experiences they had had with literature (Morrow, O'Connor, & Smith, 1990).

STRATEGIES FOR CHANGE

Motivating Change

Now that we had selected an overall strategy for the program and had researched the effectiveness in literacy development of specific methods and activities, we needed to promote change in a way that would not threaten or overwhelm the teachers. We had already started fostering change by providing them with a library for professional growth. We had also been holding regular sessions for discussion. Thus, many of the teachers were already informed on various aspects of the proposed approach. They even had a basis for evaluating what they thought would work with their children (Myers, 1991). In addition to these in-house activities, arrangements were made for teachers to attend professional conferences dealing with current issues, and speakers were brought into the district to make presentations.

Equally important would be long-term support for professional enrichment, both from someone within the district and from someone outside. Leslie Morrow served as the "outside" consultant, working with the teachers over a period of time, carrying out workshops, and organizing support sessions. As Chapter I supervisor, I assumed the "inside" support role within the district.

Teachers need to be collaborators, decision makers, and curriculum designers in the change process (Saracho & Spodek, 1983). They need to discuss strategies they like and those they don't, to brainstorm ideas, try them out, discuss how they work, and make decisions about going forward. They need to be researchers, formulating questions about new teaching strategies and classroom environments. Daily experiences become the generating force behind research questions. When teachers reflect on their own teaching, they identify their own strengths and weaknesses, clarify issues, and generate new ideas (Cooper, 1991). When they have decided on an area of inquiry, they need to collect data by observing and recording anecdotes; videotaping children engaged in literacy behaviors; collecting samples of children's work; interviewing children, other teachers, and parents; and administering both informal and standardized tests. Data provide the teacher with an objective basis for interpreting and resolving research questions. Collaboration on projects with other teachers helps refine methodology and interpretation of findings (Nixon, 1987).

With these strategies and those outlined earlier, we were ready to begin to work toward effecting change in literacy instruction in the district.

Effecting Change

We began implementing our process of change with discussions of professional materials we had shared. Leslie Morrow then led a workshop designed to stimulate enthusiasm by presenting a great variety of practical ideas for classroom use. We videotaped the workshop, as we did all ensuing workshops in the district. These videos have become a growing collection of resources to review and to share with new teachers.

We then outlined the proposed program and asked for input. Were teachers willing to try the program? Yes, though their sense of enthusiasm as a group came with a hint of caution.

Strategies and techniques described in the plan were introduced to the staff gradually, over a period of time. Teachers were encouraged to begin using them at their own pace. Most teachers seemed comfortable trying about one new technique or strategy a week. We held weekly meetings to discuss successes and failures.

We learned from each other by sharing how things worked. Teachers altered strategies to suit their individual teaching styles or their children's needs. Encouraging teachers to select and modify activities to suit their own patterns helped them make the program of change their own.

In addition to our weekly meetings, we visited teachers' classes once a week, though it was made clear from the start that the visits were not intended as opportunities to criticize, but to learn for ourselves what seemed to work and what aspects required rethinking. The visits were a time for all to offer constructive support, and to determine whether or not individual teachers were carrying out strategies in ways that were intended.

Certain changes that teachers felt needed to be made in the original plans were initiated. For instance, instead of initially working with small groups of children in activities such as story retelling and interactive story reading, it was seen as more beneficial to work with entire groups. Once children had become accustomed to the activities, perhaps then more productive small group sessions would be feasible.

During periods for independent reading, children could choose what they would like to do and with whom they would like to do it. But some extremely active youngsters had difficulty staying on task. They needed to be introduced more gradually to materials in the library corner. Time for independent work was shortened from the original projection until such time as the children would be better able to handle themselves more productively.

Teachers kept journals, recording successful activities as well as failures. They recorded exciting anecdotes of classroom occurrences, then shared them in our weekly sessions. We involved teachers as researchers, each teacher selecting the kinds of data he or she would like to collect, such as samples of children's work, interviewing children, recording dialogue between children engaged in literacy activities during independent reading periods, and videotaping different elements of the program. The data were collected over a period of time. Teachers shared their findings with the rest of the group, and conclusions were drawn about various components of the program. We encouraged teachers to let us videotape them engaged with their children in the storybook reading program. Each tape was viewed only by the particular teacher unless he or she agreed to share it with colleagues.

The question was often raised as to whether or not the program could stand alone without using more standard and traditional instructional materials. Even after a research study had demonstrated that children in the storybook reading program had scored significantly better than children in a control group on traditional tests of comprehension and concepts about books and print, the teachers generally still preferred to use commercially available materials as a supplement to the storybook reading program, primarily as an organizational tool. Their preference was respected and the teachers selected the materials they wished to use (O'Connor, 1989).

THE PROGRAM TODAY

As of this writing, the Chapter I storybook reading program has been in operation for four years. It has grown and changed since it began. There is now a stronger emphasis on collaboration between regular classroom and Chapter I teachers. The Chapter I initiative has caused district leaders and personnel to look more closely at the practices in their regular classrooms.

Teachers continue to meet regularly to share techniques and experiences and to iron out problems. Since their grade assignments are changed from time to time, and because they meet children with different kinds of problems from one year to the next, regular meetings are necessary even among the most experienced teachers. Teachers experienced in the program now take roles that we initially shared as mentors and facilitators of the program. The more seasoned teachers work with new teachers, helping them design classroom libraries, introducing them to storybook reading strategies, and offering general support. The program has expanded into the district's prekindergartens as well as into the first, second, and third grades.

A district summer program has extended the school year for Chapter I teachers, a setting in which those teachers use the storybook reading program exclusively, with no supplementary commercial materials. They also see the summer as a time to experiment with new ideas. A thematic approach was recently added, with children and teachers choosing the themes they want to follow for the summer (for example, transportation, food, America, music, and Disney characters). All literacy activities relate to the particular theme chosen.

Writing has become an important part of the program, primarily because the children themselves started to draw and write about the stories they read and began creating their own stories. Journal writing has been incorporated into the program and children make daily entries. Depending on a child's individual stage of development, the journals might be made up primarily of original drawings, dictated stories, scribble writing, letter strings, invented spellings, conventional writing, or a combination of some or all of the above.

ASSESSING THE CHANGE PROCESS

We find it necessary and important to have continual feedback from the teachers to assess the program. We also seek to determine if new strategies should be added or established ones deleted. We evaluate the progress of children within this nontraditional learning context. In questionnaires, interviews, and informal discussions with their teachers, they have discussed their concerns, likes, and dislikes about the program. Such feedback provides us with important program assessment as well as with information about the change process. Following are some of the specific questions posed of teachers, and sample responses.

1. What were your concerns when confronted with making changes in your reading program?

   • I liked the way I had been doing things and felt the changes might be an imposition on what I presently had in place.
   • Although we were a part of the change process, I still felt that I was being pressured a bit.
   • I didn't feel I had the space in my classroom for the library corners we were to design in them.
   • I felt that the reading program that we had been using was important for skill development. I didn't see how I could fit in the new program and carry out the other program as well.
   • Since the new program did not have definitive data on its effects on the literacy development of children, I was concerned about how well my youngsters would do.

2. What strategies for change do you perceive as having been successful?

   • Change was fostered slowly and at a pace we could adjust to. Therefore, we didn't feel like it was being imposed.
   • Teachers' input was respected and accepted, and programs were changed as a result of our suggestions.
   • I liked the exposure to the professional books and workshops, in

and out of the district. This exposure made me feel like a true professional who was on the cutting edge of the latest strategies in literacy instruction.

- Collaborating with peers about successes and failures was an important strategy for change. We had partners in this endeavor; we were not alone. We learned from each other and taught others as well.
- The strong roles that the supervisor, school administrators, and university personnel played in the development of the new program meant that there was district support and interest, which was a motivating factor for most of us.
- The university personnel who participated in this change endeavor motivated me to return to school for a master's degree.

3. What did you like best about changes you made in your program?

- I enjoyed the opportunity to share good children's literature with my students and felt that the stories were valued and enjoyed by my class.
- The program motivated children to enjoy reading and want to read more. This was very exciting for me to see.
- I enjoyed the wide variety of literature materials for us to use, such as roll movies, felt stories, tape stories, etc.
- I was surprised and delighted that space could be made in my room for a library corner and that so many materials could fit into such a small area.
- The library corner became a place where children of all reading ability levels mingled together. There were children who had never interacted with each other before. It was a place where enthusiasm for books and literature activities became infectious.

4. What did you learn from participating in the program?

- The social family atmosphere created during the independent reading period was conducive to learning.
- I realized when I utilized independent reading periods that children were capable of cooperating and collaborating independently of me.
- In the atmosphere that provided choice of activity and with whom one worked, children of all ability levels chose to work together, a situation that did not normally occur.
- There seemed to be something for everyone during this independent reading period, more advanced children and slower children alike.

- This program made me more flexible and spontaneous and a facilitator of learning rather than always teaching.

5. What promise does this program have for your at-risk kindergartners?

- The variety of materials available, the ability to select activities to participate in and with whom you would like to work, motivated the children to voluntarily read and write.
- The social atmosphere improved the children's ability to work with each other in a cooperative fashion. They seemed to get more done together than they could do alone. There was great satisfaction in completed projects done together.
- I always believed that programs for at-risk children needed to be different from those used with children who were not classified as such. The children needed to be provided with the skills they were missing. I was concerned about imparting strategies only. I never realized that motivation, enthusiasm, and the desire to want to read and write was as important a skill as an initial consonant sound. Good programs are good for all children.
- My children came back to visit my room after they had moved on to first grade, to sit and read in the library corner, and to borrow books to take home. This verified that the program had been a success. When their first grade teacher commented, "I never had a group that were so eager to read as your kids," I knew for sure we had made a difference.
- The test scores improved significantly for the children who participated.

WHERE DOES THE DISTRICT GO FROM HERE?

Since the teachers now tend to view themselves as change agents and researchers, it is likely that the program will continue to reshape itself as new theories, philosophies, and strategies emerge in the field of literacy learning. Change is not viewed as something that is threatening or bothersome; rather, it is seen as a way of life. It is initiated by teachers, supervisors, administrators, and university personnel, all working together for a common goal: to improve instruction for the children in their district. It is carried out gradually, with appropriate resources for reading, in-service training, collaborative support groups, and supervisory personnel taking an active role.

Can change occur without some disruption? Not likely. But with appropriate strategies, change can occur in a professional and organized manner.

REFERENCES

Beckman, D. (1972). Interior space: The things of education. *National Elementary Principal*, *52*, 45–49.

Bissett, D. (1969). *The amount and effect of recreational reading in selected fifth grade classes*. Unpublished doctoral dissertation, Syracuse University.

Bloome, D. (1985). Reading as a social process. *Language Arts*, *62*, 134–141.

Bowman, M. (1981, April). *The effects of story structure questioning upon reading comprehension*. Paper presented at the annual meeting of the American Education Research Association, Los Angeles, CA.

Boyd, W. (Ed. and Trans.). (1962). *Rousseau's Emile*. New York: Teachers College, Columbia University.

Burroughs, M. (1972). *The simulation of verbal behavior in culturally disadvantaged three-year-olds*. Unpublished doctoral dissertation, Michigan State University.

Chomsky, C. (1972). Stages in language development and reading exposure. *Harvard Educational Review*, *42*(1), 1–34.

Clay, M. M. (1979). *Reading: The patterning of complex behavior*. Auckland, New Zealand: Heinemann Educational Books.

Coody, B. (1973). *Using literature with young children*. Dubuque, IA: Wm. C. Brown.

Cooper, L. R. (1991). Teachers as researchers. *The Kappa Delta Pi Record*, Summer, 115–117.

Dewey, J. (1913). *Interest and effort in education*. Boston, MA: Houghton Mifflin.

Durkin, D. (1974–1975). A six-year study of children who learned to read in school at the age of four. *Reading Research Quarterly*, *10*, 9–61.

Eastman, P. D. (1960). *Are you my mother?* New York: Random House.

Fletcher, S. S. F., & Welton, J. (Trans.). (1912). *Froebel's chief writings on education*. London: Edward Arnold.

Flood, J. (1977). Parental styles in reading episodes with young children. *The Reading Teacher*, *30*, 864–867.

Fodor, M. (1966). *The effect of systematic reading of stories on the language development of culturally deprived children*. Unpublished doctoral dissertation, Cornell University.

Gambrell, L., Pfeiffer, W., & Wilson, R. (1985). The effect of retelling upon comprehension and recall of text information. *Journal of Educational Research*, *78*, 216–220.

Gordon, C., & Braun, C. (1982). Story schemata: Metatextual aid to reading and writing. In J. Niles & L. Harris (Eds.), *New inquiries in reading research and instruction. Thirty-First Yearbook of the National Reading Conference* (pp. 262–268). Rochester, NY: National Reading Conference.

Heath, S. B. (1980). The functions and uses of literacy. *Journal of Communication, 30*, 123–133.

Hiebert, E. H. (1981). Developmental patterns and inter-relationships of preschool children's print awareness. *Reading Research Quarterly, 16*, 236–260.

Hoban, R. (1960). *Bread and jam for Frances.* New York: Harper & Row.

Huck, C. (1976). *Children's literature in the elementary school* (3rd edition). New York: Holt, Rinehart & Winston.

Huey, E. B. (1908). *The psychology and pedagogy of reading.* New York: Macmillan.

Irwin, O. (1960). Infant speech: Effect of systematic reading of stories. *Journal of Research in Reading, 3*, 187–190.

Mandler, J., & Johnson, M. (1977). Remembrance of things parsed: Story structure and recall. *Cognitive Psychology, 9*, 111–151.

Martinez, M. (1983). Exploring your children's comprehension through story time talk. *Language Arts, 60*, 202–209.

Moon, C., & Wells, C. G. (1979). The influence of the home on learning to read. *Journal of Research in Reading, 2*, 53–62.

Morrow, L. M. (1982). Relationships between literature programs, library corner designs and children's use of literature. *Journal of Educational Research, 75*, 339–344.

Morrow, L. M. (1984). Reading stories to young children: Effects of story structure and traditional questioning strategies on comprehension. *Journal of Reading Behavior, 16*, 273–288.

Morrow, L. M. (1985). Retelling stories: A strategy for improving children's comprehension, concept of story structure and oral language complexity. *Elementary School Journal, 85*, 647–661.

Morrow, L. M. (1987). *Promoting voluntary reading: The effects of an inner city program in summer day care centers.* Presentation at the Annual Conference of the College Reading Association, Baltimore, Maryland.

Morrow, L. M. (1988). Young children's responses to one-to-one readings in school settings. *Reading Research Quarterly, 23*, 89–107.

Morrow, L. M. (1989). *Developing literacy in early years: Helping children read and write.* New York: Prentice-Hall.

Morrow, L. M., O'Connor, E. M., & Smith, J. K. (1990). Effects of a story reading program on the literacy development of at-risk kindergarten children. *Journal of Reading Behavior, 22*, 255–276.

Morrow, L. M., & Weinstein, C. S. (1982). Increasing children's use of literature through program and physical design changes. *Elementary School Journal, 83*, 131–137.

Morrow, L. M., & Weinstein, C. S. (1986). Encouraging voluntary reading: The impact of a literature program on children's use of library centers. *Reading Research Quarterly, 21*, 330–346.

Myers, M. (1991). Issues in the restructuring of teacher preparation. In J. Flood, J. M. Jensen, D. Lapp, & J. R. Squire (Eds.), *Handbook of research on teaching the English language arts* (pp. 394–404). New York: Macmillan.

Ninio, A., & Bruner, J. (1978). The achievement and antecedents of labeling. *Journal of Child Language, 5*, 1–15.

Nixon, J. (1987). The teacher as researcher: Contradictions and continuities. *Peabody Journal of Education, 64,* 20–32.

O'Connor, E. M. (1989). *The effect of story reading as an instructional strategy on kindergarten children's literacy skill development.* Doctoral dissertation, Rutgers University, New Brunswick, NJ.

Piaget, J., & Inhelder, B. (1969). *The psychology of the child.* New York: Basic Books.

Roser, N., & Martinez, M. (1985). Roles adults play in pre-schoolers' response to literature. *Language Arts, 62,* 485–490.

Saracho, O. N., & Spodek, B. (1983). Preparing teachers for bilingual/multicultural classrooms. In O. N. Saracho & B. Spodek (Eds.), *Understanding the multicultural experience in early childhood education.* Washington, DC: National Association for the Education of Young Children.

Smith, F. (1978). *Understanding reading.* New York: Holt, Rinehart and Winston.

Spiegel, D., & Whaley, J. (1980, December). *Elevating comprehension skills by sensitizing students to structural aspects of narratives.* Paper presented at the annual meeting of the National Reading Conference, San Diego, CA.

Stein, N., & Glenn, C. (1979). An analysis of story comprehension in elementary school children. In R. Freedle (Ed.), *New directions in discourse processes* (Vol. 2) (pp. 53–120). Norwood, NJ: Ablex.

Sulzby, E. (1985). Children's emergent reading of favorite storybooks. *Reading Research Quarterly, 20,* 458–481.

Teale, W. (1984). Reading to young children: Its significance for literacy development. In H. Goelman, A. A. Oberg, & F. Smith (Eds.), *Awakening to literacy.* London: Heinemann Educational Books.

Teale, W. H., & Sulzby, E. (1987). Literacy acquisition in early childhood: The roles of access and mediation in storybook reading. In D. A. Wagner (Ed.), *The future of literacy in a changing world.* New York: Pergamon Press.

Vygotsky, L. S. (1981). The genesis of higher mental functions. In J. J. Wertsch (Ed.), *The concept of activity.* White Plains, NY: M. E. Sharpe.

Wells, G. (1982). Story reading and the development of symbolic skills. *Australian Journal of Reading, 5,* 142–152.

Wells, G. (1985). Preschool literacy-related activities and success in school. In D. R. Olson, N. Torrance, & A. Hildyard (Eds.), *Literacy, language, and learning: The nature and consequences of reading and writing* (pp. 229–255). Cambridge, England: Cambridge University Press.

Yaden, D. B., Jr., & McGee, L. M. (1983, December). *Reading as a meaning-seeking activity: What children's questions reveal.* Paper presented at the annual meeting of the National Reading Conference, Austin, TX.

CHAPTER 6

Reducing Retention and Learning Disability Placement Through Reading Recovery: An Educationally Sound, Cost-Effective Choice

CAROL A. LYONS
Ohio State University
JOETTA BEAVER
Upper Arlington City School District

The number of students classified as learning-disabled has grown from a relatively small population of American schoolchildren to a significant segment of today's student body. This has subsequently changed not only our schools' instructional support programs but our general education programs as well. As more and more students—especially primary children—acquire a learning disability label, these changes will become more accepted and permanent. There is substantial evidence that this phenomenon is already occurring. Recent figures from the U.S. Office of Special Education and Rehabilitative Services (1990) document that since 1976, the number of children between the ages of six and twenty-one classified as learning-disabled (LD) has more than doubled. These classifications are on the increase for several reasons.

First, school districts are required to label children as either learning-disabled (under the 1975 Education for All Handicapped Children Act [EHA]) or economically disadvantaged (under Chapter I of the 1965 Elementary and Secondary Education Act) in order to qualify for federally funded assistance. Second, federal guidelines do not present a clear definition of what a learning disability is or how to identify students as LD (Allington & McGill-Franzen, 1990), so the decision to classify or not classify a student is generally determined by a team of school psychologists and district personnel. Third, national and local laws require schools to meet the learning needs of remedial and/or mildly handicapped special education students. Fourth, school district administrators, influenced by state legislators and school boards demanding higher test scores, are increasingly supporting early identification of a learning disability. Once labeled, these children can be removed from the regular education classroom, thus increasing the chance of higher test scores for the school district (McGill-Franzen & Allington, 1993). Fifth, parents support earlier identification and labeling practices because they want their children to receive special services as soon as a learning problem becomes apparent. Finally, classroom teachers, feeling increased pressure to teach all first graders how to read, do not generally feel that they have the specialized training needed to teach the low-progress students effectively and therefore support early referral to the LD resource rooms (Martin, 1988).

Since the number of children classified as LD is increasing and students are being identified and labeled in preschool, kindergarten, and first grade, most often because of reading difficulty, it follows that more educational programs are needed to meet the demands of this growing population. Our present educational system, however, fails to address the needs of children who do not make average progress in reading. In order to remediate the increasing number of low-achieving students, public and private schools from preschool through the college level and private clinics throughout the United States are offering a variety of learning disability programs.

There is an extensive body of research, however, that documents the general ineffectiveness of these programs (Gartner & Lipsky, 1987; Slavin & Madden, 1989; Walmsley & Allington, this volume). Furthermore, the research suggests that once elementary students are placed in instructional support programs, most often remedial (Chapter I) or special education (learning disability), they generally remain on the remedial track for a lifetime, rarely outgrowing their disability (Allington & McGill-Franzen, 1989).

Continuing to identify and place children who are having difficulty learning to read in instructional support programs is not the answer to helping these students become literate. This practice is both unfair and counterproductive. Our schools are becoming breeding grounds for failing students, especially students who are failing to learn how to read. American educators must find a way to change the trend of early identification and labeling of children as learning-disabled.

This chapter describes a program, Reading Recovery (RR), that accomplishes this goal and documents the effect of the program in two school districts. What the data reveal is that Reading Recovery significantly reduces the number of first grade students assigned to learning disability supplemental programs, and it reduces the number of students retained.

READING RECOVERY

A Brief Description

Reading Recovery, developed in New Zealand by clinical child psychologist Marie M. Clay, is an early intervention program designed to reduce first grade reading failure. The program enables the lowest-achieving students, generally the bottom twenty percent of a first-grade classroom, to catch up to the average readers in their respective first grade and continue to learn with regular classroom reading instruction. Teachers enroll in a year-long graduate course to learn the theories of learning, cognition, and literacy that form the foundation for the principles and techniques used in RR. The specially trained teachers develop skills in teaching the low-progress students how to become strategic, independent learners through weekly demonstration lessons. These live "behind-the-glass" demonstration lessons, led by an experienced teacher leader, provide teachers with opportunities to construct, interpret, and apply theories of literacy learning. Throughout the year, teachers develop competency and skill in teaching within a student's "zone of proximal development" (Vygotsky, 1978). Teachers learn how to develop a sequence of reading and writing experiences with gradually diminishing contributions of the teacher and growing contributions of the students.

Through daily thirty-minute lessons, students learn how to perform independently the same reading and writing tasks that they needed help accomplishing the previous day. This cumulative experience enables the students to learn how to construct a repertoire of strategies (e.g., self-monitoring, searching for additional cues, cross-checking one source of information with another, and self-correcting) that are used in flexible ways (Lyons, Pinnell, & DeFord, 1993; Pinnell, 1989; Pinnell, Fried, & Estice, 1990).

First Implementation of Reading Recovery in the U.S.: The Ohio Story

The RR program was first implemented in the United States in 1984–1985 in Columbus, Ohio. That year, seven Columbus teachers, two Ohio State University (OSU) faculty members, and three OSU graduate students were trained to implement the program by Professor Marie Clay and Barbara Watson, the National Director of the New Zealand program. Data from the Columbus pilot study revealed that 67 percent of the pupils who completed the program were "discontinued," reading at average reading levels. Based on these impressive results, the Ohio General Assembly appropriated $1.2 million to initiate a statewide RR program. This resulted in substantial growth in the number of teachers trained and students served (see Table 6.1).

The major reason for the continued expansion of RR throughout Ohio was the impressive research results—just over 84 percent of the 15,663 Ohio first grade pupils who completed the Reading Recovery program reached the average reading level of their first grade classrooms.

Implementation of Reading Recovery Throughout the United States

News of the research results documenting the effectiveness of the RR program spread across the United States. In a congressionally mandated study aimed at analyzing beginning reading instruction, Adams (1990) singled out RR as exemplary in teaching at-risk first graders to read. In a comprehensive study comparing RR to four other methods used to correct reading difficulties among first graders, RR was the only treatment for which there was a significant difference on four measures, Text Reading Level, Dictation Assessment Task, Woodcock Reading Mastery, and Gates

TABLE 6.1. State of Ohio Reading Recovery program

	1986-87	1987-88	1988-89	1989-90	1990-91	Total
School Districts	122	143	255	272	301	301
RR Teachers	263	531	755	832	917	917
Program Students*	1,341	2,648	3,344	3,994	4,336	15,663
Students Discontinued**	79%	86%	83%	85%	89%	84.4%

* Program students are defined as completing 60 lessons or discontinued prior to 60 lessons.
** Released from RR upon reaching the average level of the class in reading.

MacGinitie, and the only intervention program indicating lasting effects (Pinnell, Lyons, DeFord, Bryk, & Seltzer, 1994). Slavin (1987) identified RR as one of the most successful reading programs for Chapter I pupils, especially those students most at risk: the lowest 20 percent in reading ability. The research data were so convincing that RR was identified as an exemplary program by the National Diffusion Network (NDN), an arm of the U.S. Department of Education charged to investigate educational programs that work. The program has been an NDN-approved program since 1987.

From 1984 through 1988, the faculty at OSU prepared Ohio and out-of-state teacher leaders to return to their local school districts to implement the RR program. However, it became obvious that the OSU faculty could not keep up with the growing demand from school districts throughout the country that wanted teacher leader training. Additional university-based training sites needed to be established. Therefore, with support and guidance from Clay, the faculty at OSU established the first course for preparing trainers of teacher leaders—a year-long postdoctoral sequence. In 1993, twenty universities throughout the United States offered teacher leader training. By 1994, the RR program had been implemented in forty-seven states.

National data documenting the percentage of low-achieving children reaching the average reading level in their respective first grade classrooms are presented in Table 6.2. These data are especially impressive because they document the program's effectiveness in helping students achieve average reading levels in a variety of communities.

TABLE 6.2. National Reading Recovery Program statistics

	1987-88	1988-89	1989-90	1990-91
RR Teacher Leaders	44	54	64	99
RR Teachers	531	808	1,195	1,982
Program Students*	2,648	3,639	5,678	9,486
Students Discontinued**	86%	83%	84%	87%

* Program students are defined as completing 60 lessons or discontinued prior to 60 lessons.
** Released from RR upon reaching the average level of the class in reading.

Reading Recovery Children Further
Classified as Learning-Disabled

In the state of Ohio, a considerable number of the low-achieving first grade students are classified as learning-disabled (LD) prior to entering first grade by interdisciplinary teams of school professionals and/or psychologists and physicians practicing in private clinics (Lyons, 1991a). School district personnel generally place these LD first graders on a waiting list and assign them to receive special instruction in the learning-disability resource room as space becomes available.

Since the RR program identifies the lowest achievers in reading, excluding no one, there are a considerable number of these students selected to receive RR instruction at the beginning of first grade. Research (Lyons, 1989) comparing two groups of Ohio first grade RR students (LD and not LD) revealed that the group identified as learning-disabled tended to rely on visual cues and to ignore supporting meaningful language structures, while the group not identified as learning-disabled tended to overrely on meaning and language structure and underemphasize visual cues. In an average of less than thirteen weeks of RR instruction, a substantial majority of both groups had been released from the RR program using meaning, structural, and visual/auditory information in an integrated way. The RR students considered learning-disabled at the beginning of the school year were now reading at a level comparable to their classmates. The data further suggested that a student's learning disability may be the result of inadequate instruction in the LD program (Lyons, 1991b). For instance, the instructional program one LD student received in kindergarten and summer school overemphasized drill in letter/sound correspondence and visual/auditory skills. The exclusive drill on isolated letters and words established a context that fostered the student's learning disability (Clay, 1987). Through intensive one-to-one support in the RR program, the student lost his label and returned to the classroom reading with the average group. Today this fifth grader is reading with the high average readers in the classroom.

In summary, five years of research has documented that the RR program:

- Reduces the number of low-progress first grade students classified as learning-disabled in the State of Ohio
- Prevents low-progress students from acquiring a learning disability
- Enables educators to identify first grade low-achieving students who have more severe learning problems and may require specialized instruction

The RR program not only had an effect on the identification and selection of first grade students for LD programs, it also had an impact on the assessment and teaching practices in Chapter I, kindergarten, and first grade programs throughout the state.

The following section describes how the RR program created district-wide reforms and unified instructional support and classroom instruction in one suburban district of Ohio.

READING RECOVERY IN THE UPPER
ARLINGTON CITY SCHOOL DISTRICT

Profile of the District

Upper Arlington is an upper-middle-class, suburban, residential community located northwest of Columbus, Ohio. The majority of its 37,000 residents are college-oriented, business, and professional people. The community has a history of continued support and commitment to the local schools. Many new residents are attracted to the community because of its long-standing reputation for having an excellent school system.

Approximately 2400 children are enrolled in the Upper Arlington City school district's five elementary schools. The remaining students are enrolled in two middle schools or the high school. There is a low student mobility rate. Approximately 80 to 85 percent of the students who begin school there graduate from Upper Arlington High School.

The school district, rated first among the sixteen Columbus-area suburban school districts in providing students (kindergarten through grade 12) with a quality education (Cook, Foster, & Pienkny-Zakin, 1991), has received national visibility (Viadero, 1990) and been recognized for providing leadership in developing and initiating excellent programs (Burton, 1991; Tierney, Carter, & Desai, 1991). Upper Arlington High School was selected as a "high school of the future" by the Association for Supervision and Curriculum Development and along with both middle schools and four elementary schools has been recognized nationally as an exemplary school by the U.S. Department of Education.

Implementation of Reading Recovery

Even though the majority of students in Upper Arlington become proficient readers in the elementary grades, approximately one out of every eight youngsters experiences some difficulty in learning to read in first grade. In the past, district administrators and teachers generally attributed the low progress of these students to the notion that they were not developmentally ready to learn to read and needed more time to mature before providing additional support or remediation. Close examination of the low-achieving students' progress, however, revealed that these students seldom caught up to their peers. In fact, they often failed to develop adequate reading and writing strategies and were destined to continue to receive supplemental help in Chapter I or learning disability tutoring programs throughout the elementary school years.

Concern for the welfare of these students by the teaching staff led to the establishment of a committee to examine effective literacy programs. The logical place to begin this type of examination was in New Zealand, because this small country had the highest literacy rate in the world. Moreover, the New Zealand educational system had implemented an intervention program, Reading Recovery, that had successfully enabled the bottom 20 percent of the New Zealand primary children to catch up to their peers and continue to learn to read with regular classroom instruction.

Needless to say, when the Upper Arlington City school district administrators and staff heard that the New Zealand RR program would be available at OSU, they made a commitment to send a teacher for Reading Recovery teacher leader training. They understood that the following year this trained teacher leader would return to their school district to teach a group of teachers how to implement the program. Once trained, the teachers would each be able to teach approximately eight to ten low-achieving first graders how to read.

District administrators and teachers believed that by implementing the RR program in the elementary schools, the students who generally "fall between the cracks" would be identified and helped. The program seemed to have the potential for reducing the number of first grade students retained or needing long-term remedial support in Chapter I and learning-disability tutoring programs. Most importantly, the low-achieving first graders would gain the confidence and feelings of pride that all youngsters need to develop in order to function as successful learners.

Reading Recovery in Upper Arlington

Five years of RR implementation results show that the Upper Arlington City school district administrators made a wise decision. A total of 157 program children were released from the RR program reading at average levels across the five years of implementation; this represents 76 percent of the students identified as at risk of failing to learn how to read in first grade. The total number of RR students served and discontinued has increased proportionately over this five-year period.

Examination of the data displayed in Table 6.3 reveals that the number of students discontinued from the program increased across time; however, there was a decrease in the percentage of students discontinued from the program in 1991. One reason for this decrease was that seven RR teachers were in their first year of training. These teachers had limited experiences in working with the lowest readers in the class and thus were new to learning how to make the most powerful teaching decisions to support accelerative growth. Recent research suggests that the more experiences RR teachers have teaching low-progress students, the greater their ability to make judicious instructional decisions in an efficient manner (Lyons, Pinnell, & DeFord, 1993). Another reason for this decrease in the number of students released from the RR program was that for the past two years, the average band in text reading level in the Upper Arlington schools was proportionately higher than the state average band. The Upper Arlington average band was determined by calculating the mean on the text reading level for a group of 150 randomly selected first grade students throughout the district. The average band was considered to be + or − .5 standard deviations above and below the mean. Twelve Upper Arlington RR students considered *not* discontinued because they did not fall within the district average band would have been considered discontinued if the state average band had been used.

TABLE 6.3. Upper Arlington Reading Recovery program

	1986-87	1987-88	1988-89	1989-90	1990-91	Total
Grade 1 Enrollment	340	369	404	391	406	1,910
Program Students	22 (6%)	36 (10%)	41 (10%)	42 (11%)	66 (16%)	207 (11%)
RR Teachers	5	5	6	6	11	11
Students Discontinued*	16 (73%)	27 (75%)	33 (80%)	35 (83%)	46 (70%)	157 (76%)

* Students are discontinued based on the district average band; figures reported are based on UA average band in text reading (1989-90, levels 20-24; 1990-91, levels 20-26).

Impact of the Reading Recovery Program on Learning-Disability Referrals. There has also been an impact of RR on the number of students classified as learning-disabled by interdisciplinary teams of school personnel using state and district criteria for identification.

As reported in Table 6.4, there has been a decrease in the number of RR program students further classified as LD. This can generally be attributed to the increased access these children have to more effective teaching. These data suggest that the RR program has the potential to reduce the number of students diagnosed as LD in the primary grades, thus enabling the learning disability program to address the needs of students with more severe learning problems. Furthermore, in the past five years, ten of the forty RR students who were identified and served in the LD program were not placed there because of reading difficulties, and one student was phased out of the LD program at the end of fourth grade. These data suggest that for these ten students, the RR program was effective in helping them develop proficient reading behaviors.

Impact of Reading Recovery on Chapter I and Retention. Upper Arlington's policy of selection of children for participation in the program reflects the New Zealand policy. The RR program serves the very lowest

TABLE 6.4. Upper Arlington School District Reading Recovery students further classified as LD

	1986-87	1987-88	1988-89	1989-90	1990-91	Total
RR Program Students*	22	36	41	42	66	207
RR Students Classified LD**	8 (36%)	16 (44%)	12 (29%)	8 (19%)	6 (9%)	40 (19%)

* Program students are defined as completing 60 lessons or discontinued prior to 60 lessons.
**RR students identified using district and state criteria as learning-disabled. No student received both programs at the same time. RR was always implemented prior to the LD program except in a few cases. Less than .05% of the children from the total population of first grade students over a 5-year period were identified to receive LD services rather than RR services prior to kindergarten and/or first grade.

children first. That is, those children identified by their kindergarten and first grade teachers as most in need of individual help and who score the lowest on the Diagnostic Survey (Clay, 1985) are placed in RR in September. The remaining low-progress students are placed in first grade Chapter I groups.

Recently the Chapter I teachers piloted a small group literacy program for students waiting to be served in RR. Utilizing practices borrowed from specific instructional techniques used in RR (e.g., reading and writing whole text and close observation of students' literacy behaviors), teachers developed a thirty-minute Chapter I lesson framework. Four days per week, during the first ten minutes of the lesson, the teacher took a running record of one student reading individually while the other students read in small groups. Ten minutes was devoted to either shared reading or shared writing experiences and during the last ten minutes students wrote in a journal. On the fifth day, the group participated in a literature extension activity. Students took one or two books home every day to read to their parents.

The instructional approaches used by the Chapter I teachers helped some children orchestrate a range of strategies in reading that enabled them to develop what Clay (1991) refers to as a "self-extending system." The majority of these students were phased out of Chapter I at the end of the year. It is important to note, however, that students with the greatest needs were removed from the Chapter I group or first grade classroom throughout the year and received RR instruction as students were released from the RR program. Due to the success of the first grade pilot program, the lesson format is now used with second grade Chapter I groups as well. Over a three-year period, a total of 330 (5%) of the grade 2 through 5 students qualified and were served in Chapter I classes. Of these 330 students, 186 (56%) were second graders, 97 (29%) were third graders, 38 (12%) fourth graders, and 9 (3%) fifth graders, reflecting a steady decrease in the number of students needing Chapter I services over time.

The RR program has not only reduced the number of Chapter I and learning-disability referrals; it has also reduced the number of children retained in first grade. Prior to RR, 2.5 percent of the first graders were retained compared to .7 percent of first graders retained after RR had been implemented. As a result of the RR program and good classroom instruction, less than 1 percent of the first grade students have been retained in first grade during the five years RR has been implemented in the district.

Impact of Reading Recovery on Primary Assessment Practices. During the first two years of RR implementation, the RR teacher leader conducted in-service sessions for all kindergarten, first grade, special education, and

Chapter I teachers. Teachers were introduced to four assessments (concepts of print, writing vocabulary, sentence dictation, and text reading) used in the RR program. These measures, part of the Diagnostic Survey (Clay, 1985), are designed to describe changes during the emergent stages of reading and writing. In addition to learning how to administer and interpret the information revealed in the four measures, the teachers observed RR lessons. The quarterly in-service sessions and observations of RR lessons and continued support from the teacher leader and RR teachers in each elementary building enabled the regular education and support teachers to understand, construct, and use specific language to describe, analyze, and assess literacy behaviors of students in their classrooms. As these teachers continued to use these informal assessment measures, their focus shifted from a discussion of what specific children didn't know or couldn't do to what these same children knew and could do.

Two years after RR was implemented, the first grade teachers piloted a preschool reading and writing survey to capture the literacy behaviors of students prior to entering first grade. This survey included the writing vocabulary, sentence dictation, and text reading measures adapted from the Diagnostic Survey (Clay, 1985). It enabled teachers to determine students' strengths and provide developmentally appropriate experiences as soon as the children started school. The teachers were also able to better determine which students would most likely need RR screening. The survey revealed differences in first grade entrants' abilities and sensitized teachers to literacy experiences specific children needed and did not need to become literate.

The insights the first grade teachers gained in developing and using the preschool reading and writing survey prompted the formation of an educational committee comprised of kindergarten through second grade teachers in each elementary building. This committee created a developmental primary assessment, which includes observation instruments to be used in kindergarten, first, and second grade. The teachers constructed a continuum of descriptors to portray the developmental stages of emergent readers and writers in order to monitor each student's literacy devel-opment and to provide goals and performance standards. Procedures for a leveled text reading assessment and a holistic writing assessment were developed for kindergarten through second grade and kept in the student Literacy Development File (LDF). The LDF was designed to capture a student's growth in reading (documented in running records of text reading) and writing (documented in writing samples). The samples of students' work helped teachers honor growth and development over time, provide developmentally appropriate instruction, share progress with students and parents, and identify students in need of additional literacy support.

Impact of Reading Recovery in the Primary Classrooms. Two major changes occurred as a result of introducing RR into the school system. First, teacher perceptions of what low-achieving students could do changed dramatically. In the past, teachers' experiences with low-progress students demonstrated that the low achievers generally did not catch up to their peers. Students who fell behind the class in first grade continued to fall further behind as they progressed through the grades. After three years of RR implementation, however, these perceptions were changed. The primary teachers are now convinced that the lowest-achieving first graders can make accelerative progress in reading and writing. Through one-to-one instruction, provided in the RR program, these children can develop a self-improving system that enables them to benefit from regular classroom instruction.

The second major change that has occurred as a result of RR is the use of RR leveled books and techniques in the reading programs in kindergarten, first, and second grade. Although teachers had used children's literature and had read aloud to children on a regular basis, they now began to deliberately apply concepts and principles learned from the in-service sessions provided by the RR teacher leader. The assessment tools and RR observation techniques helped teachers to evaluate and broaden their understanding of students' literacy behaviors and the reading and writing processes. The teachers used children's literature as a springboard for shared reading and writing. While children were engaged in independent reading and/or writing, the teachers routinely gave attention via one-to-one conferencing, occasionally taking a running record of text reading and doing some intervention teaching. The changes in teaching practices have been positive and significant.

Aggregate pretest data on the preschool reading and writing survey and the *Diagnostic Survey* (Clay, 1985) revealed a substantial increase in beginning literacy scores. For example, across a three-year period, the first grade end-of-year average text reading level increased from level 18 (beginning second grade) to level 22 (beginning third grade). Administrators and teachers agreed that primary students' growth in literacy is due to classroom teachers' increased understanding and ability to provide effective literacy instruction in the classroom setting. This knowledge was largely gained in the in-service sessions provided by the RR teacher leader.

District administrators and teachers also attributed the low retention rate in first grade and the reduced number of students in the upper grades requiring additional support services in LD or Chapter I classes during the past five years to the influence of the RR program. They generally acknowledge that these changes would not have occurred if RR had not been introduced.

The results of a survey of parents, teachers, and principals documents the extent of this support throughout the five elementary schools in the Upper Arlington City school district. All teacher respondents rated RR as a "very good program," as did the vast majority of parents (87%) and principals (4 of 5).

The positive responses from this survey along with longitudinal data evaluating them clearly indicate a continuing support for the program. Dr. John Sonedecker, the Upper Arlington City school district assistant superintendent, recently stated, "The Reading Recovery program has added an important dimension to our district's early educational opportunities for children as well as enhanced the classroom teaching practices. Reading Recovery provides a safety net for students having difficulty with reading in their early years of schooling and is well worth the investment towards each child's success in the future." The reduction in retentions in grade and referrals to Chapter I and LD special education programs represent the payoff for an investment in RR. Few districts conduct cost-benefit analyses of any interventions, but some do.

READING RECOVERY IN THE
LANCASTER CITY SCHOOL DISTRICT

Profile of the District

A cost-comparison analysis for first grade learning-disability programs, Reading Recovery, and first grade retention in one urban school district reveals that RR saves the school money. Lancaster, Ohio, is a working, middle-class city of 34,507 located thirty miles southeast of Columbus, Ohio. Recently, 6,666 students were enrolled in the Lancaster City schools. There is one senior high school, one ninth-grade school, two junior high schools, and nine elementary schools in this school district. Approximately 80 percent of the students graduate from high school, and 40 percent of the graduates attend college or seek advanced schooling. The dropout rate is 10 percent in grades 10 through 12; half of those who drop out return to complete the General Education Degree (GED) within five years. Four of the nine elementary schools have a high mobility rate; however, approximately 50 percent of those families who move stay within the Lancaster school district.

Reading Recovery's Impact in the Lancaster City School District

Impact of Reading Recovery on Retention. Although research has argued convincingly that retention has no long-term positive effect on achievement or social development, over 2.4 million students are retained annually in the United States (Shepard & Smith, 1990). If a child is to be retained, educators generally agree that it is best to hold him or her back in kindergarten or first grade (Shultz, 1989). Furthermore, the major reason students are retained in first grade is poor reading skills (Smith & Shepard, 1987). Thus, it stands to reason that if failing first graders were taught to read, the number of students retained in first grade would decrease. An examination of the first grade retention data for the Lancaster schools prior to and after the RR program was implemented supports this argument.

As reported in Table 6.5, since RR was implemented, the percentage of students retained in first grade has been reduced by half. This reduction in the percentage of primary students retained in first grade has not only prevented approximately one-half of the lowest-achieving readers from a lifetime of psychological trauma associated with school failure, it has also saved the school district a considerable sum of money. For example, in the Lancaster school district, the average annual per pupil cost of instruction is $3,853. This figure is based on the average annual teacher salary cost of instruction for one student for 5.5 hours per day, 182 days per year. Utilizing this formula, it is estimated that retaining 76 children in first grade during the three years prior to RR cost the district an additional $292,828.

The annual teacher salary cost of RR instruction for one student for thirty minutes per day, five months per year is $1,708. If the seventy-six

TABLE 6.5. Students Retained in Grade 1 Prior to and after Reading Recovery in Lancaster Schools

	1984-87 (3 yrs) Prior to RR Implementation	1987–91 (4 yrs) After Partial, Then Full Implementation*
Grade 1 Enrollment	1,772	2,123
Total Number of Students Retained	76	63
Percent Retained	4.3%	2.9%

*Partial implementation (1987-88): 8% of the first grade population was served by 9 RR teachers (1 in each of 9 elementary schools); full implementation (1988–91): 16% of the first grade population served in 1988–89, and 20% in 1989–91, by 15 RR teachers (1-2 in each of the 9 elementary schools).

TABLE 6.6. Cost-comparison analysis for grade 1 intervention programs and retention in Lancaster Schools

Intervention	Annual Per Pupil Cost	Average Years in Program	Classroom Time per Year (182 days)	Total Cost
Retention (First Grade)	$3,853	1	1,001 hrs*	$3,853
Special Education (LD)	$2,275	4	455 hrs**	$9,100
Reading Recovery	$1,708	5 months	30 hrs***	$1,708

*Annual teacher salary cost of instruction for one child retained in first grade who received 5.5 hours of instruction per day, 182 days per year.
**Annual teacher salary cost of instruction for one student classified as LD taught in pullout resource room program for 2.5 hours per day, 182 days per year.
***Annual teacher salary cost of Reading Recovery instruction for one student for 30 minutes per day, 5 months per year.

students had been served by the RR program, the school district would have spent $129,808. But this expenditure represents a savings compared to retaining the students ($163,020). This analysis of the relative costs of RR versus the costs of first grade retention provides convincing evidence that RR is cost-effective (see Table 6.6).

Impact of Reading Recovery on Learning-Disability Placement. When the RR program was first introduced into the Lancaster Schools, district administrators agreed that *every* first grade child who was in the twentieth percentile in reading and/or language-related areas, as determined by teacher judgment and a standardized test, would be eligible to receive the program. Thus students who were classified as learning-disabled were provided RR services prior to placement in LD classrooms. After full implementation of the program, the number of students classified as learning-disabled was reduced by two-thirds (see Table 6.7).

In the three years prior to full implementation of RR, 32 first grade students were classified as learning-disabled and placed in LD classrooms at the end of first grade or during the first few months of second grade. During the three years after RR was implemented in the nine elementary schools, only ten first grade students were classified as LD. This dramatic reduction prompted district administrators to establish RR as a prevention program for all first grade students at risk of reading failure, including children thought to be learning-disabled. In establishing RR as a prevention program, the Lancaster school district has dramatically reduced the number of students incorrectly and unnecessarily diagnosed and labeled LD and placed in costly and ineffective programs.

A very conservative estimate of per pupil cost for educating one LD student is $2,275 per year. This figure is based on the annual teacher salary cost of instruction for one student taught in a pullout resource room for 2.5 hours per day, 182 days per year. In the Lancaster city schools, students generally remain in the elementary LD programs for an average of four years. Thus the school district has spent approximately $9,100 to educate one LD student for four years ($2,275 × 4 years), or $291,200 to educate 32 students over a four-year period.

As reported earlier, the per pupil cost for RR is $1,708 per year. If the 32 students had received RR, the district would have spent $54,656. This figure represents a one-time expenditure because the program is temporary and students are released when they can learn to read with regular classroom instruction. In the past four years, the average amount of time it took to discontinue RR students in Lancaster was five months. It is conceivable that the school district could have saved a total of $236,544 ($291,200 − $54,656) if the program had been implemented three years earlier.

Ann Decker, who prior to becoming an RR teacher leader for the Lancaster city schools was a learning-disability consultant for the Ohio Depart-

TABLE 6.7. First grade students (aged 6 & 7 yrs) classified as LD in Lancaster City Schools

	1985–88 Prior to Full RR Implementation	1988–91 After Full Implementation
Grade 1 Enrollment	1,781	1,573
Number Placed in LD Classrooms	32 (1.8%)	10 (.63%)

ment of Education Division of Special Education for three years and the supervisor of learning-disability programs in the Lancaster city schools for ten years, sums up the impact of the program this way:

> The cost effectiveness of the Reading Recovery program is very clear when compared to the long-term remedial programs. Placing children in the Reading Recovery program for 15–20 weeks of one-to-one intervention is far less expensive than placing them in a special education program for one year. Most children who end up in a special education program remain there for the duration of the school experience. The frustration of working with the learning disability programs in Lancaster and at the Ohio Department of Special Education proved to me that LD placement did not remediate the child's learning problems and equip him/her to go back into the regular education setting at grade level expectancy. Most educators don't realize that the original goal of LD programs was the same as the Reading Recovery program: to accelerate children to average levels in their class so that they could be dismissed from the special class. Instead, LD has become a "terminal" placement. Reading Recovery provided a hope that a high percentage of the "LD" students could be given the instruction they needed before they became failures. Administrators in the Lancaster City Schools realized that RR had the potential for reducing the number of LD referrals and retentions and therefore they were committed to making the program available to at least 20% of first-grade children. This goal was achieved in a three-year period. During the 1990–91 academic year, 20% of the first graders (including potential LD students) received a full Reading Recovery program and 88% of those children were discontinued reading with the average students in their class. In my opinion, however, you can never put a price tag on the real benefits of Reading Recovery. The success of the children, the joy of their parents, the improved instruction in regular primary classrooms . . . these are the real benefits of Reading Recovery in Lancaster and these benefits cannot be measured by dollars and cents.

CONCLUSION

Longitudinal program evaluation data clearly demonstrate that when school district administrators choose to implement the RR program, they can expect significant reductions in the number of first grade students retained and placed in learning-disability or remedial programs. Furthermore, a cost-benefit analysis comparing RR with alternative interventions designed to help the lowest-achieving first grade readers suggests that the school district will also save a considerable sum of money by:

- Reducing the number of first grade retentions
- Avoiding special education testing and diagnostic practices, which generally lead to misclassification and placement of children in LD programs
- Reducing the number of students assigned to long-term remedial reading programs

The Reading Recovery program is an educationally sound and cost-effective intervention program that provides primary students once considered reading failures with opportunities to enjoy a lifetime of school success and save the American taxpayers millions of dollars in the process (Dyer, 1992).

Dr. John Sondecker, assistant superintendent of schools for Upper Arlington, recently commented, "Reading Recovery has had a positive effect on our entire educational system . . . teachers, parents, and children. It has been the catalyst for unifying our instructional support programs and prompted schoolwide reforms. It is definitely a cost-effective preventive intervention program that our school district cannot afford to do without."

Acknowledgment: The authors gratefully acknowledge the assistance of Ann Decker for the Lancaster City school district data collection and analyses.

REFERENCES

Adams, M. (1990). *Beginning to read: Thinking and learning about print.* Cambridge, MA: MIT Press.

Allington, R. L., & McGill-Franzen, A. (1989). School response to reading failure: Instruction for Chapter I and special education students in grades two, four and six. *Elementary School Journal, 89,* 529–542.

Allington, R. L., & McGill-Franzen, A. (1990). Different programs, indifferent instruction. In D. Lipsky & A. Gartner (Eds.), *Beyond separate education: Quality education for all* (pp. 75–94). Baltimore, MD: Paul Brookes Publisher.

Burton, F. (1991). Reflections on designing a K–2 whole language curriculum: Implications for administrators and policy makers. In K. Goodman, W. Hood, & Y. Goodman (Eds.), *Organizing for whole language* (pp. 364–372). Portsmouth, NH: Heinemann.

Clay, M. M. (1985). *The early detection of reading difficulties.* Auckland, New Zealand: Heinemann.

Clay, M. M. (1987). Learning to be learning disabled. *New Zealand Journal of Educational Studies, 22,* 155–173.

Clay, M. M. (1991). *Becoming literate: The construction of inner control.* Portsmouth, NH: Heinemann.

Cook, H., Foster, E. , & Pienkny-Zakin, L. (1991). Rating the suburban schools. *Columbus Monthly, 17,* 28–40.

Dyer, P. C. (1992). Reading Recovery: A cost-effectiveness and educational-outcomes analysis. *Spectrum, 10,* 10–19.

Gartner, A., & Lipsky, D. (1987). Beyond special education: Toward a quality system for all students. *Harvard Educational Review, 57,* 368–395.

Lyons, C. A. (1989). Reading Recovery: A preventative for mislabeling young "at-risk" learners. *Urban Education, 24,* 125–139.

Lyons, C. A. (1991a). Reading Recovery: A viable prevention to learning disability. *Reading Horizons, 31,* 384–408.

Lyons, C. A. (1991b). Conversations about informal assessment procedures designed to inform instruction of a first grader identified as learning disabled. In J. Roderick (Ed.), *Context-responsive approaches for assessing children's language* (pp. 86–99). Illinois: National Conference on Research in English/ National Council of Teachers of English.

Lyons, C. A., Pinnell, G. S., & DeFord, D. E. (1993). *Partners in learning: Teachers and children in Reading Recovery.* New York: Teachers College Press.

Martin, A. (1988). Teachers and teaching. *Harvard Educational Review, 58,* 488–501.

McGill-Franzen, A., & Allington, R. L. (1993). Flunk 'em or get them classified: The contamination of primary grade accountability data. *Educational Researcher, 22,* 19–22.

Pinnell, G. S. (1989). Reading Recovery: Helping at-risk children learn to read. *Elementary School Journal, 90,* 161–183.

Pinnell, G. S., Fried, M. D., & Estice, R. M. (1990). Reading Recovery: Learning how to make a difference. *The Reading Teacher, 43,* 282–295.

Pinnell, G. S., Lyons, C. A., DeFord, D. E., Bryk, A. S., & Seltzer, M. (1994). Comparing instructional models for the literacy education of high risk first graders. *Reading Research Quarterly, 29,* 8–38.

Shepard, L. A., & Smith, M. L. (1990). Synthesis of research on grade retention. *Educational Leadership, 47,* 84–88.

Shultz, T. (1989). Testing and retention of young children: Moving from controversy to reform. *Phi Delta Kappan, 71,* 125–129.

Slavin, R. E. (1987). Making Chapter I make a difference. *Phi Delta Kappan, 69,* 110–119.

Slavin, R. E., & Madden, N. A. (1989). What works for students at risk: A research synthesis. *Educational Leadership, 67,* 4–13.

Smith, M. L., & Shepard, L. A. (1987). What doesn't work: Explaining policies of retention in the early grades. *Phi Delta Kappan, 69,* 129–134.

Tierney, R. J., Carter, M., & Desai, L. (1991). *Portfolios in the reading/writing classroom*. Norwood, MA: Christopher Gordon.

U.S. Office of Special Education and Rehabilitative Services. (1990). *Twelfth Annual Report to Congress on the Implementation of the Education of the Handicapped Act* (pp. 33–34). Washington, DC: U.S. Department of Education.

Viadero, D. (1990). New Zealand import: An effective, but costly, way to teach reading. *Education Week, 10*, 11.

Vygotsky, L. S. (1978). *Mind in society*. Cambridge, MA: Harvard University Press.

CHAPTER 7

Eliminating Ability Grouping and Reducing Failure in the Primary Grades

DOROTHY P. HALL
CONNIE PREVATTE
Winston Salem/Forsyth, NC Schools
PATRICIA M. CUNNINGHAM
Wake Forest University

One pervasive feature of most first grade reading instruction has been the presence of three or four within-class ability groups. Children were generally placed in these groups during the second month of first grade and usually remain in the same group for the rest of the school year—and often for the rest of their elementary school years (Hiebert, 1983; Juel, 1988; Shannon, 1985). Being placed in a bottom group can hinder reading development. For example, Allington (1983) has demonstrated that the reading instruction given to children in the bottom group is qualitatively different from that provided to average and high groups. First grade teachers recognize how different children are when they enter first grade and use ability grouping as a way of organizing to meet the needs of a diverse first grade population. Unfortunately, children who are placed in the bottom group almost never achieve grade-level reading and writing skills. In addition to almost ensuring failure for the bottom-group children, there is another major problem with ability grouping: In order to work with one group of children, the teacher must provide some quiet "seat work" to occupy the children she is not working with. There is no evidence that completing worksheets increases reading achievement; thus in many classrooms children have been spending two-thirds of their reading instructional time in activities not apt to increase their reading and writing abilities (Allington, 1983). Ability grouping, as a response to the differences of the children, is not a very good solution.

In this chapter, we will describe a three-year, two-school effort to meet the needs of a diverse population of children without assigning them to any ability groups. We will go back and forth between the two schools as we discuss the changes. The changes evolved over time and were different depending upon the needs of each school. The goal in both schools was to eliminate ability grouping and substantially reduce reading failure in the primary grades.

CLEMMONS ELEMENTARY SCHOOL

Clemmons Elementary School is a large, suburban elementary school in Winston-Salem/Forsyth County, North Carolina. The student population is diverse. Most students come from homes surrounding the school. The remaining students are bussed from the inner city. Twenty percent of the students receive free or reduced-price lunches. Twenty-seven percent are minority students. Clemmons had consistently scored in the upper half of the school system (30 elementary schools) on standardized tests, with a wide gap between what students in the top and bottom groups scored. The top group traditionally carried the school and although the school did well on standardized tests, many students in the bottom groups were nonreaders in the first and second grades. Eventually, most of these students attained a second-grade reading level and remained at that level and in the bottom group for the remainder of their elementary school years. In addition to their regular classroom instruction, these children received help from a learning disabilities or Chapter I teacher—and some received help from both!

Because Clemmons scored relatively well and because only a small percentage of the children failed to learn to read, the staff at Clemmons was quite satisfied with their three-group basal approach to reading instruction. However, change was in the air. Teachers were hearing about and trying out some of the whole language literature-based methods and were beginning to question the notion of ability grouping. Teachers at upper grade levels were doing much less grouping, but teachers in the primary grades were wary of giving up their groups.

The school was gearing up for a new basal adoption and many of the basals under consideration recommended whole-class reading instruction. Rather than launch full-scale into the unknown of a non-ability-grouped approach to reading, the decision was made to work with one first grade teacher in one first grade classroom to see how to provide reading instruction that met the needs of this diverse population of children without ability grouping.

Approaches to Reading Instruction

In developing the program, various approaches to reading instruction were considered and discussed. The most commonly used approach to reading in this country has been the basal reader approach. Basals teach both phonics and comprehension and, while they differ in their emphasis, basals have in common the gradually increasing levels of difficulty and the emphasis on teacher-guided reading of short selections. While basal readers do contain some phonics instruction, many pro-phonics advocates recommend that reading instruction begin with a much heavier dose of letter–sound practice so that children can learn to "break the code." Throughout the years, many reading experts have advocated a literature or trade book approach to reading. In the 1960s Jeanette Veatch (1959) popularized what she called an "individualized reading" approach. The emphasis in this approach was on children selecting real books that they wanted to read and on teachers conferencing with children and providing individual help if needed. Currently, the literature approach is once again "hot." Another approach, widely used in England, Australia, and other countries, is also "in" right now. This approach, which can be labeled "language experience/ writing," is based on the idea that the easiest material for children to read is their own writing and that of their classmates.

Throughout the years, four major approaches—phonics, basal, literature, and language experience/writing—have been in and out of favor (Cunningham & Allington, 1994). Generally, one approach has predominated just long enough for people to recognize its shortcomings and is then abandoned in favor of a different approach with different shortcomings. The question of which method is best cannot be answered, because it is the wrong question. Each method has undeniable strengths.

Phonics instruction is clearly important because one of the big tasks of beginning readers is to figure out how our alphabetic language works. Adams (1990) reviewed decades of research and concluded that while some children can figure out the letter–sound system without instruction, directly teaching this system speeds up literacy acquisition. The need for some explicit phonics instruction is particularly clear for at-risk children who have not had much exposure to reading and writing and thus have had fewer opportunities to figure out how our alphabetic system works.

Basal instruction provides teachers with multiple copies of reading material whose difficulty level is gradually increased, which the teacher can use to guide children's comprehension and strategy development. Because basals contain a wide variety of all types of literature, children are exposed to many genres and topics they might miss if all their reading was self-selected. In addition, basals outline the major goals for each year and provide an organized curricular plan for accomplishing those goals and ways of evaluating which students are meeting those goals.

The reading of real books is the ultimate aim of reading instruction, but one that has in the past taken a back seat to phonics and/or basal instruction. Children were expected to read when they finished their work or read at home. Of course, children who came from homes where books were available and reading was valued were much more likely to engage in real reading than children whose homes lacked these advantages. The literature approach to reading has once again reminded us that the purpose of learning to read is to read real books.

Writing is an approach to reading that allows children to figure out reading "from the inside out." As children write, they spell words they later see and recognize in their writing. Even when they can't spell a word perfectly, they try to sound it out to spell it and actually put to use whatever phonics they have learned. Clarke (1988) found that encouraging invented spelling was especially helpful to children who came to school with lower levels of reading and writing ability. Children who write are more avid and more sensitive readers (Tierney & Shanahan, 1991).

In the 1960s, the federal government spent hundreds of thousands of dollars to find out what the best approach to beginning reading really was. Data were collected from first and second grades around the country that used different approaches to beginning reading. The results of this study were inconclusive. Some approaches did better in certain schools, but others did better elsewhere. Virtually every approach had good results somewhere and poor results somewhere else. How well the teacher carried out the approach seemed to be the major determinant of how well an approach worked. Some teachers used what the researchers called "combination" approaches, such as language experience and basal or phonics and literature or literature and writing. The study concluded that in general, combination approaches worked better than any single approach (Bond & Dykstra, 1967). Adams (1990), in her review of research related to beginning reading, also concluded that children—especially if they are at risk—need a rich variety of reading and writing experiences as well as some direct instruction in letter–sound patterns.

Clemmons Pilot Program

In considering the various approaches, we decided that the question we should be asking was not, "Which approach?" but rather, "How can we organize classrooms so that we can 'have it all'?" The model we developed included the four competing beginning reading approaches organized into four instructional blocks—Basal, Self-Selected Reading, Writing, and Working with Words. We divided the two hours of reading/language arts time into four thirty-minute blocks and built as many links as possible between the different blocks so that the approaches complemented and supported each other.

During the implementation year, we developed and refined this four-block model in one first grade classroom. During the first four to six weeks of first grade, shared reading with big books and language experience activities were daily occurrences. Writing process was begun and children learned to see themselves as readers and writers. After a few weeks of school, daily instruction with the four blocks was initiated.

Basal Block. During the Basal Block, all children were included in instruction from a basal reading series. The teacher used suggestions in the manual, adapting them as necessary. The children were not ability-grouped but read and did workbook activities with a partner. Most basal instruction began with a whole-class format, then moved into partner format for reading or workbook activities, then back to a whole-class format for discussion of what was read or feedback on workbook pages. During partner reading, children took turns reading pages of the story. For partner workbook activities they "played school." On one page, partner A was the teacher and partner B the student. On the next page, the partners switched roles. The partners were changed from time to time, but the goal was to have children paired with children they liked and to have the less proficient readers working with someone who could support their reading. The instruction was paced to finish the entire first grade basal program by the end of the school year. In addition to reading in the adopted basal, the basal block also included teacher-guided reading of a variety of other materials—big books, easier basals, *Weekly Reader* selections, and easy trade books (when these were available). The major purposes of Basal Block instruction were to teach important comprehension skills/strategies, develop word knowledge and vocabulary, develop children's listening and speaking skills, and expose children to a wide variety of literature and genres.

Self-Selected Reading Block. During the Self-Selected Reading Block, children chose what they wanted to read from a wide variety of books and other reading materials. Children chose to read trade books (including big books), books they had published, and even occasionally a favorite story from basal readers. For each science or social studies topic studied, the teacher gathered a variety of informational books that were popular choices during self-selected reading. Children read by themselves or with a friend. Occasionally, the teacher called a small group of students and supported them through the repeated reading of a familiar book or challenged them with a new piece of literature that was hard but could be read with the teacher's guidance. Time was provided for some children to share what they were reading at the end of this self-selected reading block. In addition, several times each day, the teacher read aloud to the children.

Writing Block. The Writing Block followed a writing process format. The writing block began with a five- to ten-minute mini-lesson during which the teacher modeled writing. The teacher wrote a short piece on an overhead transparency. As she wrote, she thought aloud about what she was writing and how she was writing it. Writing conventions and invented spelling were modeled daily. Next, the children wrote about whatever they chose and spelled words as best they could. When the children had several pieces written, they chose one to publish. Peers and the teacher helped them to edit and revise the chosen piece, which they then made into a book. The daily Writing Block ended with some time in which children shared what they had published or a piece in progress in an author's chair format.

Working with Words Block. During the Working with Words Block, children developed a store of high-frequency words they could automatically read and spell and learned how to use spelling patterns to decode and spell unknown words. Two major activities took place during the daily Working with Words block: Word Wall and Making Words (Cunningham, 1991). The Word Wall was a bulletin board to which the teacher added approximately five words each week. These were common words that had been introduced in the basal reading lesson or words that the children used frequently in their daily writing. The words were written on colored pieces of paper attached to the wall so that they were in alphabetical order (by first letter only). New words were added each week and children practiced learning to read and spell these words through a daily chanting, clapping, writing activity. Each day, the teacher selected and called out five words from the entire wall. After a word was called and pointed to, the children rhythmically chanted and clapped the letters in the word. They then wrote the word and chanted and clapped it again to check what they had written.

Making Words (Cunningham & Cunningham, 1992) is an every-pupil-response letter-manipulative activity. The children were given a limited number of letters and manipulated these letters to make words. The teacher called out the word to be made, children made the words with their individual letters at their desks, and one child made the word with large letters in a pocket chart. The fifteen-minute activity started by having the children make small words and ended with bigger ones. For example, from the letters *e*, *i*, *d*, *f*, *n*, *r*, and *s*, the children made the two-letter words *if*, *is*, and *in*, the three-letter words *fed*, *red*, and *rid*, the four-letter words *ride*, *fire*, and *fine*, the five-letter words *rides*, *fires*, and *fries*, and finally the six-letter word *friend* and the seven-letter word *friends* (not coincidentally, the subject of the story they were about to read during their basal block). After using the letters to make words the teacher led the children to sort the words according to a variety of semantic and letter–sound relationships and patterns.

Assessment. Assessment was an ongoing part of the daily instruction. In addition to district-mandated basal tests, the teacher kept portfolios of the children's writing and the children kept logs of self-selected reading. The teacher also focused on four or five children each day and made notes about those children as they moved through the four blocks. In addition to the ongoing assessment, an Informal Reading Inventory (IRI) (Johns, 1988) was administered in the last month of school to determine the instructional reading level for each student.

Results of the IRI demonstrate that the four-block, multimethod, multilevel instruction was effective both for children who would have been in the bottom group and children who would have been in the top group. Half of the children who would have been in the bottom group read at or above grade level. All children who would have been in the middle group read at or above grade level. All children who would have been in the top group read at least at the third-grade level, with more than half reading at the fifth- or sixth-grade level (Cunningham, Hall, & Defee, 1991). Everyone, including the other first grade teachers in the school, realized that the children who had participated in the multimethod, multilevel classroom were reading and writing much better than children in previous years, when they had been grouped. The success of the pilot led to changes at Clemmons and other schools.

Next we will visit an at-risk school that had observed the pilot class and was ready to make some changes based on the multimethod, multilevel model.

EASTON ELEMENTARY SCHOOL

Across town, another school in the Winston-Salem/Forsyth County system was in trouble. The students consistently scored lower on achievement tests than any other elementary school in the system and had the worst attendance record. Parents were not a part of the school and often viewed the school with belligerence and hostility.

Easton was a school in which nearly three-quarters of the students were members of a minority group. Many of the students came from homes with limited book experiences and difficult home situations. Poverty was common, with 79 percent of the children qualifying for free or reduced-price meals. The majority of the students in both first and second grade were reading below grade level. Although the teachers were working hard, their instruction seemed fruitless. Behavior problems consumed valuable teaching time. Many students had tuned out learning, and their behavior became disruptive as they plodded through the elementary grades.

Even though the status of the school seemed bleak and the needs too great to tackle, the school staff were determined to initiate some changes. The instructional model used by the teachers was quite traditional. Teachers used a skills-driven basal reader and divided the students into three ability groups. The bottom groups were usually the largest of the three reading groups and students tended to maintain their place in this group throughout the elementary grades. Grouping necessitated independent seatwork, which turned into a management nightmare. Many students found it difficult to complete assigned seatwork independently and they were often off-task. In addition, these children could not afford the nonproductive time they were spending on seatwork.

In addition to classroom instruction, the lowest-achieving students also received support in a Chapter I resource setting. Students who were experiencing the least success in reading were pulled out of the classroom for thirty minutes of additional reading instruction each day. They often had difficulty returning to work upon their return to the classroom. Many of the students resented being singled out as problem readers, and these students accounted for many of the discipline problems. Little growth in reading was measured, and children remained slotted into remedial services as they progressed from grade to grade.

Upon looking closely at the model of instruction used at Easton, the school determined that neither reading ability groups nor pullout remedial programs were currently facilitating learning to read. At the end of the year, 40 percent of the first grade students were still struggling at the preprimer level and were having little or no success. In second grade, 18 percent of the students were still nonreaders, unable to read anything but the very simplest text.

After observing the multimethod, multilevel instructional program in one classroom at Clemmons Elementary, Easton decided to try to adapt the model for its high-risk population. Reading groups would be abolished and pullout programs would be eliminated. While teachers would have been more comfortable implementing the new model on a limited basis the first year, the extreme needs of the school led to a full implementation of multimethod, multilevel instruction in all classrooms. The risks were great for the teachers. They were implementing a program that had worked in one classroom where many, but not most, children were at risk. Would this approach work with large numbers of at-risk children? A commitment was made by the staff to fully implement the new model until Christmas. If the model proved to be unsuccessful, the staff agreed they would not return to their previously unsuccessful model, but would continue the search. Easton was ready for change, and multimethod, multilevel instruction seemed like a good choice as long as some small-group support for the large number of at-risk students could be found. The curriculum coordinator at the school set out to find a way to do just that. Thus both Clemmons and Easton were ready for the next school year with a new plan for the reading instruction of first grade students at both schools.

We continue this story of change by revisiting Clemmons.

CLEMMONS ELEMENTARY—YEAR 1

Following the pilot testing year, the multimethod, multilevel approach was implemented by all four first grade teachers at Clemmons. These first grade teachers had watched the pilot classroom and, noting the successes of the students, had tried one or two of the blocks with their classes before the end of the pilot testing year. Now they were ready to teach using the new approach with the support of the pilot teacher and the curriculum coordinator. All children were included in all four blocks. Teachers taught the blocks in a variety of orders that fit their teaching styles. Most teachers were more comfortable and felt more confident with two or three blocks and usually found one block challenging because of the management or "newness." The four teachers worked well together, sharing their successes, problems, and solutions.

In April of this first year of full implementation, an IRI was given to all first graders (see Table 7.1). Since the IRI was given near the end of first grade, it could be argued that either first reader or second grade level would be an on-grade-level score. If you consider scores at both first reader and second grade as grade level, 90 percent of the students read at or above grade level. Ten percent of the students read below grade level with an instructional level of preprimer or primer. There were no children who could not read at preprimer level. The veteran first grade teachers were pleased with the successes of their students. Having taught first grade at this school for many years, they knew that it was remarkable to have so few students reading below grade level. They marveled at the fact that even those who hadn't yet made it to grade level were all reading and writing.

Perhaps just as impressive were the results with very able children. One teacher noted that Josh, who came to first grade with *Call of the Wild*

TABLE 7.1. Percentage of children achieving IRI Levels for Clemmons School

IRI Level	Year 1 Grade 1	Year 2	
		Grade 1	Grade 2
6	9	14	35
5	16	14	28
4	18	23	15
3	20	10	9
2	20	18	13
1	7	7	0
P	3	5	2
PP	7	9	0

tucked under his arm, had participated in all four blocks daily. When Josh was asked which block he enjoyed the most, he responded, "The Basal." The teacher was surprised at his choice and would have predicted that he would have chosen Self-Selected Reading, during which Josh was always reading a chapter or two from his latest library book or investigating some area of interest through the reading of informational books. But Josh explained his reasoning. During basal block he got to read and talk about his reading with his friend! The responses of Josh and other accelerated students demonstrate that it may not be the basal but rather all the seatwork and the individual isolation that go along with basals and reading groups that is such a turnoff for capable students. Josh spent one-quarter of his time with the basal but equal amounts of time in self-selected reading and writing. Neither Josh nor his parents ever complained that he was bored!

In considering the success of their high-risk students, the teachers realized that they were providing multiple and diverse opportunities for these children to succeed. During the Basal Block, their children could all participate in the reading and discussions with the help of a partner. The first grade teachers became experts at selecting the best peer "teacher" for each student who needed support. During self-selected reading, they filled their classroom libraries with many easy, familiar books and allowed their students to read, reread, and "play"-read through the books using the picture clues for help. Sometimes the teachers pulled a small group and read easy books with them for ten minutes during their self-selected reading time.

During Word Wall, all children could say the words, chant the words, and write the words. Most of the high-risk students used the Word Wall to help them with the spelling of the high-frequency words they needed during the Writing Block. During Making Words, some students began by matching their letter cards to those of a neighbor. As they developed some phonemic awareness, they would listen for the sounds they could hear in words and then try to find the letter–sound match. As the year went on, most high-risk children were able to change just a letter or two to make a new word and were learning how to spell. The children could see the spelling patterns being produced and were encouraged to transfer that knowledge to the Writing Block. After making the words *Ed*, *red*, and *fed*, teachers would ask, "If you were writing about playing in the snow and needed to write the word *sled*, how would thinking of the words we just made—Ed, red, and fed—help you spell *sled*?"

Modeling invented spelling during the mini-lesson was critical for *all* students. It taught them what to do when they came to a word they could not spell. It gave all students permission to use invented spelling when writing. With the Word Wall for support and teacher modeling and encouragement of invented spelling, even the children who were most at risk could and did write.

The first grade teachers were especially pleased with the unexpected but much-noticed difference in student behavior. Visitors always commented that all first grade students were "on task" reading and writing and that the children and teachers seemed happy. "Where do you get kids like this?" they often asked.

As the year neared its end, however, the first grade teachers began worrying about their students next year. Even though everyone could read and write to a certain extent, a few children in each classroom were still not able to read at grade level. The first grade teachers felt that their children would all benefit from another year of the four-block multimethod, multilevel instruction and arrangements were made to have the second grade teachers visit first grade. The second grade teachers visited and talked and liked what they saw, but they did not embrace overall the notion of doing the four blocks in second grade. It was spring of the year and the first grade teachers at Clemmons were often seen looking at a particular child shaking their heads and saying, "If only I had these children one more year!" So it was decided that the first grade teachers would do just that and become second grade teachers for their classes.

EASTON ELEMENTARY—YEAR 1

Meanwhile, across town Easton was ready to try multimethod, multilevel instruction in first and second grade. The curriculum coordinator had also worked out a plan for forty-five minutes of daily small-group instruction. Staff development for teachers began the week before school started and continued all year long as the curriculum coordinator supported the teachers in this change. Many teachers were anxious about trying new ideas. They had always ability-grouped before and wondered how the students would respond. After all, Easton was a school in which nearly half of all their students were below grade level, and the students would now be reading grade-level material and be expected to complete the material by the end of the school year. The curriculum coordinator reminded the teachers that they were exposing the students to the grade-level materials and that the basal was just one part of the reading program now. During the Basal Block, the teacher would first build the necessary background knowledge and then help the students preview and predict what would happen in the story. Finally, the teacher read the story aloud. The students then read the story with a partner and completed any assignments they were to do cooperatively. Multimethod, multilevel instruction also included self-selected reading (for most students time to read and reread predictable or easy books), writing, and Word Wall. Each student would also have an opportunity to be part of a small group of students participating in Make Words.

Bobby, a rising second grade student at Easton Elementary, had completed first grade the previous spring as a nonreader. He had not experienced any success as he spent month after month in the Turtle reading group, reading the preprimer basal. Psychological testing suggested that Bobby was a slow learner—success was not to be expected. Illiterate parents were not able to come to his rescue. Implementing the new multimethod, multilevel model at Easton meant that Bobby would not continue to be subjected to continued failure. Instead, Bobby would be exposed to a second grade basal reader and self-selected reading. But could Bobby and the other 80 percent of the students who were at risk experience success in reading with this classroom model alone? Easton felt that these students would need the additional support of some daily small-group instruction. Therefore, FROG, *Facilitating Reading for Optimum Growth*, was developed for first and second grade students.

"FROG"

FROG was designed to provide the daily small-group instruction needed to assure the success of all students. The roles of existing personnel in the school were redefined to provide the necessary number of teachers to implement the program. Chapter I and other special teachers converged upon each classroom for forty-five minutes each day. The students in each class were divided into small heterogeneous groups that included one strong student, two or three average students, and one weak student. These groups received daily intensive instruction with one of the FROG teachers or the classroom teacher. This instruction included those components of the four blocks that the teachers felt could be better carried out in small groups. Each FROG session included four ten-to-twelve-minute components.

All children participated in self-selected reading as part of their classroom instruction. The FROG time began with a literary discussion based on these self-selected books. This discussion focused on a particular literary element, such as author, character, plot, setting, mood, style, theme, or illustration. Children read or discussed parts of their own book related to the literary element.

The second component of FROG, shared reading using predictable big books, strengthened and supported the students' reading in the Basal (guided reading) Block. The students were taught to use a variety of reading strategies including semantic, syntactic, and letter–sound cues. Punctuation, vocabulary, predictions—all teachable elements found in a particular book—became a part of the instruction as the teacher led the students to read the predictable big book.

The third component supported the Working with Words block. Children were given letters and instruction on how to manipulate those letters to make a variety of words. The emphasis was on learning that words are made up of predictable letter patterns.

The final component of FROG supported the classroom Writing Block. In the classroom, all children wrote on self-selected topics. During the FROG time, the predictable big book provided a model for teacher-directed writing instruction, allowing the children to make the reading–writing connection. There was a prewriting activity, followed by writing, revision, editing, and sharing.

When the forty-five minute FROG time ended, the FROG teachers moved to another classroom while the classroom teacher continued instruction with the whole class in the four blocks. Reorganizing the special teachers into FROG teams provided the small-group support needed by many of the children in this high-risk school to assure their success in the four blocks.

Here is a typical classroom schedule showing how FROG time and the classroom four blocks worked together.

8:45	Opening activities
9:00	FROG
9:45	Math
10:15	Basal Block
10:45	Self-Selected Reading Block
11:15	Lunch

11:45   Working with Words Block
12:15   Writing Block
12:45   Teacher Read-Aloud
 1:00   Music
 1:30   Integrated Science/Social Studies
 2:00   Physical Education
 2:30   Computer Technology
 3:00   Dismissal

Results

In addition to ongoing observation and portfolio assessment, students in grades one and two were administered an IRI at the end of the school year. Table 7.2 shows the growth that occurred during the first year of implementation.

Since the IRIs were given in May, we considered first reader or second grade–level scores as on-grade-level scores for first graders. Fifty-seven percent of the students were reading on or above grade level, while 43 percent read at the primer or preprimer level. There were no children who could not meet the instructional-level criteria at the preprimer level.

In second grade, considering scores of second or third grade as grade level, 73 percent of the students were reading on or above grade level and 27 percent read below grade level. While significant numbers of children still read below grade level, there were no nonreaders and the number of children reading at or above grade level showed a dramatic increase from previous years. According to these test scores, the multimethod, multilevel

TABLE 7.2. Percentage of children achieving IRI Levels for Easton School

| IRI Level | Year 1 | | Year 2 | |
	Grade 1	Grade 2	Grade 1	Grade 2
6	0	8	0	15
5	6	17	2	0
4	4	8	7	15
3	13	23	15	21
2	13	17	33	31
1	21	17	25	11
P	13	0	2	0
PP	30	10	16	6

model was making a difference. But far more meaningful changes occurred at Easton. Parents who had been reluctant to be a part of the school began to trickle in. PTA membership increased 120 percent. Parent volunteers and grade parents increased from five to eighty. Behavior problems, although still in existence, decreased dramatically. Easton no longer had the poorest attendance in the Winston-Salem/Forsyth system. Most significant, however, was the change in the students. Chaotic classrooms had been replaced by classrooms filled with excited students involved in reading and writing. Adding the FROG component to the multimethod, multilevel instruction gave these at-risk students some small-group instruction. Making the FROG groups heterogeneous allowed at-risk children to read, write, and share with others who were good models.

Like Clemmons, Easton decided to have the first grade teachers take their classes to second grade and continue this multimethod, multilevel instruction along with FROG for another year.

CLEMMONS ELEMENTARY—YEAR 2

The school year at Clemmons began with many changes. The first grade teachers who had been worried about the students who still were not reading at grade level took their own children to second grade. After a week, the second graders had settled back into multimethod, multilevel instruction, and the children were where they had left off in June!

The new first grade teachers (three were former second grade teachers and one teacher was new to the school) began doing the four-block multimethod, multilevel instruction. The former second grade teachers, though hesitant to change grade levels, were assured that they too could move with their classes to second grade the following year if they chose to do so. They had been impressed with how well last year's first graders were reading and writing, and most of them had tried some of the blocks with their second graders toward the end of the previous year. In making the change, they had support from the four former first grade teachers and the school curriculum coordinator. Before long, they were marveling at "how much these little first graders could learn" and "how enthusiastic they were!"

During the previous school year, a local teacher had gone to Clemson University in South Carolina to be trained as a Reading Recovery Teacher Leader. The school system hired another Teacher Leader from Australia and plans were made to begin training some Reading Recovery teachers. Clemmons made it a priority to get in that pool and had two teachers in the training group and working with the lowest-achieving first graders.

The two teachers who were being trained as Reading Recovery teachers had an impact on instruction immediately, as school personnel watched the eight "lowest" students being transformed into readers and writers. The kindergarten teachers were amazed that former students, who had been their discipline problems, were behaving better as they met with success in Reading Recovery and in their first grade classrooms using the four-block instruction. The administrative staff noticed the change also. Reading Recovery students were not only improving their literacy; their self-esteem was improving just as rapidly.

One day the four first grade teachers returned from a Reading Recovery informational meeting. Excitedly, they announced that they felt multi-method, multilevel instruction "fit Reading Recovery." They invited the two Reading Recovery teachers into their classrooms to watch all the blocks. Not only were the Reading Recovery students having success in their one-on-one tutoring, but the strategies they were learning in these sessions were put into practice as they, along with everyone else, participated in partner reading during the Basal Block, self-selected reading during which many predictable and easy books were available, and writing with Word Wall and Making Words activities. (Their Reading Recovery tutoring session was on a staggered schedule so that they missed a different classroom block each day.)

As the end of the second year neared, everyone was excited to observe how well first and second graders were reading and writing and eager to see what results the IRI testing in May would yield. Results of the IRIs given in May (see Table 7.1) showed that 86 percent of the first graders were reading on or above grade level. There were no children who could not meet the instructional criteria for the preprimer level.

The whole school was eager to see how the second graders who had the same teacher and two years of multimethod, multilevel instruction fared. The second grade teachers reported that their best students were reading chapter books and good literature daily. The writing of all students was longer and more complex and showed growth in spelling, mechanics, and sense of story.

Results of the IRIs given in May showed that 98 percent of the second grade students were reading on or above grade level. There were no non-readers. Of the ten second grade students who had not read on grade level at the end of first grade, eight were reading at or above grade level at the end of second grade. Two of these students whose tested instructional level had been preprimer at the end of first grade now had instructional levels at the third grade level (at the end of second grade). After years of using ability groups to teach first grade classes with many accelerated and many at-risk children and two years of doing the four-block multimethod, multilevel instruction with the same children, these four teachers are convinced they have found a better way.

EASTON ELEMENTARY—YEAR 2

The new year began with enthusiasm and positive anticipation. The teachers had a successful year behind them and were anticipating the implementation of several additional innovations. Students exhibited the same confidence and enthusiasm. On the first day of school, second grade students walked down the halls with a knowing smile: They knew they would be returning to the same classroom and the same teacher they had in first grade. Another major innovation had occurred: Easton had become a Schoolwide Chapter I Project and the federal monies were now used to reduce class size (see Winfield, this volume, for information on Schoolwide Projects).

Classroom instruction in the four blocks continued, as did FROG instruction. Smaller class size and teachers with more instructional expertise contributed to accelerated learning in the classroom. The students were on task and involved in reading and writing. Learning was their primary concern, leaving little time for discipline problems. Teachers had to work hard to keep the students supplied with books as they devoured all put before them. By the end of the year, all first and second grade students were reading and writing.

Results were indicative of the growth that occurred during the second year with multimethod, multilevel instruction and FROG and the first year with smaller classes. Based on the results of the IRIs given in May of first grade, (see Table 7.2), 82 percent of the students were reading on or above grade level and 18 percent read at the primer or preprimer level. There were no children who could not read at the preprimer level. In second grade, 83 percent of the students were reading on or above grade level and 17 percent read below grade level. There were no nonreaders and the number of children reading at or above grade level showed a dramatic increase from previous years. In addition, Easton School students no longer had the lowest achievement scores in the district!

Easton will continue to have students who are just emerging on the reading continuum. But these students have self-esteem, pride, and a love for reading and writing. Easton has a vision for a brighter future for the children, and the magic of learning happening is seen daily.

WHAT WE KNOW NOW THAT WE DIDN'T
KNOW THREE YEARS AGO

For decades, experts have argued about the best approach to beginning reading instruction. A variety of methods—phonics, basal, linguistic, language experience, whole language, writing, individualized, literature-based, and so forth—have come in and out of fashion, and each approach has had its advocates and its critics. In addition to the argument about which approach is best, the question of how to meet the needs of a diverse population of children has received a great deal of attention. Besides within-class ability grouping, other organizational plans such as tracking, multi-aging, transition classes, team teaching, and a variety of pullout programs for both remedial and gifted children have been implemented. Much time, effort, and money have been expended on trying to find the best approach and the best organization to teach all children to read and write. In spite of this enormous effort, our schools are still not succeeding with large numbers of children. The children whose needs we have not met very well are those at the top and bottom ends of the continuum. Children who come to school from low-literacy homes are often unprepared for literacy and fail to learn to read and write. Children who come from high-literacy homes are often not challenged, and their parents feel that the needs of their capable children are ignored.

In this chapter, we have described the results of a three-year, two-school effort to restructure literacy instruction. The impetus to restructure came from the teachers and from their frustration in trying to use ability groups and pullout special classes to meet the needs of a diverse population of children. The restructuring took place gradually, at first in only one first grade classroom in one school. During the first year, the remaining first grade teachers worked with the multimethod, multilevel instruction—refining and adapting the blocks to their own teaching styles and to meet the needs of their children. Also, during that year, the model was adapted and tried in a school in which most of the children were at risk for failure. In this high-risk school, pullout programs were replaced by the FROG component, allowing for intensive small-group teaching. In the second year, in both schools we had the additional variable of first grade teachers taking their own classes to second grade. The original school with a wide range of children added the Reading Recovery component, and the high-risk school used Chapter I funds to reduce class size. In both schools, all children remained in the regular classrooms and no children were removed for special education or Chapter I programs. Furthermore, referrals for special education decreased by 60 percent, and retentions, which had previously been 30 percent of first graders, dropped to less than 1 percent.

Results from the IRI and other observational data indicate that after two years of multimethod, multilevel instruction, no child remained a non-reader. Most children, including those at high risk for failure, read at or above grade level. Accelerated children who entered first grade already reading and writing continued to make accelerated progress and became sophisticated readers and writers.

When making any kind of change, it is important to collect data from a variety of sources. The first grade teachers who made the change to four-block instruction seemed quite satisfied with the results. We decided, however, to collect some data in a format that would allow them to express their personal opinions. To determine why these veteran first grade teachers changed to the non–ability-grouped model and how they felt about the change, a questionnaire was developed and administered to them. Teachers were asked questions designed to elicit information about how they had taught in previous years, why they made the change, and how they felt their instruction and the learning of their children had been affected.

The six teachers were all women and included three African-Americans. Five of these teachers had taught a variety of grade levels from kindergarten to sixth grade during their careers. One teacher had experience only in first grade. Their years of experience ranged from six to twenty-nine years.

All teachers reported that they had previously grouped their first grade students for reading, meeting daily with either three or four groups. To keep their students busy while they met with the other reading groups, they had assigned seatwork. All teachers reported using workbook pages, worksheets, and copying from the board. Some teachers also reported the use of voluntary reading, voluntary writing, and "centers." Research has shown that time on task has a direct correlation to student performance (Rosenshine & Stevens, 1984). Teachers were asked what percentage of their students had been on task during seatwork activities. One teacher reported that 90 to 100 percent of her students had been on task. Two teachers reported that 75 to 90 percent of their students had been on task. Two other teachers reported that 50 to 75 percent of their students had been on task, and one teacher reported that less than 50 percent of her students had been on task during seatwork activities. Teachers at the high-risk school reported fewer students on task than the teachers at Clemmons before the implementation of multimethod, multilevel instruction.

The teachers were then asked how they felt about the change before and after the school year. Four of the teachers reported that they were enthusiastic about the change at the beginning of the year, while two teachers felt apprehensive. At the end of the year, all six were enthusiastic.

Teachers were asked to compare this multimethod, multilevel instruction with ability-grouped instruction for their top, average, and bottom students. All six teachers reported that students of all ability levels did better with multimethod, multilevel instruction.

Finally, teachers were asked to imagine that they were transferred to a school where reading was taught in ability groups. Would they return to ability grouping or continue to teach using the multimethod, multilevel approach? All six teachers indicated that they would not return to ability grouping for reading instruction. Comments on the questionnaire indicated that these teachers were seeing results. They wrote things such as, "My students are enthusiastic and have greater self-esteem" and "You can't tell me that this method doesn't work!"

Teachers in one school chose to change after seeing the results of the change made by one teacher. The two teachers from the high-risk school were getting burned out because they were working hard and getting no results, so they were willing to try an instructional change. Once the decision to change was made by the teachers, they had support in making that change. This support came from each other and from an instructional leader in each school. However, the change would not have been so enthusiastically implemented had it not been for the response of the children they taught. As the year went on, these veteran first grade teachers observed their children's progress in reading and writing. From these observations and past experiences they knew that the children—particularly the lowest- and highest-achieving children—were reading and writing better than their counterparts had in past years.

From the performance of the children and the enthusiasm of the veteran teachers, the conclusion can be reached that replacing ability-grouped basal instruction with multimethod, multilevel instruction was successful in eliminating failure. In addition to the teacher choice, involvement, and support, we feel that there are three other critical variables that might account for the success of the children. The first variable is the virtual nonexistence of seatwork. In our six first grades, the children spent almost no time working alone at their seats on a worksheet or other traditional seatwork activity. Workbook pages were done occasionally, but they were done with a partner and then immediately self-checked in a whole-class activity. Thus the entire two hours allocated for language arts instruction were actually used for instruction and for reading and writing. The fact that this is unusual in most primary classrooms can be summed up by the comment of a second grader who transferred in from another school and after three days asked the teacher, "When do we work around here?" Upon further questioning, the teacher figured out what the child meant by "work"—"Worksheets!" The child was incredulous when the teacher explained that the daily partner reading, self-selected reading, writing, and working with words *was* the reading and writing work they did in this classroom!

The second variable we consider crucial is the fact that the instruction was multilevel—it provided for a variety of ability levels. During the Basal Block, much of the guided reading was done in grade-level materials. Children who were not able to read the material on their own were supported by their partners and were able to profit from the before-and-after reading discussions and strategy lessons. Some of the basal block time each week, however, was devoted to the reading of easier materials, and the teachers often pulled a small group for ten minutes of the self-selected time and read easy books with them.

During self-selected reading, children chose from a variety of books, including the simplest, most predictable books as well as sophisticated chapter books and informational books. During the third year, when the lowest students were being tutored in Reading Recovery, a duplicate set of some of the easiest books were ordered and distributed among the book baskets so that Reading Recovery children could, if they chose, reread these familiar books.

The daily Making Words activity always began with two- and three-letter words that provided opportunities for overlearning the simplest spelling patterns and ended with big words that challenged the spelling abilities of even our most sophisticated readers. All children could write as long as whatever they wrote was appreciated and encouraged and could turn their first drafts into books with help from their friends and teacher. The belief in individual differences is sacred to most educators but is given only lip service in most schools. Individual differences refer not only to differences in ability but also to differences in the ways in which children learn.

The inclusion of major elements of four historically popular approaches to teaching beginning reading is the third variable we believe played a key role in our success. In these six classrooms, all children participated in all four blocks of instruction. These blocks—Basal, Self-Selected Reading, Writing, and Working with Words—represent vastly different approaches. When questioned about which block was most effective, the six teachers were in total disagreement and each block was chosen by at least one teacher. The teacher who responded to the question with a question of her own, "For which child?" summed up the variable that seems most responsible for the success of the children.

Change in the instructional program was accomplished with no added cost to the school system or schools. The changes did require a good deal of work by the curriculum person in each school and support from the administration. In-service for all teachers was provided and the teachers were supported and encouraged as they learned new instructional strategies. Every effort was made to secure the materials the teachers needed (mainly big books for shared reading and easy books for self-selected reading).

Effective instructional change has created a learning environment in which children and teachers have an opportunity to reach their potential and has also eliminated failure in these two schools—Clemmons and Easton—which are mirror images of each other. The change has been exciting, rewarding, and on-going.

REFERENCES

Adams, M. J. (1990). *Beginning to read: Thinking and learning about print*. Cambridge, MA: MIT Press.

Allington, R. L. (1983). The reading instruction provided readers of differing reading abilities. *Elementary School Journal, 83*, 548–559.

Bond, G. L., & Dykstra, R. (1967). The cooperative research program in first grade reading instruction. *Reading Research Quarterly, 2*, 5–142.

Clarke, L. K. (1988). Invented versus traditional spelling in first graders' writings: Effects on learning to spell and read. *Research in the Teaching of English, 22*, 281–309.

Cunningham, P. M. (1991). *Phonics they use: Words for reading and writing*. New York: HarperCollins.

Cunningham, P. M., & Allington, R. L. (1994). *Classrooms that work: They can all read and write*. New York: HarperCollins.

Cunningham, P. M., & Cunningham, J. W. (1992). Making words: Enhancing the invented spelling-decoding connection. *The Reading Teacher, 46*, 106–115.

Cunningham, P. M., Hall, D. P., & Defee, M. (1991). Non-ability grouped, multilevel instruction: A year in a first grade classroom. *The Reading Teacher, 44*, 566–571.

Hiebert, E. H. (1983). Research directions: The development of word-level strategies in authentic literacy tasks. *Language Arts, 69*, 234–240.

Johns, J. L. (1988). *Basic reading inventory*, 4th ed. Dubuque, IA: Kendall Hunt.

Juel, C. (1988). Learning to read and write: A longitudinal study of 54 children from first through fourth grade. *Journal of Educational Psychology, 80*, 437–447.

Rosenshine, B., & Stevens, R. (1984). Classroom reading instruction. In P. D. Pearson (Ed.), *Handbook of reading research* (pp. 745–798). New York: Longman.

Shannon, P. (1985). Reading instruction and social class. *Language Arts, 62*, 604–613.

Tierney, R. J., & Shanahan, T. (1991). Research on the reading–writing relationship: Interactions, transactions, and outcomes. In R. Barr, M. D. Kamil, P. B. Mosenthal, & P. D. Pearson (Eds.), *Handbook of reading research*, Vol. II (pp. 246–280). New York: Longman.

Veatch, J. (1959). *Individualizing your reading program*. New York: Putnam.

CHAPTER 8

First Grade Teachers Provide Early Reading Intervention in the Classroom

BARBARA TAYLOR

University of Minnesota,
Minneapolis

RUTH SHORT

University of South Florida,
Tampa

BRENDA SHEARER

University of Wisconsin,
River Falls

BARBARA FRYE

University of South Florida,
St. Petersburg

A few years ago we became excited about the possibility of providing extra reading help, early in the school year, to low-achieving first graders to help them develop as readers by June. At that time reports on Reading Recovery and Success For All were beginning to circulate, and the results were very promising (Pinnell, DeFord, & Lyons, 1988; Slavin, Madden, Karweit, Livermon, & Dolan, 1990). By working with children before they failed in reading, and by focusing on reading and writing and the development of reading strategies to foster independence, these early-intervention programs were demonstrating that many at-risk first graders could learn to read quite well (Pinnell, 1989; Slavin, Madden, Karweit, Dolan, & Wasik, 1993).

Although the results of Reading Recovery and Success For All have been very impressive, each program uses individual tutoring provided by special reading teachers. Since it may be difficult to reach enough children through tutoring, we asked ourselves: Could first grade classroom teachers who were willing to spend an extra fifteen to twenty minutes a day working with their lowest-achieving readers provide effective early reading intervention and get good results? Since most children are with their regular classroom teacher every day for all or most of the day, we believed classroom teachers represented the most important resource in achieving the goal of all first grade students learning to read.

At the time we became interested in early reading intervention, two of the authors were working as program evaluators for the St. Louis Park, Minnesota, schools, a district implementing a whole language approach to literacy education. Instead of a basal reader, teachers used picture books for reading instruction in first grade. Children were not ability-grouped. Teachers often used whole-class instruction, such as when everyone in the class was reading the same book. Sometimes children were placed in groups when different stories were being read at the same time. Typically, children would be engaged in repetitive reading of simple stories. Phonics instruction was provided through teacher-directed experiences with big books, stories, and poems written on charts. Children also wrote daily about the stories they were reading, and through this writing they received incidental instruction in sound–symbol correspondences and how to sound out words.

When we asked teachers about special provisions for low-achieving readers, they said they spent more time with these students. They often retaught skills and listened to them read one-on-one. In one school, a special reading teacher provided about thirty minutes of daily supplemental instruction to the lowest-achieving readers in the fall. In the other school, a special reading teacher provided thirty minutes a day of supplemental instruction to the lowest-achieving readers over a six-week period, spread out over the first six months of school.

By the end of the first year of this whole language approach, one of the teachers' greatest concerns was how to meet the needs of their lowest-achieving readers. Many primary-grade teachers, in particular, felt that they needed a more systematic approach to developing these children's word-recognition abilities. Since the teachers and district were interested in providing additional in-class support to children who were not learning to read independently by the end of first grade, they were quite willing to pilot our Early Intervention in Reading (EIR) program.

We had developed the EIR program to accelerate the learning of the lowest-achieving readers by providing them with twenty minutes of daily supplemental reading instruction by the classroom teacher, in addition to the regular heterogeneous classroom reading lessons. We based the program on what has been found to be effective in promoting first grade reading development and in helping low-achieving readers. EIR involves children in the repetitive reading of and writing about stories. Instruction is provided within the context of stories being read, focusing on phonemic awareness and on strategies to foster independence in word recognition. This instruction in strategies differs from a more traditional "slow it down and make it more concrete" approach to remedial programs (Allington,

1991), often characterized by whole-word and phonics drill and round-robin reading with little attention to decoding strategies, text reading opportunities, or fostering reading fluency.

There is a high correlation between low phonemic awareness upon entering first grade and poor reading progress by the end of first grade (Juel, Griffith, & Gough, 1986; Liberman, 1973; Share, Jorm, Maclean, & Matthews, 1984; Stanovich, Cunningham, & Feeman, 1984; Tunmer & Nesdale, 1985). Researchers have stressed the importance of phonemic awareness training for low-achieving emergent readers (Juel, 1988; Stanovich, 1986), and such training has been found to improve children's reading ability (Ball & Blachman, 1991; Bradley & Bryant, 1983; Cunningham, 1990; Lundberg, Frost, & Peterson, 1988). In our program, phonemic awareness was specifically and regularly developed through teacher modeling of the sounding and blending of words in stories and through the writing of words and sentences by the children.

Research indicates that phonics instruction is also important in beginning reading (Adams, 1990; Bond & Dykstra, 1967; Chall, 1983). Recent literature reviews have argued for the teaching of phonic skills to children in concert with the reading of actual stories (Adams, 1990; Anderson, Hiebert, Scott, & Wilkinson, 1985). In our EIR program, teachers talk about the common sounds for particular letters as stories are read from charts. They also frequently refer to a short vowel chart when children have difficulty decoding words in stories with short vowel sounds. Teachers assist children in sounding out words as stories are read from the charts. Additionally, children are encouraged to think about what would make sense in the story as they attempt to read unknown words.

Writing is another important component of the program. On two out of three days spent on a story, children write a sentence about the story with help from the teacher. The importance of writing by emergent readers has frequently been noted (Adams, 1990; Clay, 1985). Typically, children begin to write letters and words at about the same time they begin to recognize printed words (Clay, 1975; Mason, 1980). Furthermore, writing words and sentences helps children learn about phonemic segmentation, blending, and letter–sound correspondences (Chomsky, 1979; Ehri & Wilce, 1987).

Repeated reading is also an important part of the EIR program, as it has been found to improve students' reading rate, phrasing, and word recognition accuracy (Herman, 1985; Hoffman, Roser, & Battle, 1993; Samuels, 1979). Children in our study read stories repeatedly with the teacher, to the aide, to one another, and to parents. They are asked to reread "old" stories as well as the ones they are currently working on with the teacher.

THE EIR PROGRAM IN THE ST. LOUIS PARK DISTRICT

St. Louis Park, a small suburban school district outside of Minneapolis, has been using the EIR program for three years. Below we describe the program, present results from Years 1 and 2 in St. Louis Park, and describe ways in which the program has been modified over the years. We also discuss the effects of the program in another suburban district using a systematic phonics program for basic first grade reading instruction and in a rural district using a basal reader program in first grade.

Description of the Program

What is unique about the EIR program is that it was designed for and has been carried out by, for the most part, classroom teachers. The first grade teachers who have used the program have demonstrated that within the classroom setting, teachers can make an important difference in the reading ability of their lowest-achieving readers by providing daily small-group, quality supplemental reading instruction.

Teachers engage in kid-watching in September. They look for children who do not know many sounds for consonants or perhaps not even the names of the letters. They notice which children do and do not recognize high-frequency words like *and* or *the* or who do or do not remember these words following instruction. By early October the teachers identify children who appear to be the lowest in emergent reading abilities. Children's knowledge of consonant sounds, basic sight words, and performance on a twelve-item individually administered phonemic awareness test (Taylor, 1990) are also considered. On this test children are asked to blend together into a word the sounds the teacher pronounces (i.e., t-a-p) and to say each sound they hear in a word (i.e., teacher says "tub" and child guesses sounds for "t", "u", and "b"). Six or seven children in each first grade class who are the lowest-ability emergent readers as determined by their teachers are selected for the EIR program.

These children spend fifteen to twenty extra minutes a day as a group with the teacher receiving supplemental reading instruction. The children also read individually to an instructional aide, volunteer, older student, or partner for an additional five minutes a day.

One goal of EIR is that children experience success in reading from the very start of the program. For this reason, reading materials are kept quite short, so that by the end of three days children can independently read them. Retellings of picture books prepared by the authors and teachers have been used as the reading material in the first half of the EIR program. Actual books, such as *Marmalade's Nap* by Cindy Wheeler or *Sheep in a Jeep* by Nancy Shaw, can be used for the reading material as well. What is important is that stories, whether actual books or story retellings, be short enough so that the children can be successful. We have found the following story lengths to be effective: about 40- to 60-word stories (Group A) from October to December; about 60- to 90-word stories (Group B) from December to February; about 90- to 120-word stories (Group C) from February through March; and about 120- to 200-word stories (Group D) from April to June.

Story retellings were made of picture storybooks that appeal to first grade children and that lent themselves to being shortened. Many of the stories we have used have repetitive episodes, some of which were eliminated in the retelling. Most of the stories listed under Group A and many listed under Groups B and C have such a repetitive pattern (see Figure 8.1).

No attempt was made to control the vocabulary in these retellings. Key phrases from books were often included in the retellings (e.g., "Just for you," "You'll soon grow into them," "I wish I could _____ like you"). Our retellings were placed in an appropriate level after they were written. That is, we retold the story, counted the number of words in the retelling, and placed it in Group A, B, or C if it had the appropriate number of words for a given level. Some retellings had to be discarded because they were too long and we felt they could not be shortened without altering the original story line.

We developed the retellings so that appealing picture storybooks could be read to and enjoyed by the children, and yet their reading experiences would remain successful. In addition to being quite short, an added advantage of the use of story retellings at first is that reading materials are fairly inexpensive. It costs much less to duplicate seven copies of a story retelling than to buy seven copies of a particular book. (See Figure 8.2 for an example of a retelling.)

Since some teachers interested in an approach like EIR may not want to use story retellings, we have identified examples of actual picture storybooks that could be used as the reading material at Groups A–D (see Figure 8.3). The placement of these books in the various levels is based on length. If these books are used, however, the teacher will need to come up with a way to teach to the group of six or seven children using one book so she can keep all six or seven pairs of eyes with her. Some books will have large enough type so all can see it. Big books can be used if they are short enough. Stories can perhaps be put on an opaque projector so all the children in the group can see the print.

FIGURE 8.1. Stories used in the Early Intervention in Reading (EIR) program

Group A—40-60-word summaries (October-December)

Five Little Monkeys Jumping on the Bed—Eileen Christelow

Ask Mr. Bear—Marjorie Flack

You'll Soon Grow into Them, Titch—Pat Hutchins

Herman the Helper—Robert Kraus

Milton the Early Riser—Robert Kraus

I Wish I Could Fly—Ron Maris

All By Myself—Mercer Mayer

Just for You—Mercer Mayer

Who Took the Farmer's Hat?—Joan Nodset

Imogene's Antlers—David Small

The Carrot Seed—Ruth Krauss

Group B—60-90-word summaries (December-February)

Charlie Needs a Clock—Tomie dePaola

Across the Stream—Mirra Ginsburg

Three Kittens—Mirra Ginsburg

Good Night, Owl—Pat Hutchins

Geraldine's Blanket—Holly Keller

Round Robin—Jack Kent

Owliver—Robert Kraus

Stone Soup—Ann McGovern

If You Give a Mouse a Cookie—Laura Nemeroff

The Farmer and the Noisy Hut—folktale

Rosie's Walk—Pat Hutchins (actual book used)

Big Brother—Charlotte Zolotow

Group C—90-120-word summaries, 100-150-word books (February-March)

A Dark, Dark Tale—Ruth Brown (actual book read by students)

Freight Train—Donald Crews (actual book read by students)

School Bus—Donald Crews (actual book read by students)

Hattie and the Fox—Mem Fox

The Monkey and the Crocodile

The Three Billy Goats Gruff

The Chick and the Duckling—Mirra Ginsburg (actual book read by students)

The Doorbell Rang—Pat Hutchins

The Very Worst Monster—Pat Hutchins

Group D—120-200-word books, actual books read by students (April-May)

You'll Soon Grow into Them, Titch—Pat Hutchins

Herman the Helper—Robert Kraus

All By Myself—Mercer Mayer

Just for You—Mercer Mayer

The Bear's Toothache—David McPhail

There's a Nightmare in My Closet—Mercer Mayer

Planes—Anne Rockwell

If You Look Around You—Fulvio Testa

If You Take a Paintbrush—Fulvio Testa

Noisy Nora—Rosemary Wells

Figure 8.2. An example of a story retelling from Group B

The Farmer and the Noisy Hut

A man lived in a hut with his mother, his wife, and six children.

It was very crowded and noisy in the hut.

The man went to see a wise man. The wise man told him to put his chickens, goat, and cow in the hut.

Now it was *very, very* crowded and noisy in the hut.

The man went to see the wise man once again.

The wise man told the man to take the animals out of the hut.

At last, it didn't seem crowded and noisy in the hut any longer.

The Daily Schedule

Day 1. Three days are spent on a story. The teacher first reads the actual picture book aloud to the entire class. She then reads the book or story retelling with the EIR group of children. If a book is used, it should be in a big book format or have large enough type that the group of six or seven children can follow the teacher as she reads and tracks. If a story retelling is used, it can be printed on a chart.

As the teacher and children read the story or story retelling, the teacher tracks the words with her finger as the words are read. The teacher stops at five or so readily decodable words (i.e., three-letter words with short vowel sounds at Group A) to model how to sound and blend them. A short-vowel

FIGURE 8.3. Other books to use in the Early Intervention Reading (EIR) program

___

A. 40–60 words (actual books used)

Ten, Nine, Eight	Molly Bang	(59 words)
Rosie's Walk	Pat Hutchins	(32 words)
The Baby	John Burningham	(60 words)
Sam's Cookie	Barbro Lindgren	(52 words)
Marmalade's Yellow Leaf	Cindy Wheeler	(49 words)
I Like Books	Anthony Browne	(55 words)
School Bus	Donald Crews	(51 words)
Things I Like	Anthony Browne	(61 words)
Sleepy Bear	Lydia Dabcovich	(50 words)
Flying	Donald Crews	(49 words)

B. 60–90 words (actual books used)

Marmalade's Nap	Andy Wheeler	(67 words)
Rose	Cindy Wheeler	(79 words)
Sheep in a Jeep	Nancy Shaw	(83 words)
Three Cheers for Hippo	John Stadler	(89 words)
Boat	Anne Rockwell	(83 words)
Two Bear Cubs	Ann Jonas	(92 words)
Molly	Ruth Radlauer	(91 words)
The Dog	John Burningham	(67 words)
Freight Train	Donald Crews	(60 words)

C. 90–120 words (actual books used)

Dark Dark Tale	Ruth Brown	(116 words)
Carrot Seed	Ruth Krauss	(95 words)
Hurray for Snail	John Stadler	(110 words)
The Chick and the Duckling	Mirra Ginsburg	(108 words)
Growing Vegetable Soup	Lois Ehlert	(110 words)
Herman the Helper	Robert Kraus	(99 words)
If You Take a Paintbrush	Fulvio Testa	(95 words)
Animals Should Definitely Not Wear Clothing	Judi Barrett	(120 words)

D. 120–200 words

Good Night Owl	Pat Hutchins	(188 words)
The Happy Day	Ruth Krauss	(130 words)
Just for You	Mercer Mayer	(150 words)
If You Look Around You	Fulvio Tests	(112 words)
All By Myself	Mercer Mayer	(155 words)
Noisy Nora	Rosemary Wells	(204 words)
There's a Nightmare in My Closet	Mercer Mayer	(153 words)
You'll Soon Grow Into Them, Titch	Pat Hutchins	(191 words)

___

picture chart (i.e., pictures and vowels for apple, elephant, insect, octopus, umbrella) is referred to as necessary to help the children remember the short vowel sounds. The teacher also points out the use of context clues as an aid in decoding as the story or retelling is read (e.g., "What word would make sense here?"). The teacher also models the strategy of self-checking. After decoding a word, the children are encouraged to ask themselves if what they said matches the letters of the word and makes sense in the story. The first time the story is read, the teacher's voice will be the leading voice. The story might be read a second time with the children's voices taking the lead if time permits.

For Group A texts the teacher selects about three words per story for the children to write in sets of boxes (on paper or small chalkboards) to develop their phonemic awareness. For each word one phoneme is represented in each box in the set (e.g., | sh | | u | | t |). The teacher begins by saying, "What sound do you hear first in *shut*? Does anyone know how we would spell /sh/? Put 'sh' in the first box."

On Day 1, the children spend about five minutes rereading an "old" story (not the one just covered or to be covered by the teacher in the small group) with an aide, volunteer, or older student (or partner if no one else is available). The aide (or other person) listening to the children reread needs to be shown how to provide the right amount of help to the children. He or she should not help much on words children are likely to be able to figure out but should help quite a bit on words they are likely to be unable to decode. Paired rereading is better than no follow-up rereading, but adult supervision of this rereading of texts from Groups A, B, and C is preferable. This independent rereading with an aide or other skilled reader should occur each day but does not have to be adjacent to the time the teacher has provided the small group instruction.

Day 2. The children and teacher either chorally reread the story or story retelling or take turns rereading parts of the story or the story retelling on the chart. The children receive as much help as needed from the teacher to avoid frustration but are encouraged to use context clues and sounding and blending strategies to decode unremembered words on their own. The story is usually read more than once on this day, with the children taking as much responsibility for this reading as they can. Usually the teacher tracks for the children as they read.

Children receive a personal copy of the story retelling that they can illustrate and use for rereading practice. A blank page at the end of this booklet is used for guided writing to develop children's phonemic awareness and knowledge of sound–symbol correspondences. The children agree on one sentence to write about the story (e.g., *The chick couldn't swim.*). Each child writes the sentence on the last blank page of the booklet or on a separate sheet of paper. The children basically stay together as they write, with the teacher eliciting from them the possible correct letters for the sounds in the words they are spelling. However, the teacher quickly tells the children the letters for sounds they most likely will not generate successfully. For example, the teacher might ask, "Who remembers how to spell *the*? Does anyone know how to spell /*ch*/ in *chick*? What do you hear next? How do you spell /ĭ/? What do you hear next? This is spelled with /*ch*/ in *chick*. What sound do you hear at the beginning of *couldn't*? How could you spell it? It's spelled with a *c* in this word. The rest of the word is spelled *o-u-l-d-n-'-t* . What do you hear first in *swim*? What do you hear next? How do you spell /ĭ/? What do you hear at the end of the word?" The teacher may assist the children orally or write the letters *after* they have (to avoid the children simply copying the teacher).

With the aide, volunteer, or older student (or partner if no one else is available), each child rereads his or her copy of the story or story retelling. The children are encouraged to do as much of this rereading on their own as they can. They are reminded of or they are shown how to use context clues and to sound and blend words in instances where they are most likely to be successful. The children are simply told difficult words, or much of the rereading is done for them if they are struggling with too many words in the story (i.e., decoding with less than 85–90% accuracy). It is important that children feel successful, not frustrated, in this program.

Day 3. This day is basically a repetition of Day 2. The teacher may choose to listen to children individually reread the story or their personal copies of the story retelling (depending on which has been used) as others illustrate the story. If the teacher listens to children read individually, the group rereading instead of the sentence writing should be dropped for the day.

If only one copy per child of a retelling is duplicated, children can take some of their story retellings home to read to a parent after the third day. Other story retellings should remain at school for practice reading material. If the copying budget permits, it is good to make two copies of every retelling so one can stay at school and one can go home.

At this point, the teacher, aide, or volunteer completes a running record as each child reads the most recent story or story retelling. This is used as a record of student progress. Although a few children may have some difficulty with the first few stories, we have found that children, on the average, perform with at least 94 percent accuracy in word recognition on the running records by the end of the third day on the story. If there isn't time to take a running record on every story, this can be done on every other story instead.

Transition to Independent Reading

By late February or early March, as children move into Group C and Group D books, the instructional approach changes considerably. Half of the books in Group C and all of the books in Group D no longer make use of story retellings and/or group instruction. Instead, the children read the original book. The teacher works with pairs of students over a three-day period as she helps them independently read stories that have not been read aloud first. The purpose of this approach is to help the children make the transition to independent reading. The teacher reminds the children of the strategies they have learned to monitor their word recognition and to decode words not instantly recognized. Strategies that have been stressed include asking yourself if the word you've said makes sense; thinking of what would make sense in the story; sounding out the parts of a word and blending these parts together; and using the vowel chart to remember the short vowel sounds. The teacher may not be able to work with all students on all three days. However, after the teacher has helped the children read through a particular book, the aide or volunteer assists them in rereading. Children can assist one another if an aide or volunteer is not available. Paired reading at these levels is encouraged, but adult supervision of the children's rereading is also desirable.

Teacher Training

Typically, teachers are introduced to the program in a half-day workshop in the fall. Another half-day workshop may be scheduled around November, once the program is under way, to work on problems the teachers are experiencing. Half-hour meetings, before or after school, are held about once a month to give teachers a chance to exchange ideas related to the program.

Most importantly, perhaps, a half-time resource teacher (working with up to six teachers) spends forty-five minutes twice a week in each teacher's classroom as the program is being implemented. This person listens to children read individually (instead of an aide or volunteer on these days), provides the classroom teacher with feedback and suggestions related to her teaching of the small group, and assists with dissemination of materials. During the first year of EIR in St. Louis Park, three doctoral students in reading education at the University of Minnesota served as resource people for two or three different teachers apiece.

EFFECTIVENESS OF THE PROGRAM

Thirty children from six classrooms in two schools in St. Louis Park participated in the EIR program in Year 1. In May, 67 percent of these children (who were from the lowest 20% of the class in emergent reading ability in October) were reading on at least a preprimer level (with 93% accuracy or better on an informal reading inventory); 40 percent were reading on an end-of-grade-one level or better. They were at the twenty-ninth percentile (38 NCE) on a standardized reading test in September and at the thirty-seventh percentile (43 NCE) in May. On these same measures, only 36 percent of the comparison children (28 children from 6 classes) were reading on at least a preprimer level in May, and 11 percent were reading on an end-of-grade-one level or better. These children were at the thirty-fourth percentile (41 NCE) on the standardized reading test in September and the twenty-seventh percentile (37 NCE) in May.

Prior to Year 1, 8 percent of first grade children in the two schools were placed in learning-disability.classes by the end of first grade. By the end of Year 1, 5 percent of the children from EIR first grade classes and 7 percent of the children from comparison first grade classes were placed in learning-disability classes. These numbers indicate that learning-disability placements for first grade students were down slightly during the year in which EIR was first implemented.

Children from Year 1 who participated in EIR and comparison children from Year 1 were tested again in second grade. By mid-March, 72 percent of the children who had participated in EIR were reading on a solid second grade level. Sixteen percent of these children continued in EIR or received special education services in second grade. Of the comparison children, 65 percent were reading on grade level. Half of the comparison children received special education services and/or participated in EIR in second grade. These results suggest that even when EIR interventions are delayed until second grade, children benefit. However, we would not want to suggest that EIR be postponed until second grade, since many children benefit from the program in first grade.

MODIFICATIONS TO THE PROGRAM

In Year 2, the EIR program was expanded to all thirteen first grade classrooms in the district, even though it operated without the university assistance available the year before. It was also expanded into second grade classrooms to be used with children who had not yet learned to read or who were reading significantly below a second grade level. Some teachers felt that the EIR program would blend in better with the regular reading program if the story retellings for Levels A, B, and C were based on the books read as part of the regular program. Consequently, teachers prepared story retellings to share among themselves that went with the stories they used in their whole language program. They were careful to adhere to recommended guidelines for story length (i.e., 40–60 words for Level A retellings).

The district assigned a district-funded resource teacher to work half-time in each building in Years 2 and 3 to train teachers new to the program and to listen to children read individually several days a week. In one school the first grade teachers have continued to provide the small-group instruction themselves. In the other the district-funded EIR resource teacher took over this role in all but one first grade classroom because the classroom teachers felt that they just did not have the time to provide the instruction themselves. In second grade classrooms the EIR resource teachers also provided the instruction because of classroom teachers' concerns about time. This issue of time will be raised again in a later section.

At the end of Year 2 in St. Louis Park, 78 percent of the seventy-eight children participating in EIR were reading on at least a preprimer level on an informal reading inventory. Thirty-six percent of these children were reading on an end-of-grade-one level or better on this inventory.

IMPLEMENTATION IN OTHER DISTRICTS

The EIR program has also been implemented in several White Bear Lake, Minnesota, elementary schools. This suburban district uses a systematic phonics program for its basic reading instruction for the first two-thirds of first grade. Children are not ability-grouped in this basic program.

In White Bear Lake the EIR program was carried out in the same manner as that of St. Louis Park in Year 1. During the first year of operation, a doctoral student in reading education from the University of Minnesota served as the resource person for the four classroom teachers using the program.

In May, 83 percent of the twenty-four children in the EIR program were reading on at least a preprimer level on an informal reading inventory; 54 percent were reading on an end-of-grade-one level or better. Of the twenty-one comparison children in the same district, 38 percent were reading on a preprimer level or better, 10 percent on an end-of-grade-one level or better.

A rural district in Osceola, Wisconsin, has also implemented the EIR program. This district uses a basal reader program in first grade, but children are not ability-grouped. The reading specialist in the district served as a resource person in St. Louis Park during the first year of implementation of EIR and has served as the resource teacher for EIR in her elementary building.

In May of Year 1, 93 percent of the fifteen children who participated in EIR were reading on at least a preprimer level; 73% were reading on an end-of-grade-one level or better. In contrast, 60 percent of the five comparison children were reading on at least a preprimer level, 20 percent on an end-of-grade-one level or better.

The one common element of the first grade reading programs across the three districts is that children received whole class heterogeneous instruction. However, each school had elected to use a different approach to the classroom reading program. The results from the three school districts suggest that EIR is an effective supplemental program for a number of quite different approaches to regular first grade reading instruction. Across the three districts, 30 to 50 percent more children who received the EIR assistance were reading by the end of first grade than comparison children who did not receive this supplemental help.

TEACHER REACTIONS

Generally, teachers have been very positive about the use of EIR in their first grade classrooms. Comments from teachers on end-of-year questionnaires have underscored children's excellent progress, enjoyment of the program, and positive feelings about themselves as readers. Teachers report that the program is worth the extra effort because it makes a big difference in their children's reading success.

The biggest teacher concern is finding the time to fit in the twenty minutes of daily supplemental instruction. Most teachers used the EIR program with their lowest-achieving readers while a teacher aide was monitoring the rest of the class in independent, self-selected reading or other independent reading or writing activities.

However, the fact that 100 percent of the teachers across three districts who piloted EIR have continued the program without university involvement and that 75 percent have chosen to provide this daily supplemental instruction themselves is encouraging. Authorities who have studied the effects of special education and Chapter I pullout programs for low-achieving readers have concluded that classroom teachers must assume part of the responsibility and, correspondingly, take the time to improve the reading ability of their lowest-achieving readers (Allington & McGill-Franzen, 1989; O'Sullivan, Ysseldyke, Christenson, & Thurlow, 1990). EIR appears to be a supplemental program that many first grade teachers can work into their busy schedules to help their poorest readers do better.

PROGRAM COSTS

EIR is an inexpensive program. Materials, including paper and sets of books and charts to be rotated among three teachers, cost about $100. This expense drops to $35 or so per teacher after the first year. The cost for clerical aides to reproduce the individual copies of story retellings for six classes is about $300. The cost for instructional aides to spend forty-five minutes three days a week in six classes is approximately $5,000. The cost for substitutes to release six teachers to attend two half-day in-service sessions is about $500. The greatest program expense is for a half-time resource teacher who works with six teachers, spending about thirty to forty-five minutes twice a week in each classroom to provide support and listen to children read individually. This cost runs from about $15,000 to $20,000. Overall program costs are estimated at $21,500 to $26,500 for approximately forty children in six first-grade classrooms. This averages out to approximately $600 per child to receive year-long supplemental daily reading help through the EIR program. If a well-trained instructional aide took the place of the resource teacher listening to children read individually for the additional two days a week in classrooms, overall program costs would drop to about $11,500 or approximately $300 per child. In any case, these estimates are based on the assumption that the classroom teacher provides the fifteen to twenty minutes of daily supplemental small-group instruction.

In many schools much of this cost could be absorbed by the reallocation of resource teacher and instructional aide time. Since adopting the EIR program typically seems to reduce the number of children who later need remedial assistance by 30 to 50 percent, the investment seems particularly cost-effective.

CONCLUSION

EIR involves providing children with additional classroom instruction and additional opportunities to practice reading easy material. The results of the program have been encouraging. Across the three districts, 30 to 50 percent more children who participated in EIR were reading by the end of first grade than children who were at a similar level of emergent reading ability in the fall but who did not receive the EIR help.

The results of EIR are not as dramatic as those reported for other, more intensive interventions (e.g., Reading Recovery, Success For All). This is not too surprising, however, because EIR does not provide individual tutoring, and the overall intensity of the intervention is actually quite modest. Nevertheless, EIR works well in schools with quite different approaches to first grade reading instruction and might be seen as an initial effort in rethinking beginning reading instruction in almost any school. It is a small-group approach to early reading intervention in which the instruction is provided primarily by the first grade teacher within the regular classroom. The program is inexpensive, relatively easy to implement, and has been viewed favorably by classroom teachers who have provided the intervention. Most importantly, the program has helped many low-achieving emergent readers get off to a better start in reading in first grade than would have been the case without their participation in the program.

In the second and third years in St. Louis Park, some first grade teachers requested that a district-funded reading resource teacher come into their classes to provide the EIR small-group instruction. Other teachers in this district and all teachers in the two other districts have chosen to continue providing the EIR supplemental instruction themselves. While it appears that EIR works well in both formats (classroom teacher or resource teacher providing the instruction), we remain strongly supportive of the former approach. The classroom teacher can better understand and help her lowest-achieving readers by providing this supplemental instruction herself and can readily make connections between the supplemental instruction and the regular reading instruction she provides. Also, classroom teachers can share the joy that the children feel as they are succeeding in the EIR program. Another advantage of having the classroom teacher, as opposed to a resource teacher, provide the supplemental instruction is that it is a lower-cost approach to providing extra help for these lowest-achieving first grade readers. An aide, possibly funded by Chapter I, can work with the rest of the class while the regular teacher works with six or seven children on the EIR program for fifteen or twenty minutes a day.

What we find particularly exciting about the EIR model is that classroom teachers are making an important difference in the end-of-first-grade reading attainment of many of their lowest-achieving readers. The teachers we have worked with have made a commitment to provide twenty minutes of daily, quality supplemental reading instruction to these children, and this effort has been worthwhile. These teachers have demonstrated that classroom adaptations can have substantial effects on the reading development of children experiencing difficulty in first grade. While EIR may not provide adequate intervention in all cases, the results gathered to date indicate that this classroom-based effort can provide many low-achieving first-grade students with the support they need to learn to read along with their peers.

Acknowledgment: We would like to thank all of the teachers in St. Louis Park, Minnesota, White Bear Lake, Minnesota, and Osceola, Wisconsin, who have participated in the program.

REFERENCES

Adams, M. (1990). *Beginning to read: Thinking and learning about print.* Boston, MA: MIT Press.

Allington, R. (1991). The legacy of "slow it down and make it more concrete." In J. Zutell & S. McCormick (Eds.), *Learner factors/teacher factors: Issues in literacy research and instruction* (pp. 19–30). Chicago: National Reading Conference.

Allington, R., & McGill-Franzen, A. (1989). School response to reading failure: Chapter I and special education students in grades 2, 4, & 8. *Elementary School Journal, 89,* 529–542.

Anderson, R. C., Hiebert, E. H., Scott, J. A., & Wilkinson, T. A. (1985). *Becoming a nation of readers.* Champaign, IL: University of Illinois, Center for the Study of Reading.

Ball, E. W., & Blachman, B. A. (1991). Does phoneme awareness training in kindergarten make a difference in early word recognition and developmental spelling? *Reading Research Quarterly, 26,* 49–66.

Bond, G. L., & Dykstra, R. (1967). The cooperative research program in first-grade reading instruction. *Reading Research Quarterly, 2,* 5–142.

Bradley, I., & Bryant, P. (1983). Categorizing sounds and learning to read. A causal connection. *Nature, 301,* 419–421.

Chall, J. S. (1983). *Learning to read: The great debate* (2nd ed.). New York: McGraw-Hill.

Chomsky, C. (1979). Approaching early reading through invented spelling. In L. B. Resnick & P. A. Weaver (Eds.), *Theory and practice of early reading: Vol. 2* (pp. 343–65). Hillsdale, NJ: Erlbaum.

Clay, M. (1975). *What did I write?* London: Heinemann Educational Books.

Clay, M. (1985). *The early detection of reading difficulties* (3rd ed.). Portsmouth, NH: Heinemann Educational Books.

Cunningham, A. E. (1990). Explicit versus implicit instruction in phonemic awareness. *Journal of Experimental Child Psychology, 50,* 429–444.

Ehri, L., & Wilce, L. (1987). Does learning to spell help beginners learn to read words? *Reading Research Quarterly, 12,* 47–65.

Herman, P. A. (1985). The effect of repeated readings on reading rate, speech pauses, and word recognition accuracy. *Reading Research Quarterly, 20,* 553–565.

Hoffman, J., Roser, N., & Battle, J. (1993). Reading aloud in classrooms: From modal to a model. *The Reading Teacher, 46,* 495–505.

Juel, C. (1988). Learning to read and write: A longitudinal study of 54 children from first through fourth grade. *Journal of Educational Psychology, 80*, 437–447.

Juel, C., Griffith, P. L., & Gough, P. B. (1986). Acquisition of literacy: A longitudinal study of children in first and second grade. *Journal of Educational Psychology, 78*, 243–255.

Liberman, I. (1973). Segmentation of the spoken word and reading acquisition. *Bulletin of the Orton Society, 23*, 65–77.

Lundberg, I., Frost, J., & Peterson, O. (1988). Effects of an extensive program for stimulating phonological awareness in preschool children. *Reading Research Quarterly, 23*, 263–284.

Mason, J. (1980). When do children begin to read: An exploration of four-year-old children's letter and word recognition competencies. *Reading Research Quarterly, 15*, 203–227.

O'Sullivan, P., Ysseldyke, J., Christenson, S., & Thurlow, M. (1990). Mildly handicapped elementary students' opportunity to learn during reading instruction in mainstream and special education settings. *Reading Research Quarterly, 25*, 131–146.

Pinnell, G. (1989). Reading Recovery: Helping at-risk children learn to read. *Elementary School Journal, 90*, 160–183.

Pinnell, G., DeFord, D., & Lyons, C. (1988). *Reading Recovery: Early intervention for at-risk first graders.* Arlington, VA: Educational Research Service.

Samuels, S. J. (1979). The method of repeated reading. *The Reading Teacher, 32*, 403–408.

Share, D. L., Jorm, A. F., Maclean, R., & Matthews, R. (1984). Sources of individual differences in reading achievement. *Journal of Educational Psychology, 76*, 1309–1324.

Slavin, R. E., Madden, N., Karweit, N., Dolan, L., & Wasik, B. (1993). Success for all: A comprehensive approach to prevention and early intervention. In R. E. Slavin, N. Karweit, & B. Wasik (Eds.), *Preventing early school failure: Research, policy and practice* (pp. 175–205). Boston: Allyn & Bacon.

Slavin, R., Madden, N., Karweit, N., Livermon, B., & Dolan, L. (1990). Success for all: First-year outcomes of a comprehensive plan for reforming urban education. *American Educational Research Journal, 27*, 255–278.

Stanovich, K. E. (1986). Matthew effects in reading: Some consequences of individual differences in the acquisition of literacy. *Reading Research Quarterly, 21*, 360–407.

Stanovich, K. E., Cunningham, A. E., & Feeman, D. J. (1984). Intelligence, cognitive skills, and early reading progress. *Reading Research Quarterly, 19*, 278–303.

Taylor, B. (1990). *A test of phonemic awareness for classroom use.* Unpublished manuscript, University of Minnesota, Minneapolis, MN.

Tunmer, W. E., & Nesdale, A. R. (1985). Phonemic segmentation skill and beginning reading. *Journal of Educational Psychology, 7*, 417–427.

CHAPTER 9

Scoring Well on Tests or Becoming Genuinely Literate: Rethinking Remediation in a Small Rural School

TRUDY P. WALP
North Warren Central School District, New York
SEAN A. WALMSLEY
State University of New York at Albany

North Warren Central School District is located in the Adirondacks in upstate New York. It is a small district, with one K–3 building (260 students), a 4–8 middle school (280 students), and a high school (190 students). It serves a predominantly rural, poor community that relies primarily on logging and tourism for its economic base.

In 1982, when Trudy Walp joined the faculty as an elementary reading teacher, the reading curriculum consisted of a strictly phonics-based basal series, with accompanying workbooks. There were no expectations or provisions for children to read full-length literature on a regular basis, nor were children expected to write much—writing experiences consisted primarily of completing grammar workbooks, with the occasional assigned report to be completed. The remedial program was organized around the Wisconsin Design, with a number of small components devoted to word recognition skills. It was strictly a pullout approach, completely separate from the regular classroom program, even though both programs emphasized decoding skills. As was typical in those days, the remedial reading program was entirely devoted to reading skills—writing was not part of the remedial curriculum. Children were placed in the remedial program primarily on the basis of their scores on the Gates-McGinitie Reading Test and/or the Stanford Achievement Test, which were administered to all children at least once a year. Students scoring at or below the twenty-third percentile were eligible for remedial classes. For a brief period before Trudy arrived, the previous remedial reading teacher had tried to broaden the scope of the remedial program, but she was not able to establish much of a foothold in the time she was in the school.

One of the first things Trudy did was to change the focus and content of the remedial program. Because she received her master's degree in reading from a program with a fairly traditional approach to reading (e.g., learning how to diagnose a child's reading difficulties with the Durrell Analysis of Reading Difficulty was a major part of her training), Trudy's desire to forgo a traditional approach to remediation merits an explanation. Trudy was originally trained in music education, and had been teaching music in public schools for about five years, along with a private practice. To her, the parallels between teaching music and teaching reading seemed surprisingly close. Traditionally, music teachers teach children the music skills; once these have been mastered, children can proceed to playing "real" music, in exactly the same way that once having acquired reading skills, children can proceed to "real" reading of books. In music education, there are methodologies that challenge the skills approach: for example, the Suzuki approach teaches children to start by playing "real" music, and they learn the skills in the context of these "real" pieces. In her own music classes, Trudy had always taught her students to learn music skills in the context of making music. Although she had been trained in reading with a skills approach, once in the classroom, she quickly adopted the same philosophy for teaching reading as she did for teaching music. Interestingly enough, this shift toward a skills-within-context approach did not come about through exposure to whole language philosophies, but rather through applying what she knew about the teaching of music to the teaching of reading. In music, playing "real" pieces of music is what is important, right from the beginning; in reading, reading "real" full-length literature is what is important, not only from the beginning, but also in remedial classes.

Thus, she shifted the emphasis of the remedial program from skills in isolation to skills in context, from word recognition to comprehension, and from short, artificially constructed passages designed to teach or practice a specific skill to full-length literature.

Trudy's use of literature in the remedial program quickly drew the attention of the school superintendent (who was also the elementary school principal), and he thought it would be a good idea to expose all children to a literature program. He asked Trudy to spend two hours a day pulling children out of their regular classes for what he called a "reading enrichment" program, which consisted of Trudy reading literature with nonremedial students on a regular basis.

These two programs operated outside of the core reading program, which so far remained intact, and probably would have remained so for a long time if, in 1984, a third of the students had not failed the recently instituted New York State writing test. This prompted the superintendent to discuss the situation with the faculty, and as a result they decided to bring in a university consultant, Sean Walmsley, to help improve the school's writing program. As together we progressed in our work on writing, we began discussions on how writing instruction could be better integrated with reading, and that led us to start rethinking the entire language arts curriculum. In an article in *Elementary School Journal* (Walmsley & Walp, 1990), we described the transformation of the curriculum from the perspective of the regular classroom program. In this chapter, we examine the reforms from the perspective of the remedial program. Since much has gone on since we wrote the *ESJ* piece in 1990, we will also bring the reader up to date with current progress on the project.

PHILOSOPHY OF THE REMEDIAL PROGRAM

Most remedial programs live by a very simple axiom—take in children who have scores below grade level on some measure of reading, bring them up to grade level, and graduate them back into their regular classes. Even Reading Recovery views its mission as taking in the lowest 20 percent of first graders, accelerating them up to grade level, and returning them as soon as possible to their regular classmates. Of course, it isn't surprising that most remedial programs are fixated on helping the lowest-achieving children raise their test performance. What they are doing is complying with existing Chapter I mandates, and the federal Chapter I program funds many, if not most, remedial reading efforts in the country.

Our philosophy of remediation includes meeting the requirements of Chapter I, but it goes much deeper than that. It rests on several fundamental principles that guide the whole K–8 language arts curriculum, not just the remedial component. Let's review these briefly.

Genuine Literacy

We want all our students to be genuinely literate. By this we mean that the students should enjoy reading and writing and choose to do so on a regular basis, that they read widely and deeply, that they communicate effectively in spoken and written form, that they be good listeners, and that they have substantial and growing knowledge of the world (including historical, scientific, economic, cultural, religious, and literary aspects).

Being genuinely literate entails more than simply scoring well on a standardized test, and it definitely involves more than learning a narrow range of reading and editing skills. It entails actively engaging in literate behavior. What this implies for our program is that instead of preparing our students for eventual literate behavior, we engage them in genuine acts of literacy right from the beginning and throughout their school career. It also implies that the language arts curriculum will not be fragmented into separate components for reading, composing, and editing, but rather integrate these in meaningful ways. Further, it implies that skills will be taught within the context of genuine reading, writing, speaking, and listening (what we term a *skills-through-application* approach), rather than as separate or prerequisite components of the program (what we term a *skills-to-application* approach). Engaging children in genuine acts of literacy, integrating the language arts curriculum, and teaching skills within the context of real reading and real writing are the cornerstones of our instructional philosophy, and guide the day-to-day language arts activities (Walmsley & Walp, 1990).

Long-Term View of Literacy Development

We take seriously the notion that a child's literacy development extends over a long period of time, and cannot be neatly segmented into stages that correspond with grades or years. We also accept the fact that all children develop their literacy abilities at different rates and in different ways. What this implies for our program is that it is more important that we nurture, stimulate, and facilitate children's literacy development than that we ensure mastery of specific literacy skills at the end of each year. Thus, we reject the notion of a fixed schedule for every child's literacy development, and support instead a *developmentally appropriate* approach, in which the curriculum is adjusted to the child, rather than the other way around (Bredekamp, 1987; Walmsley, Camp, & Walmsley, 1992). "Developmentally appropriate" is not a catchphrase for simply lowering expectations for less advantaged children, or simply abandoning them to drift along, doing whatever comes naturally. Our expectations for all the children are the same: to become fully literate, but not necessarily at the same time, nor by the same means. There is a big difference between lowering one's expectations for at-risk children because they can not keep pace with the schedule and building flexibility into the schedule so that all students can participate in the literacy program at their own stage of development. Having a fixed schedule is as unhealthy for children who are ahead as it is for children who are behind.

But it is hard to dislodge this notion of a fixed schedule. All basal programs are based on it, and it seems to undergird even the latest remedial approaches, including Reading Recovery. Even though we hold Reading Recovery in high esteem, we worry that the notion of accelerating children's literacy development assumes that there is an official rate of development from which the "at-risk" child has unfortunately deviated. Reading Recovery may be one of the most effective methods of keeping children on schedule, but the schedule itself is, for us, highly artificial.

Equal Opportunity

We take seriously our responsibility to offer all children, regardless of their literacy abilities, the full range of opportunities to develop their knowledge and their language strategies. This implies a core language arts program that immerses *all* children in substantive knowledge and literature, without grouping by ability, and without a separate instructional program for less able readers. Traditional remedial programs withhold intellectual and literary experiences from poorer readers deemed "not ready" to engage in them, and routinely underestimate what these less able readers are capable of learning. Our view of a remedial program is that it should help the poorer reader access and participate fully in a rich core curriculum. Our experience suggests that Stanovich (1986) is right when he talks about the "Matthew" effect: the better readers get better because they get to read the good literature, while the poor readers wither on a diet of "high-interest," low-vocabulary books. Commitment to equal access also brings with it the responsibility to give less experienced readers more assistance in choosing, reading, and responding to books. For us, equal access is not just a question of "rights"; it offers one of the best ways we know to ensure that less able readers develop into better readers. The very act of participating in a rich core language arts program is a major determinant of a less able reader's literacy development. No matter how good a remedial program is, without a strong core curriculum, there will always be limits on the progress that children can make. What is gained from a superb remedial program may well be lost on the children's return to a meager core curriculum. Thus, strengthening the core curriculum is a major element of reforming a remedial program. Sustaining effects of remediation—one of the critical indicators of the success of Chapter I programs—depends more on the quality of the core curriculum than on the excellence of the remedial program, and so we have no choice but to attend to the core curriculum as diligently as we do the remedial. It is for these reasons that early on in our collaboration we decided to pay equal attention to both the remedial and the core language arts curriculum. It is also the reason why a description of North Warren's remedial program necessitates an understanding of the reforms we made in the regular classroom.

REFORMING THE CORE CURRICULUM

Starting in 1985, we began reforming North Warren's language arts curriculum, using the principles described above as guides. We first tackled the third and fourth grade language arts programs, mostly because those teachers were the most willing to consider changes. At first the reforms concentrated mainly on introducing or strengthening the writing component. It soon became clear that we had competing philosophies for different aspects of the curriculum: The writing program was largely a process approach, using Graves (1983) as a major source, while the reading program remained largely skills-based. This conflict led us to rethink not only our approach to reading, but also how we might better integrate reading with writing. In turn, this prompted us to create content themes (see Walmsley, 1994) as the organizing framework for the entire language arts curriculum (as opposed to a basal reading series), so that reading, writing, speaking, and listening would all have a common focus. We had already learned how to tuck editing skills within the context of children's own writing, and so tucking reading skills within the context of children's own reading of full-length literature made sense to us. Putting both of these into practice turned out to be much more challenging than we thought: In fact, it took us several years to get comfortable with a theme-based approach in grades three and four, and we are still actively involved in extending the approach down to kindergarten and up to eighth grade. As we near our tenth year of work on this curriculum reform, we are beginning to appreciate the notion that meaningful reform takes a long time and a sustained effort.

In the majority of North Warren's K–8 classrooms, then, language arts instruction is organized around themes, and all language arts activities relate to these themes. In the remainder, teachers either use themes as a major instructional tool or are just beginning to try them out. (We recognize that teachers, like their students, are at different stages of their own development, and we have always taken the stance that they should be doing what they feel comfortable with. We offer support for reforming the classroom's language arts program, but do not insist that teachers make changes they are not ready for. As we write, we do not have teachers who oppose these reforms, but we do have teachers who need more time to make them.)

Whether themes are used or not, there are some critical attributes of language arts instruction that we are working toward. The first is that children are exposed (in read-alouds, guided/shared reading, and independent reading) to a wide range of literature across the grades. We do not have graded lists of required literature, but we ensure that children have been exposed to a large number of different kinds of books (e.g., traditional literature, contemporary and historical fiction, nonfiction, and so forth), a wide range of authors and illustrators, and books on a variety of topics. The second is that children write on a regular basis. Again, we do not prescribe specific topics, but we do our best to ensure that children have written on a wide variety of topics, for different purposes and audiences, and that by the time they graduate from eighth grade, their writing experiences have been substantial. The third is that children have had substantial opportunities for oral discourse (talking, speaking, discussing, debating, and so forth) among themselves as well as with their teachers.

In order for these to occur, we needed to address the issue of time. Adding literature and writing to a schedule that is already full is bound to cause problems, and we did not want to add these components at the expense of others. Part of this dilemma is addressed by integrating the components of language arts. For example, if you take the twenty minutes devoted to separate instruction in spelling each day and incorporate it into the editing phase of the writing program, then you can use the twenty minutes to increase the amount of time devoted to writing. If you merge the teaching of reading skills with the reading of full-length literature, and the teaching of editing skills with writing compositions, then you will save large amounts of time compared to treating these as separate components. The other aspect of the time dilemma is addressed by creating uninterruptible blocks of time in which all children are present in the classroom, and from which no child may be taken away for "specials." It took an executive order from the superintendent for these daily ninety-minute blocks to be created, but they are now in place, and without them it would be very difficult to have the kind of integration of language arts that a theme-based approach calls for. Integration does not mix well with pullout programs and departmentalization.

Once the language arts "blocks" have been created, teachers are now free to integrate the various aspects of language arts in their own ways, without fear that they are allowing their "reading" time to encroach on their "writing" time. It also allows them to pursue topics or books or writing activities for extended periods of time until they are completed, rather than having to fit them into prescribed, rigid schedules. Loosening up the schedule in this way also encourages teachers to think about integration across subject areas, not just within the strands of language arts. There is, we admit, a downside to this freedom: Teachers can get carried away with one aspect of language arts to the detriment of others. But our experience is that eventually a balance is maintained, and that the benefits of this open schedule far outweigh its disadvantages.

Another aspect of the language arts program we have been able to change across grades K–8 is to eliminate grouping by reading ability. There is now no ability grouping left, even in the two grades that periodically use commercial basal readers. Ability grouping is incompatible with the principle of equal access, as well as being documented in the research literature as having long-term negative effects on less able readers (Oakes, 1985). What convinced our teachers to abandon ability grouping was our willingness to increase the support for less able readers (about which more will be said below), the fact that ability grouping got in the way of effective integrated language arts instruction, and that theme-centered instruction seemed well able to meet the needs of all children in the class.

The only form of ability grouping that has persisted is the practice of retaining children, but this has decreased by about half (from eleven to six per year) over the past five years, although not without spirited debate among the primary teachers. Our real concern about retention is that if we take the long-term view of literacy development, not only do we find that retaining children has long-term negative effects (Shepard & Smith, 1989), but also that this practice conflicts with our philosophy that questions the existence of a fixed schedule of literacy development.

This is one of those issues on which we sit on one side of the fence and many of our primary teachers sit on the other. We are not yet sure how to resolve it. If we press for ending retention, then teachers respond by referring children they would have retained to special education instead. For us, that is no solution either. And it is hard to convince teachers not to retain children who are not "on grade level" or who are not "ready" for the next grade when they have seen the short-term benefits of past retentions with their own eyes (they do not see the long-term harmful effects). Given that retention is directly related to a fixed curriculum, letting go of the fixed curriculum eventually persuades teachers to let go of retention, but there is a transitional period in which teachers are neither confident enough with a developmentally appropriate approach nor sufficiently convinced of the inadequacy of the fixed curriculum. One of the techniques we think has contributed most to teachers' willingness to make this transition are the narrative report cards we have developed for K–6. Describing a student's growth and needs in language arts, instead of quantifying and comparing their performances with grades, has helped teachers see that children's language development is much broader than merely mastering a number of language arts skills in a given year.

REFORMING THE REMEDIAL CURRICULUM

Reforming the remedial program began in 1982. Up until then, the program was strictly pullout. Children who tested at or below the twenty-third percentile on the Gates-McGinitie or the Stanford Achievement tests were assigned to half-hour periods three times a week in the reading room with a Chapter I teacher. The remedial curriculum was completely divorced from the regular program and consisted primarily of drills taken from Recipe for Reading (Traub, 1982), Glass Analysis for Decoding (Glass, 1973), and Distar (Engelmann & Bruner, 1974).

The first thing Trudy did was to set these materials aside and instead to use full-length literature as the basis for all remedial instruction. Ironically, this approach separated the remedial program even further from the regular classroom program, which used the Economy Basal Series. Children in the remedial program spent their time reading books, writing compositions, responding to and discussing what they were reading, and working on reading and writing skills through the literature and the writing. In almost every respect, the approach used in the remedial room had the characteristics of what would eventually become the schoolwide instructional approach. However, it was still a pullout program; it accepted only those children who scored at or below the twenty-third percentile; and it had little or no connection with the regular classroom program. In essence, it was a self-contained, literature-based language arts program for poor readers!

This program stayed intact until we started working with the third and fourth grade teachers. At that point, it changed quite dramatically. The first thing that happened was that Trudy's responsibilities were shifted from working with seventy-five students from nine different classrooms, grades one through four, to working with thirty students in four classrooms (grades three and four), plus having responsibility for directing the language arts reforms in grades three and four. An additional reading teacher was hired to work with first and second grade students. Also, the remedial program itself changed from exclusively pullout to a combination of in-class and pullout services. For part of the core language arts block, Trudy would work in the classroom with the teacher and the remedial students; later each day, she would meet with the remedial students on their own in the reading room. While in the classroom, Trudy would do a variety of things such as observing "her" students in their language arts activities, helping them with a guided reading activity, holding book conferences on their independent reading, or holding writing conferences. Trudy's instructional activities depended on what the classroom teacher was doing at the time and on how the remedial students were responding or performing. Another new feature of this approach was that Trudy and each of the classroom teachers now had a weekly planning period in which they shared responsibility for instructional activities, as well as communicating about the progress and needs of the remedial students. This planning time also allowed Trudy to share with the classroom teachers ideas for reforming and strengthening the regular curriculum so that it met two goals, to provide more effective instruction for remedial students in the regular classroom, and to assist teachers' efforts to move their language arts program toward a literature-based approach.

In the remedial room, Trudy continued the approach she had been using for the two previous years, except now she was able to draw on what she had learned about the children as they performed in the regular classroom that morning and what she knew about the classroom teacher's instruction. In her classroom visit, Trudy may have seen that a remedial child was having difficulty understanding part of a guided reading experience. In the reading room that afternoon, she could work with the child on that particular book, so that the next day the child wouldn't fall behind. On other occasions, Trudy might reteach a reading or writing strategy that a remedial child had not quite grasped, or one that the classroom teacher had not presented in a way that the child could grasp. Because they are slow readers, remedial students frequently do not finish reading selections and fall behind. In the reading room, Trudy could help the child complete reading the selection, or reread it to clarify points, or even read ahead so that the child was prepared for the next day's lesson. If in the morning the teacher had been holding a book conference and a child was mixing up the book's characters, this could easily be sorted out in the afternoon session. Remedial students are not always having difficulties, and so the afternoon session might be devoted to extending a child's experience with a book—for example, illustrating or dramatizing a book on which a successful conference had already been held in the classroom. One of the most significant changes that has occurred by using this approach is that now the remedial child's instruction is driven almost exclusively by his or her needs, rather than according to a set curriculum of skills. This approach is particularly effective in the area of skills transfer. In a traditional remedial program, a child is taught specific skills and then is expected to take them into the regular classroom and apply them when they are needed. In our approach, the skills we work on are those that a child needs in order to participate successfully in the classroom, and what is learned can be applied immediately. Thus we not only work on strategies that apply to real classroom literacy tasks, we also ensure that there is no delay in transferring newly acquired skills to these tasks.

The major benefits of working in the classroom with the remedial students included improving the efficiency of instruction, bringing the remedial and regular programs in line with one another, and sharing the responsibility of the remedial students' literacy development equally between the classroom and remedial teachers. The lines between the regular and remedial programs quickly became blurred, and have remained so ever since.

PROFILES OF TWO REMEDIAL CHILDREN

So far we have looked at the changes from the point of view of the classroom and remedial teacher. Let's now look at the same changes from the perspective of two remedial students, one of whom graduated from eighth grade in 1985, the other graduating from eighth grade almost ten years later.

Drew's Story

Drew (not his real name) started kindergarten at North Warren in 1975. His kindergarten program was relatively uneventful. It was a typical "readiness" program, and Drew spent much of it tracing, doing worksheets, learning the names of the letters and colors, and how to form letters in writing. By the end of kindergarten, his teacher's initial suspicions were confirmed, and Drew was declared "not ready" for first grade. His second year in kindergarten was not much different than his first, except that he was a year older, and this time he did well enough on the Stanford Early School Achievement Test (SESAT) to graduate into first grade. There he was placed immediately into the bottom reading group and recommended for remedial services on the basis of his scores on the SESAT. Drew settled into his reading group, made up of poor readers like himself, and worked his way through three of the preprimers and one primer in the Economy Series. In the reading room, Drew worked with four other first graders on consonant sounds and short vowels. Back in the classroom, Drew's writing comprised copying sentences from the board, with an emphasis on correct letter formation. By the end of first grade, Drew was reading at a 1.1 grade-equivalent reading level, and proceeded to the bottom reading group in second grade, where he picked up where he left off in first grade.

This pattern continued in grades three through six, and by the end of sixth grade Drew's reading level was 5.2. In the eight years he had been in school, Drew had completed literally hundreds of dittos and spent hundreds of hours working on letter–sound correspondence, sight vocabulary, and comprehension skills. He hated reading and almost never read except to complete an assigned book report. His writing was characterized by poor spelling and almost illegible handwriting, and his compositions were brief and minimally developed. In fact, Drew regarded himself as a nonreader and nonwriter. Drew was read to in each grade level, but unfortunately much of the time that his teachers read aloud to the class, Drew was pulled out for remedial reading. He also was frequently absent from school, and somehow never managed to catch up with his work. By eighth grade, Drew had read very few books. Because he was in the low reading group, he never was able to take advantage of the independent reading time offered to children who had completed their seatwork; coupled with his dislike of reading, Drew found that most of the books in the classroom were too difficult to read, and the ones recommended to him were too babyish.

Drew's teachers did their best to help him and to improve his reading abilities, but he never seemed to respond to their efforts, and there never seemed to be enough time to take care of his needs. His remedial teacher was doing all the things that remedial teachers were supposed to do, such as diagnosing at a subskill level through diagnostic reading tests, working on one skill at a time until mastery was demonstrated, pretesting for the next skill on the checklist, and working on that until mastery. Somehow Drew never was able to apply the skills he learned in the remedial room to the real reading and writing tasks he had to do in the classroom.

From a 1995 vantage point, Drew's experiences sound somewhat depressing, and yet most of us can easily recall students whose experiences were similar to Drew's. They reflect assumptions and practices that were prevalent until the mid-1980s. Our portrait of Drew is neither unrepresentative nor exaggerated, nor is it intended to cast teachers in that period in an unfavorable light. Faced with the same circumstances, we ourselves would likely have done to Drew what others did.

Josh's Story

Josh (again, not his real name) entered kindergarten in 1986. His kindergarten experiences were similar to Drew's in many respects, but very different in others. What was the same was the basic commitment to a readiness program, with its emphasis on mastering letter recognition, colors, numbers, and social skills. What had changed from Drew's year in kindergarten was that the teachers were now beginning to incorporate ideas from the emergent literacy movement and changes they saw going on in the upper elementary grades. Process writing, including invented spelling, was now a regularly scheduled part of the kindergarten day, along with shared reading through big books. Unlike Drew, who never actually wrote a story, Josh wrote many of them, and was encouraged to write about his experiences and to share what he had written with his classmates. It didn't bother his teacher that at first neither he nor anyone else could actually read what he had written, but toward the end of the year his teacher characterized his writing as "young," and because of that, along with poor SESAT scores, recommended that he be retained. Unlike Drew, whose recommendation for retention went unnoticed and unchallenged, there was much debate about Josh's recommendation. Finally, a compromise was struck. It was agreed that Josh would be placed in first grade but receive remedial services, and a decision would be made at the end of first grade on whether to retain him then. Already, though, Drew's and Josh's literacy experiences were taking different paths. Drew had few genuine literacy experiences in kindergarten—they consisted primarily of the read-alouds—while Josh had experienced read-alouds, shared reading, and real writing. (Compared to what a current kindergartner would experience in this same classroom with the same teacher, even Josh's experiences were quite meager, but at least the importance of these early literacy experiences was recognized by his kindergarten teacher.) By the time Josh entered first grade, the first grade program had undergone several important changes. The first grade teachers had replaced the Economy Basal with Scott Foresman, but they only ordered the readers (no workbooks or practice sheets). Themes from the Scott Foresman series were used to organize the language arts curriculum, but were supplemented with teacher-made materials. For example, the "Friends" theme from the series was used as the basis for a longer unit that included the basal passages, but also drew on books and other materials developed by the teachers and remedial staff. Literature now played a much larger role in first grade, becoming the major vehicle for reading instruction. Writing was well established; children wrote daily on a variety of topics, and their editing skills were taught within the context of their own writing. Spelling was no longer a separate language arts activity.

There were no ability groups for reading, and so Josh was not placed in a low group, as Drew was. But he did qualify for remedial services, and so each day his remedial reading teacher worked with him in the classroom and again later, in the reading room. Unlike Drew, Josh's remedial program was based on needs indicated through classroom observation, running records (using the literature being used in the classroom), and analysis of his writing (for composing and editing skills). By this time, the Gates-McGinitie had been dropped, and the Stanford was now given only once a year. In the remedial room, Josh's remedial teacher worked on reading and writing strategies using the books and compositions from the regular classroom, focusing on those skills that Josh needed to participate successfully in his classroom reading and writing tasks. Josh's remedial teacher did all the things that a remedial teacher trained in the late 1980s was supposed to do. Her approach reflected the many changes that had occurred over the previous decade in the field's thinking about diagnosis and remediation, about the teaching of skills and strategies, and about the proper relationship between classroom and remedial practices.

By the time Josh finished first grade, he still was not on grade level (as measured by the Stanford Achievement Test), but running records taken across the year showed steady, although slow, development of good reading behaviors. When the teachers discussed his progress at the end of the year, retention was no longer an issue. For one thing, Josh was not going into a basal program in second grade, so being ready for the following year was no longer a factor. For another, teachers noted steady progress in Josh's reading and writing abilities, and they weighed this progress more than a grade-equivalent score on the SAT's. If the second grade teachers could take Josh from where he was and continue working with him, why hold him back another year? Josh went on to second grade.

In second grade, Josh's teachers used Holt's literature anthology as the basis for their language arts program, supplemented with trade books and organized around themes. Josh continued receiving remedial services from the same remedial teacher, providing much continuity. As in first grade, the remedial teacher worked in the classroom on a daily basis, and so Josh continued to receive help both in the classroom and remedial room. By the end of second grade, Josh was not yet at grade level on the Stanford Achievement Test, but he was closing the gap. Another thing his teachers noticed was that Josh enjoyed reading and read a large number of books during the year, both in school and at home.

In third grade, Josh's teacher organized her language arts program entirely around themes, using only trade books and other materials (e.g., newspapers, *Cobblestone* magazine, *National Geographic World*, and so forth). Josh continued in the remedial program, this time with Trudy. This year was particularly good for Josh. All of the work done in the previous years was now paying off. His use of reading strategies and skills solidified, and he became an independent reader. At the end of the year, he put in a strong performance on the state's reading PEP test; other indicators, such as his day-to-day reading and writing performance and his SAT scores, also convinced his teachers and parents that he no longer needed remedial services.

By the time Josh entered fourth grade, the reformed language arts program was fully in place, and so Josh's fourth grade experiences were in a literature-rich curriculum organized around themes, with daily reading and writing activities. Josh participated eagerly and successfully, without the remedial support he had received in third grade, and did well at this grade level. He continued to grow as a reader and writer.

Although the fifth grade curriculum is theme-based, its themes are more closely integrated with content areas, and there is both more reading and more nonfiction reading at this level. About halfway through the fifth grade, Josh's teacher noticed that he was beginning to struggle with his reading, and recommended that he receive extra help from the remedial teacher for the remainder of the year. Josh's difficulties would not have turned up on a standardized test, so he would not have been eligible for

Chapter I services based solely on test scores, but in keeping with the philosophy of helping students when they need it, the remedial teacher started working with Josh again, using the classroom materials as the basis for remediation, as before. New York State has a writing competency test at the end of fifth grade, and Josh passed it comfortably.

Josh continued receiving remediation during sixth grade, but the amount of time was gradually reduced, in preparation for phasing him out of the remedial program by the end of that year. Josh did well on the New York State reading Pupil Evaluation Program (PEP) test at the end of the year, and his SAT scores were only slightly below grade level.

Josh is now in eighth grade. He no longer receives remediation, and he is doing fine. His reading comprehension on the SAT is at the forty-seventh percentile, and his total reading is at the forty-first percentile. He passed all his courses with grades ranging from 79 to 84 (70 is passing), and passed the State Competency Exams in both reading and writing. Last year, according to his reading inventory, he read nine books (about 1,200 pages of text), including Charles Dickens's *A Christmas Carol* and Arthur C. Clarke's *Childhood's End*.

When we sit down and look at Josh's "red" folder (which contains yearly reading inventories, samples of writing, and notes on book and writing conferences), we would be hard-pressed to identify him as a poor reader. From fifth grade on, there are approximately eight books per year (about 1,000 pages) recorded on his independent reading inventory sheets (most of these have book conference notes attached to them), and he has written a large number of compositions, ranging from personal narratives to research reports, poems, letters, and journal entries. Josh views himself as a reader and likes to read. But there was never a time when he did not think of himself as a reader, even during the period in which he was receiving intensive remediation. Josh has turned out to be a better reader than Drew, we admit, but the difference between them is not that great in terms of performance on standardized tests.

What really characterizes the difference between the two boys is that Drew's literacy experiences were quite slender, while Josh's have been extensive and cumulative. A simple comparison between the two boys on the amount of their reading and writing graphically exemplifies Allington's (1977) maxim that if poor readers don't get to read much, they'll never become good readers. What Josh's folder reveals is that poor readers can read a lot if they are in a program that invites them to become readers and provides the support for doing so. But quantity is not everything. Drew didn't read much, but even what he did read could hardly be described as quality literature. (Then again, the whole curriculum at that time was somewhat literature-impoverished by our current standards.) Josh not only read a lot, but what he read was of much higher quality, and of a much broader range.

The other comparison worth noting is how the two boys were treated as readers. Drew was always treated as though he needed to be prepared for reading, while Josh was treated as a reader who needed assistance with the reading he was doing. Part of this difference is due to the shift from a fixed to a developmentally appropriate curriculum. In the fixed curriculum, children quickly get sorted into good, average, and poor reader groups. In a developmentally appropriate curriculum, especially one that abandons ability grouping, a range of individual differences is a given. What this does is change teachers' perceptions of children as readers and writers, from being ahead, at, or behind a schedule (or each other) to simply moving forward along the continuum of literacy development. It is no accident that Josh sees himself as a reader while Drew did not; Drew was "behind," while Josh was always growing. If Drew had been treated like Josh, we are sure he would have been more like him.

We paint these two portraits not to make a black-and-white contrast between traditional and current approaches to remediation, but rather to show the changes we have made in both philosophy and practice at North Warren. Also, it is important to note (as we did in Walmsley & Walp, 1990) that like others who have reformed their programs, not everything works the way we would like it to, nor have all children made the kind of progress we would like, or even that Josh made. We constantly worry about children who do not seem to be thriving in our approach, and we continually modify our practices to better meet their needs. We have made a lot of progress in the last ten years, and yet we see many challenges ahead. Solving one problem always raises the challenge of another. That is what keeps us going, and what also prevents us from declaring North Warren a "model."

REFLECTIONS ON THE NORTH WARREN REFORMS

Our experiences in North Warren over the past decade have taught us a number of things about reforming remedial approaches in elementary school, but they have also raised several issues that merit further discussion.

One thing we have learned is that you cannot view the remedial program as separate from the core curriculum. One reason for this is that there are limits on how much time a child can be placed in remedial services; most of a child's time in school is spent in the regular classroom. Even the best remedial program cannot compensate for a low-quality core curriculum. Indeed, a poor core curriculum may cause poor reading and writing performances, making a remedial program necessary. In recent years, Chapter I regulations have mandated that the remedial and core curriculums be "congruent." This was intended to improve the quality of remedial programs. Unfortunately, many remedial educators have interpreted this mandate by simply attaching the remedial program to the core curriculum without examining the quality and content of the core curriculum (Walp & Walmsley, 1989). More of the same of something that is low quality has little chance of improving remedial services. Therefore, reforming the remedial program necessitates reforming the core curriculum. Interestingly, from the point of view of an at-risk learner, it may be more important to reform the core curriculum than the remedial one.

Remedial programs (including special education) are, when you think about it, forms of ability grouping. To reform the remedial program as an entity separate from the core curriculum maintains the separateness of the two programs, and perpetuates the notion that children need to be sorted into programs according to their literacy abilities. In contrast, if the remedial program is seen as an integral part of the core curriculum, the sorting notion gives way to a support model, in which children are given help according to their core curriculum needs. Chapter I has always admonished remedial educators to "supplement, not supplant" the core curriculum; we would argue that remedial services should support, not supplement or supplant. "Supplement" implies either that the core curriculum is inadequate for the remedial child's needs, or that it is fine and should be left alone. This leaves the remedial program either standing off by itself or possibly aligning itself with an inadequate core curriculum. "Support" implies that the remedial program is an integral part of the core curriculum, and that its role is to help students participate successfully in that curriculum. However, the quality of the remedial program depends on the quality of the core curriculum, so any improvements we seek for the remedial services have to involve consideration of the core curriculum, and vice versa.

Another thing we have learned is that our approach places heavy demands on the teachers, and requires teachers with considerable expertise. The reforms we have made to both the regular and remedial programs involve replacing largely commercial instructional materials, in which the teacher guides the children through someone else's program, with an approach that relies much more heavily on the teacher's knowledge and experience. For example, North Warren teachers create their own themes; read and select appropriate literature for read-alouds, shared reading, and independent reading; and then develop the instructional activities to go along with them. As a consequence of this preparation, teachers have an enormous fund of knowledge about the themes and about the books and about instructional strategies, all of which can be brought to bear in the classroom. This preparation is a great deal more thorough than a quick glance at the teacher's manual in preparation for tomorrow's reading lesson, and helping teachers reach this position has taken several years.

In the remedial room, too, we have shifted the emphasis from an approach that uses commercially prepared materials to one in which the teacher draws on her own expertise and experience to create the activities and teach strategies to children. In order to provide instruction that is responsive to a child's needs, the teacher must be knowledgeable about literacy development, children, the core curriculum, and the materials and activities best suited to the task at hand. For example, while the remedial teacher is in the regular classroom, she is carefully observing both the remedial children and the classroom activities, and making decisions about what would best help a child in the classroom and what needs to be done later, back in the remedial room. It takes a long time to develop this expertise, and the degree of intensity can be exhausting. But it is a critical component of our approach, and without this expertise it simply would not work. As our colleagues involved with Reading Recovery have also discovered, quality of instruction rests on very thorough preparation.

A final issue involves the criteria for placing children into Chapter I programs, monitoring their progress, and releasing them back to the regular classroom. Chapter I regulations have traditionally required that children be selected, monitored, and released on the basis of standardized test scores. Recently Chapter I has welcomed other indicators to be used for these purposes, but still requires standardized test scores for reporting student progress, effectively rendering alternatives moot. Describing a child's literacy status and growth solely in terms of changes on standardized tests is very troubling to us. Not only do standardized tests measure a very narrow band of literacy behaviors, they also treat literacy development as though it were simply the linear acquisition of a set number of literacy skills. These measures may—barely—be adequate for selecting, monitoring, and releasing students within a traditional, fixed, skills-based approach to literacy; they are hopelessly inadequate for describing a student's status and progress toward genuine literacy.

There are plenty of high school and college graduates whose standardized test scores define them as proficient readers, but who are not literate. Conversely, there are students who do not measure up on standardized tests but are literate in the sense that they have had substantial literary experiences, they read books on a regular basis, they enjoy reading, they have gained and continue to gain useful knowledge of the world around them, and they are thoughtful about what they have read. Most importantly, these children regard themselves as literate—in Frank Smith's (1987) terms, they are members in good standing of the Literacy Club. Their standardized test scores give few if any clues about their genuine literacy. We argue this not to be excused from state and federal standards and definitions of literacy, but rather to suggest that such definitions are much too limited, and stand in the way of meaningful reforms in remedial services. If we are allowed to make whatever changes we like to remedial programs but have to comply with existing measures for determining a child's status and progress, the net effect is that we make no reforms. If we are required in the Annual Review of Effectiveness to describe the success of our remedial efforts in terms of positive gains on standardized tests (even though we may be encouraged to also use alternatives), then we have no choice but to focus our program on raising standardized test scores. Since a child's literary knowledge is not measured by any currently available standardized test, our efforts to deepen and broaden a child's literary experiences—a major goal of genuine literacy—are not reportable, and therefore do not count. As far as "effectiveness" is concerned, we have been wasting both our time and the children's. We are not willing to compromise our goals in this way, because we now have a generation of children in North Warren who clearly have benefited from our commitment to genuine literacy. But we also are not politically naive, and we are aware of the consequences of poor standardized test scores. And so some of our time and energy is devoted toward ensuring that children do in fact perform well on the tests used for reporting to Chapter I. Indeed, they do. In the years in which we have been reforming the language arts program, sixth grade reading scores on the New York State Pupil Evaluation Program test have never fallen below 92 percent passing (the range is 92–100% passing); fifth grade New York State Writing Test scores were 86 percent passing in the first year we began the reforms; they have been steadily increasing, and have only fallen below 100 percent passing once since 1988 (96% passing in May 1991). These numbers include our remedial reading students, and most of the special education students as well (excluded are children receiving full-time services outside the school).

We call this "rendering unto Caesar." It is a necessary price to pay so that we can pursue what is really important to us, which is creating the conditions under which children like Josh can come into genuine literacy.

REFERENCES

Allington, R. L. (1977). If they don't read much, how they ever gonna get good? *Journal of Reading, 21*, 57–61.

Bredekamp, S. (1987). *Developmentally appropriate practice in early childhood programs serving children from birth through age 8*. Washington, DC: National Association for the Education of Young Children.

Engelmann, S., & Bruner, E. C. (1974). *Distar Reading I: An instructional system*. Chicago: Science Research Associates.

Glass, G. G. (1973). *Teaching decoding as separate from reading*. Garden City, NY: Adelphi University Press.

Graves, D. H. (1983). *Writing: Teachers and children at work*. Portsmouth, NH: Heinemann.

Oakes, J. (1985). *Keeping track: How schools structure inequality*. New Haven: Yale University Press.

Shepard, L. A., & Smith, M. L. (Eds.). (1989). *Flunking grades: Research and policies on retention*. Philadelphia: Falmer.

Smith, F. (1987). *Joining the literacy club*. Portsmouth, NH: Heinemann.

Stanovich, K. E. (1986). Matthew effects in reading: Some consequences of individual differences in the acquisition of literacy. *Reading Research Quarterly, 21,* 360–407.

Traub, N. (1982). Reading, spelling, handwriting: Traub systematic, holistic method. *Annals of Dyslexia, 32,* 135–145.

Walmsley, B. D., Camp, A.-M., & Walmsley, S. A. (1992). *Teaching kindergarten: A developmentally-appropriate approach*. Portsmouth, NH: Heinemann.

Walmsley, S. A. (1994). *Children exploring their world: Theme teaching in elementary school*. Portsmouth, NH: Heinemann.

Walmsley, S. A., & Walp, T. P. (1990). Integrating literature and composing into the language arts curriculum: Philosophy and practice. *Elementary School Journal, 90,* 251–274.

Walp, T. P., & Walmsley, S. A. (1989). Instructional and philosophical congruence: Neglected aspects of coordination. *Reading Teacher, 42,* 364–368.

CHAPTER 10

Improving Early Literacy: Vermont Stories of Educational Change from the Bottom Up and the Top Down

SUSAN CAREY BIGGAM
NANCY TEITELBAUM
Vermont Department of Education
JAN WILLEY
Addison Northeast Supervisory Unit, Bristol, Vermont

In Vermont, as in many other areas, the need for improved literacy instruction is compelling. Too many students have been identified as eligible for compensatory and special education services because of lagging reading achievement. Too few of these students have been able to catch up with their peers and benefit fully from classroom literacy instruction. In many schools, the focus of literacy instruction itself has been variable, with teachers often torn between a basal tradition and newer whole language emphases. Remedial and special education services have been variable as well, and often "thinned out" because of diminished resources.

We have been particularly concerned with early literacy development, the population of at-risk primary students, and the process of change in schools. Our interest in Marie Clay's (1985) educational philosophy and her strategies for preventing early reading failure led us to initiate an effort to enhance awareness of her work across Vermont. At the same time, we hoped this effort would improve our capacity for addressing the instructional needs of young children who found learning to read difficult. All the while we attempted to observe and support the changes that would be necessary to implement early intervention efforts. We knew that change was complex, and that state initiatives and our optimism would not be enough to accomplish what needed to be done. But by attempting to observe the factors at work and paying attention to relevant research on the process of educational change, we hope to see change that is effective and sustained for both students and teachers.

In this chapter we describe some of the encouraging trends in early literacy instruction—trends influenced by Clay's work. First, we note some of the key ideas concerning educational change that have guided our efforts and shaped our thinking. Next, we explain the educational context in Vermont from a statewide perspective. Then we relate three stories of school sites where change involving early literacy is unfolding, and we comment on some of the factors that seem to be influencing change at each site. Naturally, our observations are limited by the "lenses" we wear and the factors that we choose to notice.

WHAT IS THIS THING CALLED CHANGE?

Songwriter Cole Porter wrote, "What is this thing called love?" His lyrics speak of the enigmatic, unwieldy, changing nature of love. If Mr. Porter were alive today, he could deftly rewrite the lyrics to read, "What is this thing called change?" For many of us, educational change has been just as baffling and variable. Change efforts frequently become failed affairs, despite promising beginnings with exciting innovations.

Fortunately, current perspectives on educational change can help us chart a more effective course for initiating and sustaining change efforts. Fullan (Fullan & Stiegelbaner, 1991) underscores the need to look beyond the innovation itself to the other factors involved. He stresses that the change process is multidimensional in nature and often messy. But we can learn quite a bit by looking at phases of the change process—how change is initiated, shared with school personnel and others, implemented, supported through staff development, combined with other school elements, and absorbed into the life of the school.

We have also been influenced by Fullan's (Fullan, Bennett, & Rolheiser-Bennett, 1990) view that a good idea, despite impressive research evidence, is not enough. The implementation process can make or break an innovation. Internal, local factors such as characteristics of teachers and principals, as well as those of districts and communities, are key elements contributing to the success or failure of an innovation. When these factors work together efficiently, they mesh like cogs or gears in a machine, producing positive outcomes for students.

External factors, such as pressures from the "top down" (directives or mandates from federal and state departments of education), and outside influences (work of consultants, research findings, and so forth), are important as well. These influences must work in consort with local efforts in order for change to be successful. Ultimately, the student, of course, must be the beneficiary of the change efforts. Often it has been all too easy to lose sight of this.

In summary, we have been trying to look at change efforts in Vermont through a lens that recognizes the dynamic, interactive, and complex nature of change. Such a framework, even though it is complex and nonlinear, has prompted us to keep a watchful eye on the process as we observe and promote change in literacy support for at-risk first graders.

THE CONTEXT

Recently the Vermont State Board of Education, after extensive discussion around the state, adopted four goals:

- Vermonters will see to it that every child becomes a competent, caring, productive, responsible individual and citizen who is committed to continued learning throughout life.
- Vermonters will restructure their schools to support very high performance for all students.
- Vermont will attract, support and develop the most effective teachers and school leaders in the nation.
- Vermont parents, educators, students, and other citizens will create powerful partnerships to support teaching and learning in every community. (Vermont Department of Education, 1990)

A set of statewide initiatives, the "Green Mountain Challenge," has been developed and revised annually to help accomplish these goals. Special education reform, known as Act 230, has been implemented, portfolio assessment begun, and planning steps taken toward full literacy for all Vermonters. Several of these (and other) efforts have directly affected primary-level education and contributed to the educational climate of openness to new ideas.

Act 230, passed by the Vermont Legislature in 1990, was designed to implement a comprehensive system of education services that would afford all students the opportunity to succeed in the regular classroom. As part of this effort, every school (K–12) developed an Instructional Support Team to provide a forum for supporting classroom teachers and discussing interventions for students who require additional classroom assistance. Because of this, responsibility for success of all students began to shift toward classroom teachers. Act 230 was a consciousness-raising mechanism, prompting teachers with a more diverse student population in their classrooms to include all students in their classroom instruction.

Curriculum and assessment in Vermont were also being rethought. In 1992, as part of Vermont's statewide assessment program, fourth and eighth grade student math and writing portfolios were implemented and assessed according to criteria drawn up by statewide committees of teachers (Hewitt, 1993). Curriculum in Vermont has a long tradition of local control and an absence of state guidelines. Hence, reading and writing curricula and instruction vary widely from school to school, even from classroom to classroom. At the primary level many teachers had recently moved toward more extensive use of children's literature within a more integrated language arts approach — away from an isolated skills curriculum. Many teachers had become uneasy with traditional approaches to accountability/ assessment. Many primary-level teachers, even though not part of the statewide assessment of writing and math portfolios, were influenced by the growing trend toward performance assessment and ready to investigate new evaluation methods that more closely linked assessment and instruction.

In the late 1980s many Vermont administrators and teachers had begun to learn of Marie Clay's work with at-risk first graders. In 1988 several well-attended informational sessions on Reading Recovery, sponsored by the Vermont Department of Education, were offered for administrators and teachers. Clay's emphasis on early intervention, with a focus on student independence and high-quality teacher training, seemed to hold great promise for achieving the goals set for Vermont educational programs.

It soon became clear that even though the research was compelling, Vermonters were not about to leap into implementing Reading Recovery. The initial high costs were a factor, and many educators remained satisfied with "business as usual" for meeting the needs of remedial students. Also, there was a need for systemwide support. In a rural state such as Vermont, it was evident that the only way Reading Recovery could be implemented was through the collaborative efforts of several school districts.

Thus a small team of teachers and state education staff developed an implementation strategy. This involved working toward implementing Reading Recovery in Vermont and fostering more effective classroom literacy support for at-risk first graders through awareness-level teacher training, supportive classroom sessions, and orientation sessions for administrators.

The first effort, an awareness-level training program called PIERS (Providing Intensive Early Reading Support), provided over 150 teachers with an introduction to Clay's philosophy and strategies. This was done over a three-year period and included teachers from most districts in the state. The PIERS teachers, who received three days of training in the summer, three follow-up sessions, and peer coaching, were asked to try out some of the strategies adapted from Reading Recovery with individual students on a daily basis. It was repeatedly stressed to the teachers and their administrators, however, that the purpose of PIERS was to improve beginning reading instruction and work *toward* implementing Reading Recovery, and that their training was simply introductory and not a substitute for full implementation of the program.

In addition, another 300 teachers and paraprofessionals attended a two-day seminar called "Strategies for the Supportive Classroom: Applications of Marie Clay's Approach." They saw a video introducing the Reading Recovery program and then were introduced to strategies for observing students' concepts of print, taking running records, and expanding their questioning. They also learned how to build student independence in reading by developing use of multiple cues (print, language, and meaning) while reading. Eight weeks later they gathered again to share their explorations and discuss what they had written in their reflective journals.

Several different effects from the PIERS and Supportive Classroom staff development efforts became apparent. Many teachers found that even with this limited exposure, they had deepened their awareness of the process of learning to read and their role as teachers in supporting strategy use, and saw some impact upon students. One teacher noted, "Michael began to cross-check by himself, using both the picture and the first letter of the word!" Another commented, "I never realized how often I interrupt kids as they read!"

Others found ways to adjust classroom teaching methods and noticed a shift in the evaluation strategies they employed. The following reflection by a PIERS teacher illustrates this:

> As we began our work in the classroom this year, it became very clear that we were looking at readers very differently as a direct result of the PIERS program and reading research on the Reading Recovery program. We in the primary unit began to look at what readers could do rather than what difficulties they were having. We then began to analyze what strategies the children were using and introduce them to ones they were not yet using but were ready for.

Many teachers began to introduce concepts about print such as voice–print matching, return sweep, and the concepts of "letter" and "word" more consciously. One second grade teacher noted, "We found that at least two of our second graders had concepts-of-print confusions, and we were then able to address their needs immediately and see clear progress in reading confidence."

Most participants tried to balance their teaching more effectively so that students would learn to use multiple cues while reading and become more independent. One wrote, "I find I need to bite my tongue at times and step away!" Another commented in her journal, "I now use a much more balanced approach to prompts—more of 'does it make sense . . . what *would* make sense?'—combined with 'what letter would you expect to see?' Before I was harping on 'sound it out . . . '" Such comments were encouraging and showed evidence of some teachers shifting beliefs toward inclusion of all students and greater teacher responsibility for all learners.

In many cases parents became distinctly more involved because of the success of their youngsters. Quite a number of teachers sent books home every night so that students could read to family members. One teacher wrote in her journal, "With the help of a Chapter I grant we instituted an emergent readers' Book Bag program. Now high quality literature is made available to the students to take home and share with parents . . . with a journal that is passed back and forth between teacher and parent."

Several teachers began knocking on principals' and superintendents' doors with the message that their PIERS or Supportive Classroom training was not enough. One PIERS teacher wrote, "This is hard! . . . I can see why you need a year's training to really make a difference for hard-to-teach students!" They were impressed with the power of Clay's approach but knew that a systematic approach was needed—one with extensive training, systemic support, and availability for all students in need. Another PIERS teacher commented, "I am looking forward to being trained as a Reading Recovery teacher . . . if PIERS training has stimulated this much interest and change already, Reading Recovery will take us even further." Several administrators became advocates for the program, and by the following fall one training site for Reading Recovery was in place in southeastern Vermont, and two additional sites were forming in the northern part of the state.

Once Reading Recovery training was available in the southeastern part of the state, it again became clear that broad-based support would enhance full implementation of the program. Clay (1985) has noted that systemwide support is essential and stresses that good teaching in the regular classroom—"the backdrop of a sound general programme"—must be the first priority for educators. Johnston and Allington (1992) raise the same issue in a different manner:

> If failure is produced in part by the comparative nature of the classroom, then taking some students from the bottom and moving them to the middle simply places other students at the bottom as the new normative failures. In other words, early intervention is not enough. (p. 1002)

In an effort to build supportive classrooms and a hospitable environment, a one-credit, after-school "Reading/Writing Seminar" course was offered to forty-six primary-level staff within the Reading Recovery consortium area—a blend of classroom teachers, remedial reading teachers, and special educators. This course was co-taught by the Reading Recovery teacher leader and the State Education Department consultants. The course provided participants with strategies both appropriate for the regular classroom and congruent with the philosophy and approaches used in Reading Recovery. Teachers learned to level books, take running records, support cross-checking behavior, and consider changes in their language arts block to maximize time spent reading and writing using authentic literacy tasks.

In reflecting on the process of educational change, several observations come to mind. First, within Vermont's climate of statewide systemic reform, Reading Recovery has been framed as a systems-change approach, and not as an isolated add-on program affecting only those who receive the specialized assistance from specially trained teachers. From our perspective (as state Department of Education consultants and district administrator), we see ourselves as "instigators" (Fullan, 1990) and have provided teachers, administrators, and support staff with opportunities to learn about and experiment with Clay's strategies. Finally, we have been able to maintain a collaborative relationship with a number of local districts over a three-year period. Presently, in each of the three Reading Recovery consortia we are considered active members who have a shared voice in the planning, implementation, and constant monitoring of the Reading Recovery initiative. It is clear to all the parties involved that meaningful change is long-term and will require sustained efforts.

In the remainder of this chapter several examples will be shared to illustrate how local changes in literacy support for at-risk students have evolved. Each example is different from the others, and should illustrate some of the internal and external factors influencing change.

EXAMPLES OF CHANGE IN VERMONT SCHOOLS

Starksboro

Anne and Jodi's Story. This story takes place at Robinson School, a small rural K–6 school with a strong history of innovation and collaboration. Anne is the Chapter I teacher and Jodi teaches a grade one to two multiage class. Even before Act 230 required it, Robinson had a support team for teachers to help other teachers meet the needs of students. At

Robinson the traditional barriers between Chapter I, special education, and the classroom had been minimized through collaborative efforts. Even before the term became in vogue, the school district was one that embarked on restructuring and developed a district philosophy and vision statement to undergird change efforts.

In spite of these positive factors, there had been a record number of student referrals for Chapter I at Starksboro, especially from second grade teachers who reported that students were experiencing considerable reading difficulty. In addition, a special education "referral binge" was occurring, with a significant number of students who appeared to require intensive remediation in phonics and related basic skills. Finally, about 15 percent of students in grades one and two were being retained at some point in the primary-level program.

It became obvious that Chapter I and special education alone, as presently organized, could not solve these problems. Anne and Jodi reflected on the instructional program in the primary grades at Starksboro. They hypothesized that in the school's current literature-based program, considerable emphasis had been placed on helping students use meaning and structure cues, while visual or print cues—and cross-checking among cues—had not been as strongly emphasized.

The next summer, 1990, Anne and Jodi received introductory training in Marie Clay's philosophy and strategies through the PIERS program. In the fall they were able to apply these with students, and soon became excited as they saw students applying multiple cueing strategies and self-correcting. They sent books home nightly to parents with comment sheets and received positive responses.

Jodi and Anne soon began sharing their enthusiasm and using a common language to solve problems during weekly primary team meetings. Other primary-level teachers soon became interested. Intermediate-level teachers, too, became curious, because Anne began adapting some of the strategies with older Chapter I students who were still not independent readers.

In the winter of 1992, Jodi and Anne began a series of after-school staff development sessions for all of the primary level staff, instructional assistants, and the school's special educator. As a result, the special educator now takes running records on each of the second graders she works with, and a first grade teacher has made "browse bags" containing books children have read previously, which children use for rereading in order to warm up for reading instruction. Jodi and Anne both continually use the instructional strategies gained from the PIERS experience, and are anxious to learn more.

Some schoolwide trends can be seen as well. Although the criteria and guidelines for considering retention of students in grade has remained the same, there has been a distinct drop in retentions over the past two years. Referrals to Chapter I also decreased. In first grade, referrals decreased by 50 percent, in second grade by 38 percent, and in third grade by 75 percent. During these years the standards for referral remained the same, and there was little change in the characteristics of school population.

Reflections. When we look at Jodi and Anne's school, a number of factors that have positively affected change in literacy support come into focus. Rosenholtz (1989) defines a variety of features that tend to make teachers more successful in implementing new practices. These include opportunities for teachers to interact, to communicate, and to receive support from one another. These factors enable teachers to build trust, as Jodi, Anne, and the other staff members did for each other. Robinson School provides an environment where teachers can test out ideas and share experiences. Over time a shared commitment to new instructional practices has begun to develop. Teachers now have a keener understanding of the beginning reading process, and the need to help students use multiple cues and gain independence. They also have additional tools to observe and support students when needed.

Strong administrative support at the district and building level is essential for setting high expectations and sustaining interest in the innovation, as well as providing ongoing training and support as practices are implemented (Huberman, 1983). Jodi and Anne were encouraged by their principal, Chapter I coordinator, and superintendent to take on teacher training and coaching roles. School faculty became interested in new reading practices when they heard Jodi and Anne share their successes using strategies developed by Marie Clay. District and school administrators enabled teachers to learn from one another over an extended period of time. This environment allowed for teachers to make new practices their own.

Bellows Falls

Cathie's Story. In the fall of 1990 Cathie, previously a kindergarten and first grade teacher, became principal of Central School in Bellows Falls, a midsized town in Vermont with much unemployment, a high percentage of children eligible for free/reduced lunch, and many students classified as eligible for special education services. Teachers at Central had previously used a basal program as the core approach. They had recently begun to implement whole language strategies and were struggling to accommodate the needs of an increasingly diverse student population with widely ranging reading abilities. Chapter I and special education teachers and paraprofessionals helped with special services, but scheduling was difficult. There just did not seem to be enough instructional intensity in the support programs to make a difference for many students. Quite a number of primary-level students (an average of 20% from a school population of 260) were being recommended for retention each year, and referrals for special education evaluations were also high.

Cathie's arrival as principal followed an initiative by the superintendent, strongly supported by the school board, to join a consortium of school districts to implement Reading Recovery in their schools. During the following school year a teacher leader was being trained at Ohio State University so that the training of Reading Recovery teachers could begin the following year. Cathie agreed to be the Reading Recovery contact person for the district.

One of the first things Cathie did, as part of an effort to build awareness and capacity on the part of teachers concerning Clay's philosophy and approach, was to arrange for a two-session "Supportive Classroom" in-service education program to be held in the district. Three-fourths of the K–2 staff at Central School participated and learned about both the Reading Recovery program and some of the strategies and adaptations appropriate for their classroom instruction.

Also during this year, a review of the district's language arts program was undertaken that resulted in two decisions: to cut back on the number of standardized tests administered, in order to encourage more performance-based assessment in the classroom (now no standardized tests are given until fifth grade, except for Chapter I purposes); and to establish an "Extended Reading Block" for the first grades.

The notion of a reading block was to provide students with a ninety-minute time period focused on language arts, with extensive adult support available. This time was held sacred for the four first grade classes. Schedules were arranged so that art, music, and physical education classes were moved outside Reading Block times. For the following fall semester (year 2), arrangements were made so that there were at least two adults present in each classroom of eighteen to twenty students, in addition to the classroom teacher. These adults included the principal, individual aides for special needs students, Chapter I teachers and paraprofessionals, special education teachers, and locally funded paraprofessionals.

During the Reading Block students are actively engaged in reading and writing text. The additional adults support this by taking running records, listening to students read, and helping children write stories or complete projects. Often one of the most important aspects of their role is to engage the children in conversation about what they are learning.

A key feature of the Reading Block is a planning session held once a month during school hours. Substitute teachers work in the classrooms, allowing the teachers and administrator an important time to focus on instruction and providing them with a clear charge to do so. At the beginning of each session the discussion focuses on program changes and then moves to individual children. At times the group functions as an Instructional Support Team, helping teachers consider possible adaptations and accommodations for students with diverse needs. The staff has begun to develop a shared philosophy and shared language around reading and writing issues.

Reading Recovery was beginning in the school as well. A number of primary-level teachers took the one-credit seminar co-taught by the Reading Recovery teacher leader and a state Department of Education consultant. As the year went on, it became possible to rearrange schedules so that the Reading Recovery teacher could spend some time in the first grades during the Reading Block when they were not teaching Reading Recovery students. And the Reading Recovery teachers began to join the monthly planning/support team sessions, where they have been able to offer valuable input.

Results from these changes have been gradual but significant. No longer can one see first graders staring off into space in midmorning; all are actively engaged in some type of literacy activity throughout the ninety-minute Reading Block. Teachers of second, third, and fourth grades are now also eager to have a similar Reading Block scheduled. There has been a significant reduction in recommendations for retention. During Cathie's first year as principal, 14 students out of 140 repeated either kindergarten or first grade; only two years later, no students were recommended for retention in grade. In addition, there has been a definite reduction in referrals to special education.

Most of the teachers now regularly send books home with children. Four teachers wrote grant proposals for book bag programs, and several Paired Reading (Topping, 1987) workshops were offered to provide parents with simple, supportive ways to help out at home. Budget requests for trade books have increased significantly. In other words, change has come to Central School.

Reflections. At Central School we see the principal as a strong change agent. Cathie understands literacy instruction for first graders and is supportive of Reading Recovery. She also knows that teachers are at different starting points of understanding and commitment to learning new teaching strategies (Crandall, 1982).

Because of her understanding of adult learners, Cathie actively supported a variety of different types of training opportunities such as the Supportive Classroom workshop and the one-credit course. Now, during Instructional Support Team meetings, teachers (including the Reading Recovery teachers) are beginning to evaluate how the practices in the primary classes are going and whether they need to be modified. At Central School primary teachers are beginning to assess the impact of their new practices on students.

Cathie actively participated in the reorganization of the first grade Reading Block, took the one-credit seminar herself, and allowed teachers to observe her in the learning process. She plans together with teachers and talks about teaching practices, thereby improving the quality of their working relationship. The teachers and principal are demonstrating many of the practices that Huberman (1983) asserts are necessary for successful implementation. Successful implementation occurs when there is "continuous pressure on teachers" (p. 24), and when resources, time, reorganization, teaming, and continuous reflection are encouraged and kept going over time. Another integral factor is the stability of the leadership. Cathie has been at the school for three years and remains an agent for change. Central School continues to implement Reading Recovery and Clay's philosophy because of the positive effects on teacher learning and student achievement, and ongoing support from an administrator who advocates for children.

St. Johnsbury

Susan's Story. For a number of years Susan had been a first grade teacher at Adams Elementary School in St. Johnsbury, a small city in the northeastern part of the state. During the late 1980s, St. Johnsbury, like many other places, had much unemployment, a high percentage of students eligible for Chapter I and speech-language services, and increased integration of special needs students into the classroom. While district teachers had traditionally followed a skills-based scope and sequence using a major basal series, some teachers were beginning to experiment with process writing and the use of literature in their classroom reading and language arts lessons.

Susan and another teacher in the district received awareness-level training in Marie Clay's strategies during the initiation of the PIERS program. They each tried some of the supportive strategies with one student and used each other for coaching and support. This teaming and collaboration was important; it helped to clarify confusions and support or question decisions made during their early experimentation.

In reflecting on this period, Susan wrote:

> We felt like pioneers in a new frontier as we met daily to map out
> and discuss our day's journey (where we were with the child, what
> we observed on the way . . .). We soon realized that we could
> not make a nice, neat map of where each child would go, but
> instead we had to make close observations of subtle progress, and
> make adjustments according to the strengths and needs of the
> child. We began to observe, watch, and ask questions rather than
> always supplying right answers.

As Susan began to see some encouraging results with the students that
she was tutoring before school, she began to transfer some aspects of the
approach to her classroom work. Consciously and unconsciously the strategy questions began to creep into her interactions with students: "Did that
make sense?" "If it were _____, what letter would you expect to see at the
beginning?" As she continued her work that fall with her first graders, she
discovered that sometimes she had been assuming too much of first graders;
often they were confused about some of the most basic concepts about
print. And many students needed the message made explicit that reading is
for creating meaning.

On the other hand, Susan also found that frequently she had been
expecting too little as a teacher; with a little gradual support students could
read and write right from the beginning of the year and read quality children's literature before long. The reading/writing connection became much
clearer for Susan as her beliefs shifted: She noticed that the better the quality
of the literature her students heard and read, the more frequently literary
phrases and quality language patterns would appear in the students' oral
language and writing pieces.

Susan found that the whole focus of her teaching and classroom evaluation was changing. She was no longer teaching a reading program through
sequential steps. Rather, she was learning to observe what the children
could do and what they seemed ready to do next. The key seemed to be
helping early readers to *think* they were readers.

As they began to see their students' progress, Susan and her colleague found themselves compelled to share what they were doing. Susan would share her students' progress with anyone she could drag into
her classroom—the second grade teacher, the superintendent, parents,
para-professionals, and so forth—saying, "Look at what this child can do
. . . you've *got* to come in and see the smiles on their faces as they are
reading."

As word of success using Clay's strategies began to filter through the district, plans were made to hold a district workshop for all primary-level staff members during the upcoming summer. The purpose of the workshop was to build awareness of Clay's strategies and inform the participants about the possibility of Reading Recovery being implemented in the district; twenty-eight people voluntarily attended.

Continued experimentation with strategic reading techniques intensified the need for teaming and support. In the fall of the second year, a support group was formed to address the needs of several staff members using similar strategies in first and second grade classes. Since all services (special education, Chapter I, and speech-language) were provided in the classroom, it was necessary for staff members to have a common language and instructional focus. Susan and several other staff members had attended a summer School Development Institute, which had focused on collaborative teaming for instruction. This provided the group with some excellent process skills to help during their Monday before-school meetings. This group practiced strategy questions, read and discussed current reading articles, and provided feedback and encouragement for each other. One paraprofessional commented that she liked the feeling that she was "part of a team and had an equal chance to contribute to the discussion and help to make decisions about ways to best help children learn."

Administrative and parent support were positive factors, too. District-level administrators encouraged cross-classroom visits as well as visits from school board members. They also disseminated reading materials and facilitated grade-level meetings by arranging for substitutes. Susan and several other teachers worked hard to bring parents into a real partnership relationship. They initiated parent contacts continuously, held parent workshops, sent out letters to parents, and encouraged parent volunteerism of all sorts.

The impact of these efforts became clearer as time went on. In reflecting on what had changed in her classroom as a result of her familiarity with Clay's strategies and a more holistic view of the reading/writing process, Susan noted some striking differences in her expectations for her first grade students, particularly for those students previously thought of as "at risk":

A few years ago, when I was using the standard basal program, I would have been happy if my Chapter I students were able to read the following kind of text by February of their first grade year:
"Have you come to see us?" the man asked.
"We have," she said.
"We have come to see what you do here."

Now this same type of student is introduced to books such as Mercer Mayer's *Little Bear* at this time of year.

And, by May or June, previously my students eligible for Chapter I might have been reading:

"I am Kim," said Kim.

"Can you find Ben and me?"

"This is a great place to play!"

"First we climb in," said Ben.

"Then we climb out."

Now by this time of the year, Chapter I students are reading trade books such as *Are You My Mother?*, and *Henry and Mudge*, normally considered to be appropriate for the end of first grade.

During the following school year (year 3) administrators joined in the formation of a four-district consortium to bring Reading Recovery training to the area. Not surprisingly, Susan applied to be the consortium's candidate for teacher leader and was accepted. A good deal of discussion continued over the course of the planning year, but the groundwork laid in the previous two years paid off: A critical mass of teachers, administrators, school board members, and parents had sufficient information and interest built to support moving toward Reading Recovery implementation. In addition, much had changed for the better during classroom reading and language arts lessons.

Reflections. We see Susan as a teacher-researcher investigating her own questions within her classroom. Loucks-Horsley et al. (1987) describe the characteristics of teacher-researchers as experienced, intelligent, and inquiring people who search for answers to self-generated questions. Susan certainly exhibited these qualities. She collected data that answered several questions she had about early literacy instruction. Then, as a teacher-researcher, she developed new understandings of literacy instruction and incorporated this knowledge into her daily teaching. She shared her data with others. When teachers and paraprofessionals observed in her classroom, they saw all children engaged in meaningful literacy experiences. In a sense, seeing was believing, and these observers were ready to learn new practices from Susan (Hargreaves & Dawe, 1989).

Administrative support played a key role in Susan's professional development as well. She was given release time to share her materials and observations with adults in her district and at state and national conferences. It was the profound change in student learning that gave Susan the impetus to share her findings.

WHAT WE HAVE LEARNED AND
WHERE WE ARE HEADED

For years we have read about and listened to speakers describing the elements that appear to make change more likely. But this only became real to us through active participation. For example, we have noticed that:

- The power of the innovation itself is critical. Marie Clay's philosophy and approach obviously can make a startling difference for youngsters. Unlike some other fleeting change efforts (fads), this one has staying power not just because of its impressive written research evidence, but primarily because teachers experienced change in themselves and their students. From our point of view as supporters of change, this initiative soon developed momentum and, in many cases, long-range planning toward institutionalization has resulted.
- Teachers often develop leadership capacity when they become reflective. As they notice significant changes in their own teaching behaviors and witness real changes in student achievement, they develop a voice. They advocate for students, instructional accountability, and systemic support.
- The "slinky" effect is real. Pressures and supports from the top down and energy from the bottom up make for movement toward change. In the cases we have seen, teachers have welcomed support from both local administrators and Department of Education staff, and have continued to sustain the momentum of change because of their experiences with students.
- Parents become extremely powerful partners when they witness the success of their own youngsters. They begin to become engaged with the school in ways that were not previously possible.

Looking ahead, we know that substantive change requires time and effort. Teachers, administrators, and others may need ongoing support in continuing to shift their belief systems. These belief systems are pivotal for changing the schools' support for early literacy. From the perspective of the Vermont Department of Education, we will also increase our support for administrators who are key players in providing systemic support for Reading Recovery—for example, offering annual summer focus sessions for principals to brainstorm what has worked and what other supports are needed. One-credit seminar courses in the Reading Recovery consortia continue, since interest remains high. Finally, we continue to try to be good observers of what we see and hear and apply our developing knowledge of the change process as we strive toward the goal of literacy for all learners.

REFERENCES

Clay, M. M. (1985). *The early detection of reading difficulties*. Auckland, New Zealand: Heinemann.

Crandall, D. P. (1982). The teacher's role in school improvement. *Educational Leadership, 41,* 6–9.

Fullan, M. (1990). Staff development, innovation and institutional development. In B. Joyce (Ed.), *Changing school culture through staff development* (pp. 3–25). Alexandria, VA: Association for Supervision and Curriculum Development.

Fullan, M., Bennett, B., & Rolheiser-Bennett, C. (1990). Linking classroom and school improvement. *Educational Leadership, 47,* 13–19.

Fullan, M., & Stiegelbaner, S. (1991). *The new meaning of educational change* (2nd ed.). New York: Teachers College Press.

Hargreaves, A., & Dawe, R. (1989). *Coaching as unreflective practice: Contrived collegiality or collaborative culture?* Paper presented at the annual meeting of the American Educational Research Association.

Hewitt, G. (1993). Vermont's portfolio-based writing assessment program: A brief history. *Teachers and Writers, 24,* 1–6.

Huberman, M. (1983). School improvement strategies that work: Some scenarios. *Educational Leadership, 41,* 23–27.

Johnston, P., & Allington, R. (1992). Remediation. In R. Barr, M. Kamil, P. Mosenthal, & P. D. Pearson (Eds.), *Handbook of reading research, volume II* (pp. 984–1012). New York: Longman.

Loucks-Horsley, S., Harding, C., Arbuckle, M., Murray, L., Dubea, C., & Williams, M. (1987). *Continuing to learn: A guidebook for teacher development.* Andover, MA: Regional Laboratory for Educational Improvement of the Northeast and Islands and National Staff Development Council.

Rosenholtz, S. (1989). Workplace conditions that affect teacher quality and commitment: Implications for the design of teacher induction programs. *Elementary School Journal, 89,* 421–440.

Topping, K. (1987). Paired reading: A powerful technique for parent use. *Reading Teacher, 41,* 608–611.

Vermont Department of Education. (1990). *Vermont education goals*. Montpelier, VT: Vermont Department of Education.

CHAPTER 11

Change in Urban Schools with High Concentrations of Low-Income Children: Chapter I Schoolwide Projects

LINDA F. WINFIELD

University of California, Los Angeles

Most elementary schools (71%) currently receive federal funds to support supplementary instruction for economically disadvantaged students from the Chapter I program. The fastest-growing Chapter I programs are schoolwide projects (U.S. Department of Education, 1992). The Hawkins-Stafford amendments (1988) to the Educational Consolidation and Improvement Act stimulated the shift to using Chapter I funding for schoolwide projects in schools where 75 percent or more of the students are economically disadvantaged. A fundamental goal of such projects is to reduce the fragmentation of instruction and instructional responsibility characteristic of so many Chapter I programs (see Walmsley & Allington, this volume). In schoolwide projects the focus is on upgrading the entire school program since the majority of children are eligible for Chapter I support. The shift is away from separateness and toward collaborative effort, from specialist teachers in separate rooms toward improving classroom instruction. Prior to 1988, federal regulations allowed schoolwide projects but required that districts provide matching funds for non–Chapter I–eligible students. This requirement prohibited many financially strapped school districts from becoming involved. The 1988 amendments eliminated the matching fund requirement but also imposed additional accountability

---

An earlier version of this chapter appeared in *Educational Evaluation and Policy Analysis* (1991, vol. 13) and some aspects were presented at the U.S. Department of Education, Schoolwide Project Meeting, Dallas, TX, February 1992.

measures to prevent Chapter I funds from becoming "general aid" to schools.

The new regulations also required a school-based planning component that involves a self-study of local needs, consensus development on the part of the school staff, and a building leadership team. The flexibility in federal regulations comes at a time when the knowledge base has been advanced concerning effective schools (Purkey & Smith, 1983), the change process (Fullan, 1982), successful programs in urban schools (Slavin, Madden, Karweit, Livermon, & Dolan, 1990), and factors contributing to resilience and persistence in disadvantaged populations (Winfield, 1991). A major task confronting urban school systems and schools is how to make use of this new knowledge and also take advantage of the increased flexibility to improve the learning outcomes of low-achieving students. These opportunities come at a time when poverty has increased dramatically in major urban school districts (Wacquant & Wilson, 1989) and contextual factors, such as size, demographics, diversity, density, a growing underclass, the underground drug economy, the politics of school boards, and an eroding tax base, create uncertainty and turbulence in most urban school environments (Englert, 1989).

LARGE URBAN SCHOOL SYSTEMS

It has been suggested that in response to uncertainty, school districts create large, complex bureaucracies (Bidwell, 1965) characterized by rigidity and a variety of dysfunctions (Levine, 1978). In large urban districts this results in a tendency toward disengagement from instruction (Meyer & Rowan, 1978). Typically, this means that staff in central administration offices pay more attention to maintenance aspects of operating the school, such as transportation and managing school facilities, than to improving the instructional program. While attention to these components is necessary, focusing on these alone also means that other systemic improvements may not occur. In addition, the governance and control of many school systems serving disadvantaged students are often fragmented by competing groups at the state and district levels, such as unions, school boards, state departments, and special programs such as Chapter I, migrant education, special education, and bilingual education. There is a high degree of role differentiation and specialization at the central office level, and individuals and groups become territorial regarding their expertise, budget, and constituencies. Services provided to the schools are seldom coordinated, and school building principals typically must deal with four or five central staff persons for many simple requests.

However, district-level policies influence coordination of efforts and instructional collaboration at the school level (Birman, 1981; Kimbrough & Hill, 1981). Urban Chapter I programs have traditionally been characterized by a high degree of centralization. Chapter I program plans are usually developed and monitored at the district level and principals and teachers have had little input in the design of service, selection of services, identification of students, distribution of resources, student scheduling, or the curriculum selection. Often Chapter I programs produced "interference" with school programs and instructional fragmentation for students (e.g., Allington, 1986). It has been rare for programs to be coordinated with classrooms, although the ECIA amendments requiring closer coordination between Chapter I instruction and the core curriculum are changing this situation. However, in schools with high concentrations of low-income children the interference and fragmentation were often more prevalent because the majority of the children were eligible for these pullout programs. This resulted in children constantly leaving the room to participate in one or more of the special programs, making coherent classroom instruction difficult to achieve.

The purpose and intent of schoolwide projects—upgrading the whole school program—may be difficult for schools to attain given the competing demands of central office groups. In general, when school districts reorganize central administration, only marginal improvements are realized and the potential benefits are confounded with other simultaneous changes (March, 1978). Tinkering with duties and position titles at central administration rarely has an impact on the instructional process in classrooms. The difference between those districts in which schools successfully change and the typical school is the concept of "connectedness" (Wimpleberg, 1989).

Wimpleberg (1989) also suggests that it is unlikely that schools will act on their own to improve or that school systems have resources needed to facilitate the process of change. Technical assistance must be provided in the form of personnel rather than through paper plans or mandates (Eubanks & Levine, 1987). For instance, in the large urban district described in this chapter, mentor teachers served in a capacity to facilitate school change. These individuals, designated as "program support teachers," did collaborative teaching, conducted staff development, advised the principal on the instructional program, and provided instruction to small numbers of students. Other positions were created that were filled by individuals who worked to support change at the school level (see Winfield, Hawkins, & Stringfield, 1992). Nonetheless, the general framework for these schoolwide projects was developed by central office staff following the general requirements in the federal program regulations. This central office initiative was important; without it, far fewer schools would have elected schoolwide project status.

Other studies have also identified examples of strong leadership by large urban school superintendents who shape districtwide conditions for improving schools within a context of broad community support (e.g., Hill, Wise, & Shapiro, 1989). District-level initiatives that work to provide needed resources to schools and seek to simplify the potential maze of red tape that school personnel encounter can have a major impact on how schools deliver instruction to students and are critically important in fostering and perpetuating school improvement.

This chapter presents a case study that describes changes in a major urban school system and schoolwide project (SWP) schools following the passage of the Hawkins-Stafford amendments in 1988. For one full year (July–July), I attended central and district office SWP meetings and staff development sessions and carried out one- to two-day site visits in eleven SWP schools. In addition, I examined school system documents, SWP proposals, and other school reports. A more thorough description of this study can be found in Winfield, Hawkins, and Stringfield (1992).

THE SCHOOL SYSTEM CONTEXT

This Chapter I program serves 162 schools and receives approximately $50 million in Chapter I funds annually. For a decade, various initiatives targeted toward improving the achievement of Chapter I schools had been initiated by the superintendent, who can be described as a demanding instructional leader. However, she places the education of the quarter-million children ahead of everything else while managing a $1 billion budget. A previous initiative had targeted the improvement of twenty-six high-poverty Chapter I schools over a three-year period beginning in 1983. Private foundation funds and Chapter I monies were used to support a school-based planning and implementation process. At the beginning of the third year of the project, the central office[1] staff felt that some schools needed additional human resources in order to change the historical patterns of low student achievement. Thus, for example, the kindergarten program was expanded to a full day in an attempt to expand opportunities to learn. Permanent substitutes were assigned to each school in order to provide more instructional consistency on a day-to-day basis. For the 1986–87 school year, the system elected to designate eleven of these schools as SWPs and to pay the matching funds then required for noneligible students who were receiving services. In 1988, when the Chapter I guidelines were changed, the school

---

[1]The urban district described had a central administration, but also seven decentralized district offices within the larger system.

system rapidly expanded the number of schools in the program. Chapter I funds were provided to each school as block grants (averaging $250,000–$300,000, or $900/pupil). Today, about half of all the elementary schools in the system are SWPs.

While these initiatives were under way, a systemwide Chapter I task force recommended expansion of SWPs, based on student outcome data. The task force was comprised of members from all of the major special-interest groups and stakeholders (e.g., central office staff from budget, special education, curriculum, compensatory programs, district superintendents, teachers, and principals in Chapter I schools). The task force was charged with developing a comprehensive compensatory education program to improve student achievement. This revised program would then be phased in over a two-year period. One former task force member said, "It was a working group. . . . It brought everybody to the table. . . . We didn't always agree but we knew that something had to be done to improve. . . . That's the bottom line."

The school system's approach to developing a SWP identified five main thrusts:

1. A whole school approach that supports students in the classroom program and provides special support for students who require it
2. School-based management requiring school staff and parents to determine the nature of the intervention, within program guidelines and contractual requirements
3. Ongoing monitoring of individual student, class, and school performance, giving particular attention to Chapter I students and those students receiving intensive services
4. Providing support from the central and district offices for parent and staff training on an as-requested basis
5. Concentration of fiscal resources so that funds beyond the minimum amounts are committed from Chapter I and district operating budgets

Of these five factors, the school-based management component was central to the legislative intent of the Hawkins-Stafford amendment and yet a very difficult process for schools to implement. The intent was to get the professional staff in each school to reflect on and analyze their local needs and plan effective instructional interventions. This was to replace the more common procedure whereby solutions were dictated from the top of the district administrative office down to schools. At the school level, one of the stumbling blocks was getting started in this initial process and doing it well. To work effectively, this process required:

- Orienting/training principals in shared decision making and creating a vision for the whole school
- Time and resources for developing the capacity of the staff
- Ongoing technical assistance and support in designing effective instructional interventions

The concept of a leadership team at the school level is not novel. However, what was distinct in these SWPs was that the teams were responsible for improving instruction of all students and had control of the Chapter I budget for the school.

An Office of Schoolwide Projects was created by the district as part of its commitment to SWPs. This office was staffed by a manager who was to develop and oversee the implementation process. Mr. D., the manager selected, had no prior central office experience but had been a successful elementary principal for some years and was credited with turning around the dismally low performance of an extremely impoverished urban school. Mr. D. indicated that educating school principals was a necessary but too often overlooked task that should initiate all attempts at changing schools.

> From my own experience, to change what's happening in schools, staff development for principals is critical because most of them don't know what to do. . . . Teachers have to be supported because many of them are scared to change, and direct services to the school have to be expanded but also coordinated.

Mr. D. developed the operational guidelines for implementing a SWP and was the role model for principals. In addition, he was the chief advocate for students, teachers, and principals in schoolwide projects. On many occasions, he indicated that schools needed to undergo an awareness and orientation phase that primed them for changes in how they traditionally delivered services to Chapter I eligible students and provides teachers, as well as principals, with training in how to participate in decision making on a schoolwide level. The creation of this office and the appointment of an experienced educator "from the trenches" were keys to the success of the implementation of the SWP in this district. If nothing else, the office provided principals with a single contact point and a sympathetic colleague who could assist in clarifying procedures. The selection of this principal also made available an administrator whose primary concern was improving the instructional process in schools serving large number of "poor" (in both the economic and academic sense) students.

SYSTEM SUPPORT FOR SCHOOL CHANGE

Virtually everyone in this district agreed that school-based planning and site-based management are processes that are not easy to carry out effectively. Principals and teachers required continual coaching, encouragement, admonishment, recognition, and incentives to buy into the process and implement an intervention schoolwide. In this district principals and teachers had traditionally selected instructional materials and made decisions about a particular program or focus. However, few professionals in SWP sites had been involved with making decisions that affected the whole school. Few had been in a situation where a consensus had to be reached concerning hiring an additional math resource teacher or eliminating the remedial reading positions so that additional classroom teachers could be hired to reduce class size.

Schools were assisted with these decisions in their leadership team meetings by specialized SWP personnel in newly created positions. These individuals were knowledgeable about change, the instructional process, and school-based management and functioned as internal change agents. A new position, titled Instructional Interventionist, served as a liaison between the district and the SWP site. Individuals in these positions were district-funded supervisors who had been part of a former division within central administration that emphasized school change and innovation through developing human resources. They attended professional meetings on topics such as organizational development and group dynamics, as well as on implementing cooperative learning and development of the new math standards. An observation of one of these meetings revealed a discussion of a *Kappan* article on change and how it related to several of the schools within their respective districts. The interventionists might be considered experts in pedagogy and organizational change and were able to act as brokers at the district level to get necessary resources to the SWP schools. They participated in principal-led monthly leadership team meetings in each SWP school and organized ongoing staff development and cross-school sharing for principals and staff. In addition, they coordinated, directed, and provided staff development for instructional support teachers, provided assistance to the principal in arriving at a workable school improvement plan, and ensured that all materials and supplies purchased were related to the school's detailed instructional improvement plans.

The Instructional Support Teachers (ISTs) were teacher-level positions in each district. Often these individuals were former program support teachers who had been promoted. Thus, their primary emphasis was on instruction. Each IST was responsible for overseeing two SWPs and worked directly with the principal and school personnel. They were in each school two to three days a week, depending on needs at the individual SWP site. They served as troubleshooters and implementation coaches for principals. In addition, they provided staff development and worked with their school-based counterparts, the Program Support Teachers (PSTs).

The PSTs were teacher-level positions based at each school and selected from the school staff by the principal. PSTs were considered master or mentor teachers by peers and the principal. They provided instruction to students ninety minutes a day, and spent the remainder of the time working directly with the principal, new teachers, and other staff in implementing the schoolwide plan. They monitored student progress, participated in leadership team meetings, and did demonstration lessons. Interviews with these staff indicated that their positions were labor-intensive, demanding, and required long hours, yet they were highly sought after, as evidenced by the number of teachers applying and taking the oral and written test. Regular classroom teachers indicated that they felt that the positions were accorded higher status and were seen as master teachers even though PSTs and ISTs received the same salaries as regular teachers. The system of specialized positions was dynamic—one in which new talent was constantly sought and veteran program support teachers were promoted into IST positions, and ISTs moved up to Instructional Interventionist. Several of the Instructional Interventionists became principals.

In some respects the newly created positions were characteristic of the system's centralized organization; however, the reorganization and newly created positions served the purpose of changing the functions and responsibilities of previous Chapter I district personnel. Most of these professionals had traditionally operated in isolation from other district-level personnel involved in supporting and monitoring instruction in the schools. They created and monitored compensatory education programs while others developed and monitored classroom instruction, bilingual instruction, or special education services. The functions of these Chapter I professionals changed to school-based action-oriented assignments with the sole function of supporting schools in improving the quality of instruction provided to all students. They referred to themselves as "facilitators, change agents, and teachers" rather than as supervisors. Although all of the various positions within the hierarchy may not be required for smaller, less centrally controlled districts, it was apparent that a school-based individual who functioned as a facilitator or internal change agent was needed here to create and maintain successful schoolwide projects. The hierarchy and system established in this district allowed these individuals to support each other in the change process and not concede to the conservative, socializing forces within the schools and subdistricts to maintain the status quo.

INSTRUCTIONAL FRAMEWORKS

While federal program support for compensatory, special, and bilingual education efforts is widely praised, it is often a mixed blessing in schools where over three-quarters of the children qualify for one or more sets of instructional support services. In such cases, classroom instruction is often difficult as a constant stream of children leave the room for the special classes and return a while later. Thus, a major objective in implementing SWPs was to change from the traditional pullout model to a whole school instructional focus. The central office staff created and provided staff development in broad instructional frameworks focused on changing classroom instruction, not just on organization and management at the school level. The frameworks were entitled "effective instruction" and "teaching thinking." Both frameworks included factors such as high expectations, monitoring, positive school climate, and teamwork. These frameworks also stressed classroom-based strategies such as cooperative learning, active teaching and learning, and effective lesson delivery and functioned as broad guidelines for improving instruction. Individual schools had to operationalize what they meant for their schools.

The reading materials in use in the schools were basal readers that had been adopted at the district level. In schoolwide project sites, most schools continued to use the existing basal; however, they had the option of upgrading and purchasing new materials with SWP funds. Most schools opted to obtain supplementary materials, but some purchased reading anthologies for classroom libraries and still others purchased a new literature-based basal series.

Attendance at SWP staff development sessions was voluntary but strongly encouraged, and teachers were paid for participating. As a result, participation in and implementation of the various frameworks was highly variable across school sites. In some sites, components of the framework adopted were not a salient part of classroom instruction or schoolwide programs. In other sites, the framework was used as a common language for staff to use to discuss students and instructional matters or served to facilitate team building. In these settings, the frameworks helped to create a sense of community among staff, allowing them to coalesce around common goals. It also bonded schools together to create a sense of esprit among principals and their staffs as they began to identify themselves as a "teaching thinking" or some other kind of school. The particular instructional framework selected did not seem as important as allowing principals and teachers to select and adapt one that they felt was most appropriate to their school.

PARENTAL INVOLVEMENT

Another goal in SWP sites was involving parents in the educational process of their children. Each school's SWP proposal had to delineate ways in which the site would conduct parent involvement activities. Schools were also required to include funding for a School Community Coordinator in their budgets. These coordinators had two basic functions. First, they initiated strategies to improve student attendance. At several sites they were responsible for implementing a daily system of identifying all absent students in order to make immediate contact with the home. Second, they also coordinated and directed parent workshops over the school year. "Parent scholars"—parents from the community who assisted in the classrooms—were also funded out of SWP budgets. These assistants were provided with a modest stipend and worked in ten-week cycles. Parent scholars worked in classrooms and assisted in the library, computer lab, and lunchroom. Each SWP site was also provided with the services of a part-time parent trainer who visited the site regularly to assist in recruiting and training community assistants and to assist in other parent involvement activities. Each site also had a trained Home Demonstrator, a trained full-time person from the local community whose sole purpose was to make home visits and work directly with parents on developing their child's learning readiness, helping their child with homework, and other school-related activities. These personnel, along with an expansion of traditional parent-school functions (e.g., parent nights, PTA, pretzel sales), worked to improve the number of parents involved in SWP school activities.

The use of community members for these staff positions facilitated parent involvement. The School Community Coordinator and the Home Demonstrator were required to live in the neighborhood and because of this had a greater awareness of community resources and access to parents and other community members. Creating parent scholars increased the number of parents who visited the school regularly and fostered better communication among teachers and parents. Each of these positions also served to forge stronger links between the community and the schools.

WHAT WERE THE MAJOR TYPES OF INTERVENTIONS?

Eleven SWP sites were studied and these schools used their Chapter I funds in a variety of ways, but three broad uses predominated. First, the SWP schools bought curriculum materials. Second, funds were used to extend the school day or the school year. Third, Chapter I support teacher positions were converted into classroom teacher positions to reduce class sizes. Typically, in the first year or two of the project, some of the funds were used to purchase needed materials such as science kits, math manipulatives, and classroom literature libraries. One site used funds to extend the school year by twenty-two days, and some added an after-school program. Nearly all of the schools used their Chapter I funds for additional classroom teaching positions to lower the teacher-student ratio during math and reading instruction. Approximately half reduced class size in classes with the lowest-achieving students. Often the additional teaching positions eliminated split-grade classes. In some schools, the Program Support Teacher, SWP reading and/or math resource specialist, and basic skills teacher provided the entire lesson to the whole class on a scheduled basis. Other schools developed team teaching models in which SWP personnel taught in the classroom with the regular teacher. In short, there were few similarities in the instructional programs delivered in most SWP sites.

At each site, the building leadership teams created programs that they felt would be more likely to enhance student reading achievement than had the traditional Chapter I pullout program. What was common across SWP sites was adherence to minimal regulatory requirements, which included the funding of one full-time School Community Coordinator, at least one Program Support Teacher, and ten to twelve hours per faculty member of paid staff development. The use of Chapter I funds for other positions, whether these were additional classroom teachers, a schoolwide project reading teacher, math resource specialist, or to purchase additional materials or resources was at the discretion of each building leadership team.

GETTING STARTED

The influential role principals play in supporting instructional improvement has been well documented, and the same was true with respect to SWP sites. The principal is accountable not just for conveying and enforcing district mandates but also for translating an educational vision and creating a sense of common purpose and collegial spirit among staff. This includes those who have typically been segregated from the regular education program, including teachers identified as Chapter I, compensatory education, bilingual education, or special education. Principals reported that one of the biggest obstacles to getting started was developing the leadership team. Principals accomplished this in a variety of ways.

In some schools a new core group of teachers came into the site and the principal recruited leadership team members from them, in addition to one or two of the older staff. In other sites, persons serving as grade-level chairpersons, union representatives, and reading specialists were invited to serve. According to principals interviewed, essential characteristics of being a team member were openness to change, knowledge about the school's instructional program, and commitment to the belief that the school could improve the instructional effectiveness of services traditionally delivered to students. Most principals indicated that in starting the process, they coalesced a group around the most pressing problem that was interfering with classroom instruction. These principals then used the initial success of the group to go on to tackle additional problems.

In some sites, the first and most pressing problem was the physical plant. One principal inherited a decrepit, decaying building that had not been maintained for years. She began a massive cleanup campaign, and eventually enlisted support from several teachers. The idea was to convey to students and parents that this was a place where someone cared. However, she did not stop with physical improvements. She wrote grant proposals and obtained funding for an innovative video communication/language arts program. Another principal began the team leadership building by getting the team to establish procedures for the orderly entrance and dismissal of over one thousand elementary students. This lead to an eventual system of student incentives and rewards not only for orderly behavior but also for attendance and for reading trade books. Another group's initial task was to transform the chaos in the lunchroom to an orderly, more controlled outlet for students' energy.

Second, principals indicated that they initially tried out ideas on one or two members of the leadership team. For example, in one site there had been a Chapter I lab at the school for over ten years. This lab served only a small percentage of Chapter I students in a minimally effective pullout program. The principal and Program Support Teacher gathered the available data on number of students eligible and number of students served, as well as student performance on a variety of measures in preparation for planning the SWP proposal. This information was presented to the leadership team to assist them in making the decision to reallocate resources and ultimately use the funds to hire additional classroom teachers.

Third, principals in the SWP sites were creative in formulating a vision or knowing what kind of school they wanted to have in the next few years. For the most part they agreed that it was important to reduce class size, if not for increasing instructional effectiveness, at least for the morale of the teachers. There was also general agreement that pullout instruction should be minimized in an attempt to create a more coherent instructional program for low-achieving children. But it was the diversity of program changes that more typified these sites.

One principal, for example, believed that an extended school year was the most appropriate solution. In this SWP site Chapter I funds were reallo-cated to provide an additional twenty-two days of schooling. This extended year effort provided both remediation and enrichment in an extremely impov-erished environment where summer reading loss was likely to occur. Another principal envisioned a whole language, literature-based curriculum for his predominantly Latino school population. He felt that the only way children learned to read was "through reading and positive interactions with a variety of meaningful texts." He started by increasing the amount of time for reading instruction from one hour to ninety minutes, emphasizing literature-based instruction and thematic unit planning. The building leadership team con-tracted with a local university to provide on-site graduate courses on whole language. Still another principal's ideas were stated as follows: "In order to show improvement, you have to give help to those most in need. So these students we call Chapter I eligible require the best teachers and the highest-quality instruction, and these teachers also need support."

In many of these sites, layers upon layers of federal and state categori-cal programs, along with special district programs, had fragmented the instructional program for large numbers of students (Allington, 1986). Cre-ating a viable, effective schoolwide project was like fitting pieces of a puzzle back together. The missing pieces of the puzzle in some schools were rele-vant knowledge of effective classroom strategies and an awareness of inter-ventions that would improve reading achievement outcomes. It was in these very areas that principals often provided the leadership needed to move the SWP forward.

WHAT DO SWP SCHOOLS LOOK LIKE?

Ames School

Ames School is a fifty-year-old building in the middle of a neighbor-hood rapidly undergoing regentrification. The school enrollment has re-cently declined from 700 to 400 in grades K–8. Ninety percent of the students in the school are eligible for free lunches. Although the school population is predominantly black (81%), there are also Asian (3%), His-panic (4%), and white (12%) students attending the school. The school has thirteen regular education classes and ten special education classes. The special education classes enroll moderately and severely handicapped chil-dren bused from outside the immediate school neighborhood. The staff have devised activities to integrate many of these students into the school day; in fact, this idea predated the schoolwide project status.

This school enjoys a good reputation and according to the current principal, parents are clamoring to enroll their children. Ames ranks among the top ten schools in math and science achievement in the district and has had a full-time science room with a science teacher for the last four years. On average, student reading achievement in the school rose by six normal curve equivalents (NCEs) (spring-to-spring) in 1989–90 (Winfield, Hawkins, & Stringfield, 1992). As one enters the school, it becomes immediately apparent from the school banner, displays of students' work, trophies, and awards that someone has fostered and maintained a sense of school pride and spirit. In the school office, a two-page handout for substitute teachers is noticeably displayed and provides essential information on lesson plans, roll book, homework, lines, classroom management, school procedures, and academic notes on each subject area. The first line reads: "We are a schoolwide project school."

The previous principal was credited by the school staff with the impetus for and direction of change in the school. Staff members indicated that her first personnel decision was not instructional but hiring a trained person who was considered a noninstructional paraprofessional to handle both discipline problems and the "lunchtime chaos." This person not only developed disciplinary techniques such as time-out rooms and in-school detentions, but initiated the idea of a climate committee to focus on visible and positive rewards for students and teachers. This committee eventually became the leadership team for the schoolwide project plan, but by that time the school had initiated awards assemblies, attendance achievement certificates, alumni day, and school jackets and had developed a host of other activities for fostering school spirit, pride, and collegiality. Prior to the school becoming a SWP site, the former principal had contacted a local educational laboratory to provide ongoing staff development in thinking skills curricula. In the SWP plan, the principal and leadership team initiated an emphasis on areas of the curriculum that had been neglected. In this case, the emphasis was placed on science. The majority of resources acquired were in this area for the first one to two years and included the purchase of classroom science kits and the hiring of a building science specialist.

Mr. A., the new principal, has been a principal in urban schools for the past twenty-two years. He credits the success of the SWP to the former principal, who had developed the basic plan. He feels that the plan is "teacher-intensive" and indicated that the funds were used primarily to hire additional teachers to reduce class size during reading instruction. He said, "We're not lacking for materials, but most of the money was spent on personnel. In the lower grades, two teachers assist in the primary-grade reading cycle. One works with the upper-grade reading/language arts."

Mr. A. attributed the successful implementation of the SWP to the ongoing staff development and an active pupil support committee that meets twice a month to discuss alternative interventions for individual students having academic problems. He said, "Having paid staff development and meeting time for pupil support committee meetings has been a great advantage." He described the staff as stable and very strong-willed but capable and very caring.

Teachers at Ames School indicated that the biggest change since becoming a SWP was that all of the faculty provided input into the plan. Other teachers indicated that the increased flexibility was an advantage. One teacher said, "I never liked the pullout model. . . . The coordination makes sense. . . . They're not freight packages. . . . They're children." Another teacher noted: "Before, the classroom assistants could only teach certain students. . . . Now they can deal with all of the kids." The teacher, who also chaired the climate committee for the school, credited the paid meeting time for the pupil support committee, which he indicated "allows us to be more systematic in finding out and doing something with kids who are having problems. . . . These teachers here really care. . . . This place is like one big family and we support each other."

Mrs. B., the Program Support Teacher, has been at the school for twenty-two years. She noted that thinking skills was an area that staff decided to work on even prior to becoming a SWP. She indicated that their decision to adopt the framework on thinking skills was an easy one. Mrs. B. explained that although she is the teacher of record for a group of twelve kindergartners who are already reading and for fifteen of the lowest-achieving first graders, the majority of her time is spent in various classrooms conducting demonstration lessons or co-teaching with other teachers. She explained that teacher of record is a SWP concept that means that the person who provides the instruction in reading, for example, is also responsible for monitoring and improving student progress and grading. Her other responsibilities included assisting classroom teachers. She says:

> If a teacher is absent, I'll go in during the reading period so that the reading instruction is not disrupted. We have a new teacher in the school, and I was in her class conducting the reading lesson for the first month or so . . . since also, along with Mrs. G., the other reading teacher, I give an informal reading assessment to all students three times a year so that some don't fall through the cracks.

She viewed monitoring student progress and classroom instruction as important aspects of her position. She felt that SWPs require a lot of paperwork; however, "teachers have all the information on individual students in one place, the SWP record book—grades, end of unit tests, citywide tests, teacher-made tests, and homework assignments. I collect these every six weeks from each teacher and review them."

The school's integration of handicapped students as well as its commitment to teach all students was observed during the reading cycle. An excerpt from a classroom observation follows:

> Mrs. B. began her routine that apparently all of the children know. It is a song with hand motions that the children do that captures their attention and tells them to put their thinking caps on. She introduces the lesson by saying, "Today we are going to talk about beginning sounds," and draws a picture of a hat on the board and writes __at. "Now what belongs in this space?" The children respond "H" and she writes it in. She continues to introduce word families and sounds that will later be used in a "Big Book" story she reads. She is animated, moves around the room, calling on the whole group and individual children, including the handicapped students, to respond to provide the beginning sounds for the pictures and word families on the board.

One would not have recognized that some of the students in this classroom were classified as "trainable mentally retarded" except for the size and age of some of the youngsters seated and one little girl who imitated the behavior of the other children but seemed not to understand the lesson. Still, she raised her hand to respond to questions and tried to write the letters, which, upon observation, were illegible scribbles.

At Ames School, the spirit and sense of collegiality were expressed by several of the staff members. Another indication of the progress being made is seen in the improved student attendance and improved achievement. Both had steadily increased across the period of implementation of the SWP.

Bigsby School

Bigsby School is relatively new, having been built in the 1970s. It is a large factorylike structure that takes up nearly a city block and overshadows the small row houses in its immediate neighborhood. The school is bordered on one side by a large outdoor play area and in the front by a mixture of both well-kept and decrepit, boarded-up row houses. An influx of young families with small children into the neighborhood has increased the school's enrollment. At the time of the visit, the school enrolled more children than the 900 student capacity of the building. At Bigsby, a majority (71%) of students are Hispanic, 21 percent are white, and 7 percent are black. One is immediately overwhelmed by the sheer size of the building, with its huge hallways and extremely high ceilings with exposed pipes. Nevertheless, every available space at the school is filled. One kindergarten class and a class of third graders use rented space in an adjacent church building. The science, art, and music rooms have been converted to classrooms. Thus, specialist teachers go from classroom to classroom. Despite over-capacity enrollment, entrance, dismissal, and a fire drill were quite orderly. Prominently displayed in the lobby was the Creating Success logo, the instructional framework chosen by the school.

According to the School Community Coordinator, a young bilingual Hispanic woman who has lived in the neighborhood for fifteen to twenty years, the big change in the neighborhood occurred about five years ago. "Many stable families who could afford to move left the area. . . . We have a lot of young families with many children. . . . Some who have just come over from Puerto Rico. . . . We also lose a lot of kids whose families return [to Puerto Rico]." In addition to home visits requested by teachers and parent workshops, this woman spends a substantial amount of time referring parents to community agencies, taking parents for appointments, translating for parents who don't speak English, providing clothes and emergency shelters, and interpreting report card marks. She had served as president of the Home and School organization prior to becoming a School Community Coordinator.

Because of its size and lack of stability of principals (four in the previous five years), the school had been in complete chaos, according to staff. One teacher indicated, "This structure was built for warehousing kids and that was all that was going on." She went on to say that the central administration's standardized curriculum provided some guidelines for instruction; however, there was no schoolwide instructional program per se. According to one teacher,

> The former principals hid in their offices and provided no leadership to a school that was growing increasingly large, with more and more students from increasingly poor and language-minority homes. A district-wide basal series was being used by those teachers who cared to teach reading. Each of the specialized personnel had an office, Chapter I teacher, reading teacher, bilingual, ESOL, and district reading teacher, and they all took particular students out into their offices.

The current principal, Mr. C., is a high-energy, fast-paced, organized, and task-oriented individual. He stands in the hall and greets each child by name, handing out small rewards for good behavior, for perfect attendance, and for reading. He indicated that the school as a whole is challenged to read one million pages between September and June. Since becoming a SWP, he feels, he is allowed more flexibility in how he can use his staff, and co-teaching models were stressed in the building. Here SWP teachers team-taught with classroom teachers to reduce the student–teacher ratio during language arts periods.

One example of this co-teaching and the emphasis on whole language was observed with Ms. R., who had been at the school since 1977 and had previously taught second, third, fourth, and fifth grade. She is now a basic skills teacher and spends ninety minutes each in two classrooms working alongside two classroom teachers. She meets once a week with teachers to develop a thematic unit. On the day we visited Bigsby School, the classroom teacher was out and a substitute was in the classroom. However, Ms. R. continued with the thematic unit planned with twenty-two third graders:

> Students had read *Sylvester and the Magic Pebble* and Ms. R. went over the major parts of a book report and wrote on the blackboard—Setting, Character, Main Idea, Details, and Story Problem, eliciting comments from individual students on each area. Students actively participated in the discussion bringing out details of the story. Children started the assignment in class as Ms. R. and the aide circulated to see who was having problems. She announced that the book report was to be completed as a home-work assignment. Students were then asked to take out their the-matic activities. One little boy, Victor, shared his with me. He said, "I'm doing math" . . . and showed me a graph he had plot-ted on a page. . . . I asked: "Was it hard?" "Naw," he said. "Ms. R. explained . . . and my partner and me worked on it together."
> The page read:
> *Plot Profile: Sylvester and the Magic Pebble*
> *On this chart plot the story's plot tension as they occurred.*
> *Refer to the chart below.*
> *(picture of a graph) Tension on Y axis, time on X*
> *1. Collect rocks*
> *2. Find extraordinary one*
> *3. Rock is magic*
> *4. Sets out for home*
> *5. Meets lion . . .*
> *When does the plot reach the highest level of tension?*
> *Why?*
> *What other incidents should be included on this chart?*
> Ms. R. began directing the class's attention to math word problems on the chalkboard that some children were having prob-

lems with. She said: "The tree Sylvester is sitting under loses one
leaf every two seconds. How many leaves will the tree lose in
fourteen seconds? Class, what do we have to do to find the
answer?" . . . Silence . . . someone shouted "seven" . . . "That's
right," said Ms. R. "How did you get it?" "Divide two into fourteen," the student responded.

The other activities in the teacher-made unit included additional writing activities: "You have just been hired by *People* magazine to design a magical item. Choose a partner (or work alone if
you choose). Write a TV commercial or magazine advertisement
to try and sell your item," or "Define the word *habitat* and using
an encyclopedia or dictionary describe the natural habitats of the
following animals: donkey, eagle."

Other examples of co-teaching at the school included the math resource teacher and assistant teaming with three classroom teachers to reduce the student–teacher ratio for math instruction for one hour each day.
In addition, the bilingual education teacher worked in classrooms with
bilingual students. Funds also paid for planning time for the bilingual
teacher to plan with classroom teachers.

Mr. C.'s background is in reading/language arts, and he teaches during one class period each day. He states,

> The only way children learn to read is through reading . . .
> through frequent, positive interactions with a variety of meaning-
> ful texts. They learn to construct meaning. . . . The develop-
> mental process is supported by systematic, explicit instruction in
> phonics/word attack skills. We increased the amount of time from
> one hour to ninety minutes . . . emphasizing literature-based in-
> struction and thematic unit planning. Because of SWP, we reduce
> class size and student–teacher ratio during reading/language arts
> instruction. We also have on-site staff development in implement-
> ing a literature-based reading program provided by a local univer-
> sity. Teachers received three graduate-level credits.

Classroom teachers noted other benefits of being a SWP. One teacher
indicated, "We are a big school and we have a lot of funds poured into us,
but we were told this is how you have to spend it, regardless of whether
students needed it or not." Another said, "Now we're able to get more
personnel. . . . We used to have classes ability-grouped and some classes
were not Chapter I eligible but were still in need of additional help. Before I
couldn't serve them." Other teachers noted that paid meeting times, on-site

training, and availability of funds to purchase sets of literature books and expand classroom libraries were important benefits of being a SWP.

In the year prior to initiating a Chapter I SWP at Bigsby School the average student's NCE gain in reading was −.63. Following the shift to SWP status, the average achievement gain was +1.41 NCEs. In addition, the average daily attendance increased from 85 percent to 89 percent over this period (Winfield, Hawkins, & Stringfield, 1992). Both of these shifts indicate that the decision to move into a SWP is benefiting children at Bigsby School.

CONCLUSION

The case study findings suggest that SWP schools in the process of change look much like other schools that are making conscious attempts to improve classroom instruction and improve upon existing programs. But because SWPs are located in schools with high concentrations of children who live in poverty, many of the schools are plagued by staff vacancies, budget cuts due to declining enrollments, and high student mobility. However, with the support of SWP initiatives, the schools are grappling with issues such as how to make schoolwide decisions, how to create effective working plans for improvement, how to integrate other existing categorical programs into a coherent instructional program, how to allocate the available resources effectively, how to provide ongoing support to classroom teachers, how best to monitor program effectiveness, and how to deliver higher-quality instruction to disadvantaged students.

It is important to note that in order for schools to move away from segregated Chapter I programs to a more integrated focus on improving the core curriculum instruction for all students, parallel changes must be made at the central office. Not only must these offices become more "connected" to the instructional process, they must also be reorganized in ways that provide effective coordination and delivery of direct services to schools in the process of becoming SWPs. For SWPs to effect the desired changes, school systems will also have to invest heavily in human resources and professional development at all levels. High-poverty schools create tremendous needs for direct, on-site, systematic assistance in changing existing structures and negative belief systems, more intensive professional development in collaborative teaching models and subject-matter instruction, more proven high-quality educational interventions for students experiencing academic difficulties, and strong reciprocal agreements with teacher training programs to aid in recruitment and development. Schoolwide projects have the potential for improving the learning of large numbers of disadvantaged students.

However, this potential will be met only if adequate support for change is provided at the central or district level, and if sufficient resources are devoted to providing human resources and professional development.

In schools where teachers and principals have had little influence on decisions about curriculum or program organization, a major aspect of becoming a SWP is learning how to make such decisions. Nonetheless, at each SWP site changes had been made, changes that have benefited the low-income students who attend the schools. Change was not easy, not always successful, and never smooth. Change required substantial investment of time and energy by building staff and shifts in attitudes, beliefs and roles (Winfield, 1986). But change was accomplished.

REFERENCES

Allington, R. L. (1986). Policy constraints and effective compensatory reading instruction: A review. In J. Hoffman (Ed.), *Effective teaching of reading: Research and practice* (pp. 261–289). Newark, DE: International Reading Association.

Bidwell, C. E. (1965). The school as a formal organization. In J. G. March (Ed.), *Handbook of organizations* (pp. 972–1022). Chicago: Rand McNally.

Birman, B. F. (1981). Problems of overlap between Title I and P.L. 94–142: Implications for the federal role in education. *Educational Evaluation and Policy Analysis*, 3, 5–19.

Englert, R. M. (1989). *Understanding the urban context of schools in large cities.* Paper presented at the convention of the University Council for Educational Administration.

Eubanks, E. E., & Levine, D. U. (1987). Administrative and organizational arrangements and considerations in the effective schools movement. In D. S. Strickland & E. J. Cooper (Eds.), *Educating black children: America's challenge* (pp. 66–81). Washington, DC: Bureau of Educational Research, School of Education, Howard University.

Fullan, M. (1982). *The meaning of educational change.* New York: Teachers College Press.

Hill, P. T., Wise, A. E., & Shapiro, L. A. (1989). *Educational progress: Cities mobilize to improve their schools.* Santa Monica, CA: Rand Corporation R-3711-JSM/CSTP.

Kimbrough, J., & Hill, P. T. (1981). *The aggregate effects of federal education programs.* Santa Monica, CA: Rand Corporation.

Levine, D. H. (1978). The social context of urban education. In D. A. Erickson & T. L. Reller (Eds.), *The principal in metropolitan schools* (pp. 106–129). Berkeley, CA: McCutchan Publishing Corporation.

March, J. G. (1978). American public school administration: A short analysis. *School Review*, 86, 217–250.

Meyer, J., & Rowan, B. (1978). The structure of educational organizations. In J. W. Meyer & W. R. Scott (Eds.), *Environment and organizations* (pp. 79–109). San Francisco: Jossey-Bass.

Purkey, S. C., & Smith, M. S. (1983). Effective schools: A review. *Elementary School Journal, 83,* 427–454.

Slavin, R. E., Madden, N. A., Karweit, N. L., Livermon, B. J., & Dolan, L. (1990). Success for all: First-year outcomes of a comprehensive plan for reforming urban education. *American Educational Research Journal, 27,* 255–278.

U.S. Department of Education. (1992). *National assessment of the Chapter I program: The interim report.* Washington, DC: U.S. Department of Education.

Wacquant, J., & Wilson, W. (1989). The cost of racial and class exclusion in the inner city. *The Annals, American Academy of Political and Social Sciences, 501,* 8–25.

Wimpleberg, R. K. (1989). The dilemma of instructional leadership and a central role for the central office. In W. Greenfield (Ed.), *Instructional leadership: Concepts, issues, and controversies* (pp. 100–117). Boston: Allyn and Bacon.

Winfield, L. F. (1986). Teacher beliefs towards academically at-risk students in inner urban schools. *Urban Review, 18,* 253–267.

Winfield, L. F. (1991). Resilience, schooling and development in African American youth: A conceptual framework. [Special issue]. *Education & Urban Society, 24,* 5–14.

Winfield, L. F., Hawkins, R., & Stringfield, S. (1992). *A description of Chapter I schoolwide projects.* Baltimore, MD: The Johns Hopkins University, Center for Research on Effective Schooling for Disadvantaged Students.

CHAPTER 12

The Implementation of the Accelerated School Model in an Urban Elementary School

STEPHANIE L. KNIGHT
JANE A. STALLINGS
Texas A&M University

The publication of *A Nation at Risk* in 1983 focused national attention on problems associated with the process and outcomes of public schooling. At least one-third of elementary and secondary students in the United States have been identified as high-risk (Levin, 1987; McDill, Natriello, & Pallas, 1985), because their underachievement in school often results in a high dropout rate and inadequate preparation for later employment. One out of every four students in school will eventually drop out.

Despite widespread emphasis on the problem, reform efforts using models based on effective schools research have had minimal impact on at-risk children (Cuban, 1989). Although some instructional interventions have shown promise in reducing the achievement gap between disadvantaged students and their more advantaged peers (e.g., Slavin, Karweit, & Madden, 1989; Slavin & Madden, 1989), these programs have had only modest impact (Levin, 1987). The failure of many of these reform efforts may be due to faulty assumptions underlying their basic approaches (i.e., deficit models that focus on remediation) and lack of an integrated approach to the problem (Hopfenberger & Levin, 1993). Furthermore, many programs for disadvantaged students neglect variables associated with student engagement or psychological investment in learning (Newmann, 1989). As a result, educationally disadvantaged students enter school behind their peers and fall further behind as they progress through school. Although the problems are complex, part of the difficulty can be attributed to school organizations that provide little support for responsibility and decision making by the professionals in the schools who could best meet the needs of students, learning environments that provide "drill and kill" approaches to remediation, and low expectations for at-risk students (Levin, 1990).

The Accelerated School Model provides an approach designed to address many of these problems. Henry Levin and his colleagues at Stanford University based the model on the following premises (Hopfenberger & Levin, 1993):

- Learning environment characterized by high expectations and status
- A deadline for eliminating the achievement gap (usually set as the end of elementary school)
- A fast-paced curriculum focusing on student engagement
- Involvement and empowerment of teachers and parents

These instructional, curricular, and organizational elements are integrated to further the vision determined by teachers, administrators, and staff of individual schools (Levin, 1991a). In particular, language is emphasized in all aspects of the curriculum. Through this process, disadvantaged students can be brought up to grade level before entering middle school and teachers can assume professional responsibility for student learning.

The purpose of this chapter is to trace the implementation and evaluation of the Accelerated School Model (ASM) in an urban elementary school during the initial implementation. The project was part of a Satellite Center Project directed by Henry Levin at Stanford University to establish Accelerated School Models in several sites across the United States. The chapter includes a description of the implementation of ASM principles in general and in the site school specifically, a description of the evaluation plan associated with the project, and the preliminary findings from the study.

OVERVIEW OF THE ACCELERATED SCHOOL MODEL

The Accelerated School Model focuses on three principles, which faculty, administrators, staff, parents, and students working together operationalize in their school: unity of purpose, building on strengths, and empowerment with responsibility (Hopfenberger, 1990). *Unity of purpose* involves determining the kind of school participants would want their own children to attend; taking stock of their school using a number of indicators related to desired outcomes; identifying the gap between where they are and where they would like to be; and using the inquiry process to change curricular, instructional, and organizational features of their school to enable them to move closer to their vision of the ideal school.

Building on strengths reflects the need to identify and build on the strengths of all involved. In this manner, it is the antithesis of the deficit model, which often prevails in discussions of at-risk students and urban schools. Questions center on the characteristics that students bring with them to school (natural curiosity, language, varied cultures) as well as what teachers, parents, and administrators are already doing that is successful. While the challenges emerge as schools take stock, the strengths are used as a basis for meeting the challenges.

Empowerment with responsibility provides the means by which the group realizes the common vision. The taking-stock process yields a number of priorities identified by the group to move the school closer to their vision. These priorities become the basis for the establishment of cadres or task groups that use the inquiry process to propose, implement, and evaluate changes. Each teacher belongs to at least one cadre, depending on interests and expertise. Cadres also may include administrators, staff, parents, and students. The governance structure highlights participatory decision making through establishment of a Steering Committee with representation from each cadre. Activities and decisions of the cadres are brought to the Steering Committee for discussion and approval. Decisions that influence the entire school are brought to periodic School-As-A-Whole meetings for discussion and action.

Keeping the three principles in mind, participants change the curriculum, instruction, and organization of the school to address their priorities and to reflect the model's major premises (see Table 12.1). The preferred curriculum of an Accelerated School focuses on higher-order skills and activities and interdisciplinary, integrated content related to the experiences of students in the school. Language development is a primary emphasis in all subjects. Instruction is student-centered and hands-on to produce active student involvement. As a result, pair and group activities are common and tracking of students is avoided. Organization of the school draws on parent and community involvement with teachers, staff, and administrators in participatory decision making. The principal acts as a facilitator for the processes and activities of the Accelerated School.

IMPLEMENTATION OF THE ACCELERATED SCHOOL MODEL AT URBAN ELEMENTARY

The concept of the Accelerated School Satellite Center Project was designed by the Accelerated Schools staff at Stanford University and funded by Chevron Corporation (Levin, 1991b). The model involves partnerships between schools and universities to develop Accelerated Schools around the

TABLE 12.1. Comparison of conventional and Accelerated School practices

Conventional	*Accelerated*
ORGANIZATIONAL PRACTICES	
Parents uninvolved	Parents in partnership
Subject area departments	Teams, schools-within-schools
Faculty involved in decisions	Committees for inquiry
Principal as manager	Principal as coordinator and facilitator
Central office as monitor	Active central office support of site
Fixed scheduling	Flexible, creative scheduling
Isolation of teachers	Staff interacts with, coaches, and supports each other
CURRICULAR PRACTICES	
Remediation	Enriched approach
Emphasis on factual knowledge	Critical thinking, social skills
Concepts in abstract	Concepts applied to real world and personal experience, concrete problem solving
Disciplinary focus	Interdisciplinary approach (language across the curriculum)
Remedial track	Common curricular objectives
Core subjects only	Full range of electives (e.g., arts, physical education, and career information)
Limited access to extracurricular activities	Universal access to extracurricular activities
INSTRUCTIONAL PRACTICES	
Rote learning and drill	Active discovery learning
Textbooks	Literature, primary sources
Worksheets and workbooks	Personal, community, and real world experience; student construction of materials
Lecture-style teaching	Projects, expressive modes, hands-on activities, educational technology
Teacher-centered classrooms	Cooperative learning, peer and cross-age tutoring, student responsibility
Homogeneous grouping	Heterogeneous grouping

country. Texas A&M University was one of four universities charged with the task of initiating and facilitating the model in an urban elementary school with a high at-risk population. Stanford provided initial training involving more than forty hours of workshop participation for university and selected school personnel during the summer prior to implementation of the model and additional training during follow-up sessions throughout the following year. University participants subsequently provided training in the model for school-based personnel, facilitated implementation on-site several days per week, attended cadre and School-As-A-Whole meetings, and designed and conducted research and evaluation activities to investigate the processes and products of implementation of the Accelerated School.

Two elementary schools from a large urban district were identified for the project based on similar demographic characteristics and principal leadership style. The principals of the two schools were identified by district personnel using Accelerated School guidelines and both expressed a willingness to participate in the development and implementation of the Accelerated School Model, through a collaborative decision-making process involving teachers and administrators. One school (Urban Elementary) was chosen as the site for implementation of the Accelerated School Model, while the other served as a comparison school for evaluation purposes. Each school enrolls approximately 500 students and has similar ethnic compositions (approximately 60% black, 25% Hispanic, and 15% white and others), with more than 60 percent of the student population eligible for free or reduced-price lunches. In addition, both have after-school magnet programs for students in the district who qualify. Scores on the Texas Educational Assessment Measure indicate that the two schools exhibited similar student achievement prior to implementation of the model.

Teachers and administrators at Urban Elementary participated in a summer training session prior to implementation of the model in the fall. Using a combination of small-group discussions and whole-group brainstorming led by project facilitators, the school forged a vision statement to define their joint purpose. The underlying components of the vision statement include:

- Development of a collaborative team of students, staff, parents, and community working toward common goals
- Empowerment of students, teachers, and parents
- Student achievement of academic excellence
- Student social growth

Four priority areas emerged from preliminary "taking stock" activities: discipline, staff development to enable teachers to implement curricular and instructional features of Accelerated Schools, heterogeneous grouping, and parent involvement. Teachers volunteered to join one of four temporary task groups formed around these areas and began the process of taking stock in each area, determining the gap between the vision and current status in the area, and implementing pilot programs to address identified challenges.

Throughout the first year, teachers met weekly in their cadres. Surveys were devised to determine needs and resources of faculty. As a result, activities and new programs were implemented to address curriculum and instruction with an emphasis on reading, writing, and oral language. Teachers planned and participated in staff development workshops to acquaint them with the whole language approach and process writing and to enable them to use alternative grouping arrangements within and across classes. Since classes had previously been homogeneously formed by ability level, several teachers experimented with heterogeneous grouping by combining and cross-grouping across a few classes. Widespread adoption of heterogeneous grouping was hampered by the structure of their Chapter I program and a district requirement that students labeled as gifted and talented be taught only by teachers trained in the district's gifted and talented curriculum.

All teachers had the opportunity to observe in another model Accelerated School in the area to provide concrete examples of active teaching and learning. Cadres discussed ideas gleaned from these observations and previous workshops, related the ideas to their particular priority area, and designed pilot studies to test their value for Urban Elementary. Teams of teachers experimented with the development of themes, which they integrated across content area and grade level. For example, a question raised by a curious fourth grade student (Can a dead chicken move?) led to a thematic unit consisting of dissection of chicken feet, reading and writing about chickens, and the gathering of recipes for chicken dishes. In another example, the kindergarten and fourth grade teachers implemented a cross-age tutoring program in which the older students created books that they read to the younger ones. Prior to implementation of the model, most classes had typically been very structured in their use of seating and grouping patterns, providing little opportunity for student–student interaction and relying heavily on worksheets and textbooks as the medium of instruction. By midyear, every grade level provided model classes exhibiting cooperative grouping arrangements, within- and across-grade-level teaming and tutoring, learning centers, and less reliance on texts and greater use of authentic materials. Bulletin boards in the halls were used to display reading and writing games devised by parents to extend learning outside the classroom.

While the Staff Development and Heterogeneous cadres were focusing on pilot programs addressing curriculum and instruction, the Discipline and Parent Involvement cadres were also taking stock and implementing trial programs. Support groups for students who, in the words of one faculty member, were "once labeled bad and then always considered bad" were formed. One group of boys met weekly with a teacher to participate in social and sports activities, to discuss problems, and to try to bring up grades. They learned table manners and had dinner together in a restaurant to apply what they had learned, a first-time experience for the majority of the boys. A similar club for girls was subsequently formed. In addition, the BUG (Bringing Up Grades) Honor Roll was formed to bring recognition to students for improvement in their studies.

The Parent Involvement Cadre focused on involving parents who typically did not participate in school activities. A parent survey in Spanish was constructed to find out more about the needs and concerns of the rapidly growing Hispanic population in the area. As a result, one of the teachers began offering English classes for Spanish-speaking parents two times a month. Parents brought younger children with them and their school-age children often served as assistants or tutors for their parents, engaging in literacy activities as a family.

After the first year of implementation, teachers participated in a retreat focusing on reflection of the accomplishments and challenges of the implementation. Several changes in focus were noted, resulting in the replacement of the Staff Development and Heterogeneous cadres with cadres for Student Social Growth, Curriculum Development, and Communication. Discussions concentrated on teachers' perceptions of the most serious drawback to the model: lack of time to meet, plan, and develop curriculum. Despite the time concerns, teachers appeared to feel that their efforts had been successful. In the words of one of the teachers, "We as a staff feel tired together. It is a good tired."

EVALUATION OF THE MODEL

The primary purposes of the evaluation planned by the Texas A&M Accelerated School Satellite Center were to describe the implementation of the Accelerated School Model and to investigate its impact on classroom processes, student and teacher attitudes and perceptions, and student achievement over time. To achieve these goals, both qualitative and quantitative data were collected.

Implementation of the model was depicted by means of a case study of Urban Elementary. The processes associated with implementation were documented through minutes and participant observations of cadre and school meetings and training sessions, logs kept by university facilitators, and teacher and administrator interviews. Data from the logs and interviews were sorted into information units and grouped into categories and then into domains (Spradley, 1979, 1980). Impact of the model was investigated through surveys designed to look at intermediate outcomes such as student perceptions of learning environment and teacher perceptions of school climate; observations of classroom processes and teacher behaviors; and comparison of student achievement on criterion and standardized achievement tests with achievement of students in the comparison school. The data for the first two years of the project are currently available.

Documenting the Processes of Implementation

Results of the qualitative analysis of the implementation of the Accelerated School Model reveal that concerns about time, communication with other cadres and administrators, money, and role definition were common across cadres and at all phases of the implementation (Ferrara, 1992). Teachers had difficulty finding a common time to meet. Some teachers were assigned morning duty from 7:30 to 8:00 A.M., while others worked in the extended-day magnet program. Therefore it was difficult for cadres to meet before or after school. Since teachers in each cadre represented different grade levels, they did not share a common planning period. Teachers often felt uncomfortable with coverage of their classes by university facilitators or other teachers, since they felt a strong sense of responsibility for their students and classes. The problem was complicated by the tendency of the principal to resist innovative scheduling that represented a departure from district policies and to retain fairly tight control and strict adherence to previous administrative procedures. Cadres generally approached the problem by keeping teachers who missed cadre meetings informed about the proceedings and alternating meeting times. Similar problems arose when scheduling Steering Committee and School-As-A-Whole meetings.

Given the restrictions of time and schedules, the need for communication was obvious. Cadre members wanted to make copies of cadre notes to distribute to others, but restrictions on the amount of copying allowed often prevented this. Ultimately, the group considered the problem so severe that they formed an ad hoc cadre for communication to study the problem and implement plans to remedy the problem. Eventually, a section of the teachers' lounge was set aside for communication, and procedures for posting information before and after cadre meetings were developed.

Money for materials and staff development was also a recurrent problem despite the fact that the school received support from the project. The Chevron grant specified that a portion of the money given to the Satellite

Center be designated for use by the school site for expenditures related to implementation. In addition, the university site received support for facilitation and evaluation expenses. Nevertheless, the problem centered around priority allocation and ready availability of those funds. Discussions about budget priorities served to clarify and translate the vision into more concrete terms. Finally, teachers formed a budget cadre that established guidelines for application and allocation (potential for furthering the school vision, number of students expected to benefit, and potential for impact on student learning or behavior). Ready availability of the funds was solved by having the money transferred from the university account to a district account. However, teachers soon found that the turnaround time for reimbursement of funds was equally slow through the district.

Another problem that surfaced throughout implementation concerned the redefined roles of teachers and administrators. Previously, building-level administrators were rewarded in the district for strong leadership of a more traditional, directive nature. Teachers had expressed concerns initially in journals and interviews that shared decision making might not work at their site for this reason. Many were reluctant to make decisions and constantly deferred to the principal. University researchers and facilitators often noted in logs and journals the difficulties associated with the demands placed on all involved as more responsibility for schoolwide decision making was transferred from principal to teachers. While current logs indicate the problem still exists, a core group of teachers with strong leadership qualities has emerged over the past two years. Furthermore, teachers and administrators report that teaching and grouping practices have changed as a result of ASM.

Investigating the Impact of the Model

As previously described, quantitative data were also collected to document changes in teachers and students as implementation proceeded. The School Level Environment Questionnaire (Fraser & Fisher, 1981), an instrument designed to measure teachers' perceptions of school climate, was administered prior to implementation of the model and during the fall and spring of the first year of implementation to the teachers of Urban Elementary and the comparison school. In addition, students' perceptions of their learning environment, motivation, and achievement were also assessed in both schools.

School Climate. While differences between schools in school climate overall were not significantly different by school for any of the administrations, several differences in directions of the means of scales within and across schools were interesting (Knight & Stallings, 1992; Stallings & Knight, 1991). For both schools, climate was lower for the first survey administration than at any other time. No scales emerged as equal to or greater than 3.5 on the 5-point scale for either school. Although perceptions of climate in general were higher for both schools the following fall, they declined slightly as the year progressed. The only three scales over 3.5 for both schools in the spring analysis were Affiliation, Professional Interest, and Work Pressure. However, the comparison school had declined in perceptions of Professional Interest from fall to spring, while Urban Elementary remained constant. Furthermore, Urban Elementary's perceptions of Work Pressure increased while the comparison school's reports of workload decreased over the year. The lower means of Urban Elementary for Staff Freedom (from first to last survey and in comparison with the other school) and the lower means on the final survey in Participatory Decision Making and Resource Adequacy (in contrast with the comparison school) were somewhat puzzling given the nature of ASM. However, teachers at Urban Elementary reported in follow-up interviews that their perceptions were framed in reference to perceived needs associated with ASM and not in contrast to previous years. Implementation of the model had made them aware of how much more freedom they needed to carry out plans and had increased the need for resources such as time and materials for development of an enriched curriculum for students. Overall, the survey information lends some support to interpretation of the qualitative data indicating that a group of teacher leaders for decision making had emerged.

A related outcome supports teacher perceptions of improved school climate. Although the teacher turnover rate for Urban Elementary was not as high as the district rate of 30 to 40 percent or more yearly prior to implementation of ASM, the school experienced the loss of several teachers each year. After the first year of the Accelerated School Model, not a single teacher resigned or requested a transfer to another school. Interviews with the principal revealed that even the teachers who had been less active in implementation of the model felt that they were making progress and wanted to remain in the project.

Student Perceptions. Student perceptions of learning environment and motivation were measured for both schools during the fall and spring of the first year using the My Class Inventory (Fisher & Fraser, 1990) and the Multidimensional Motivation Inventory (Uguroglu, Schiller, & Walberg, 1981). Since most classroom pilot projects were implemented after the first survey administration, the fall survey serves as a baseline for student perceptions. Results revealed significant overall differences by school and by time of administration. Follow-up analyses indicated that although students in the comparison school initially perceived less friction and more cohesiveness, by the end of the year Urban Elementary students perceived less friction and the groups exhibited no significant differences in cohesiveness (Urban Elementary increased while the comparison school decreased). In addition, while Urban Elementary students initially perceived more instruction classified at the lower levels of Bloom's Taxonomy, in the spring the comparison students reported more lower-level instruction. These findings are compatible with the team approach and emphasis on higher-order skills associated with ASM.

Student Achievement. The Accelerated School Model aims for student performance that is on grade level by the end of elementary school. Since many students in high-risk, inner-city schools enter school behind their more advantaged peers and continue to lag behind, the goal is challenging. Despite the achievement goal, Levin (1988) maintains that achievement gains may require three to six years before they can be documented. Furthermore, many of the higher-level skills and dispositions may not be adequately captured by standardized achievement tests. For these reasons, the evaluation emphasis during the initial year of operation focused on behaviors and perceptions that might ultimately lead to changes in test scores and on documentation of the implementation of the model. Nevertheless, test scores were recorded for both the Accelerated School and the comparison school prior to and after implementation.

Initially, scores on the Texas Educational Assessment Measure, a test given to third and fifth grade elementary students based on mastery of the state's common curricular objectives in reading, writing, and mathematics, and the Metropolitan Achievement Test (MAT6), a standardized achievement test given to all grade levels, were recorded for both schools. During the first year of implementation, the TEAMS was replaced with the Texas Assessment of Academic Skills (TAAS). The MAT6 subsequently became the instrument used to track and compare the progress of both schools. Since the model emphasizes language development, the grade equivalents for reading and language were examined. Tables 12.2 and 12.3 present the grade-equivalent scores on the MAT6 for all grades in Urban Elementary and the comparison school prior to and after implementation of the model. The test is taken in April of each year and on grade level would be reflected by a grade equivalent of 1.8 for first grade, 2.8 for second grade, and so forth.

As can be seen in Table 12.2, the grade equivalents of Urban Elementary for reading prior to implementing ASM reveal that students performed below grade level in all grades. On the other hand, the comparison school, while performing below grade level in all but one grade, was outperforming

TABLE 12.2. MAT6 reading grade equivalents

Grade	1989	1991
Urban Elementary		
1	1.6	2.0
2	2.2	3.2
3	3.0	4.5
4	4.5	4.2
5	5.2	5.5
Comparison School		
1	1.7	1.9
2	2.9	2.6
3	3.4	3.1
4	5.3	5.2
5	5.1	5.2

Urban Elementary in every grade except one. The language grade equivalents in Table 12.3, while slightly higher, reflect a similar picture.

However, the achievement test performances after the first year of ASM portray a somewhat different picture. For reading, students in Urban Elementary second and third grades performed on grade level, while only the first grade students in the comparison school were on grade level. Furthermore, Urban Elementary outperformed the comparison school at every grade. For language, Urban Elementary emerged higher in the first three grades and similar to the comparison school at the upper grades.

While it may be somewhat early to draw definitive conclusions about achievement gains, especially given the rather narrow scope of the tests, the patterns are promising. Further corroboration of the outcomes of the MAT6 comes from results of the criterion-referenced TAAS test, which is given early in the fall semester and reflects the previous year's achievement. Table 12.4 presents the percentages of students passing each section of the test for Urban Elementary, the comparison school, and the state and district averages. In third grade, Urban Elementary students performed better than the state and district averages. Fifth grade results for math and reading were less encouraging, but the writing results, which were similar to the district

TABLE 12.3. MAT6 language grade equivalents

Grade	1989	1991
Urban Elementary		
1	1.8	2.3
2	2.8	5.3
3	4.4	4.6
4	5.7	4.9
5	6.7	6.0
Comparison School		
1	1.9	1.9
2	2.9	2.9
3	4.1	4.5
4	5.4	5.0
5	6.6	5.9

average and higher than the comparison school, may reflect the increased emphasis on process writing (Sperling, 1991), which emerged as a result of Accelerated School cadre activities. In addition, since the TAAS was administered seven months prior to the MAT6, the test may not represent achievement gains made during the remainder of the year.

TABLE 12.4. Percent passing TAAS mathematics, reading, and writing

Grade	Math	Reading	Writing	Math	Reading	Writing
	URBAN ELEMENTARY			COMPARISON SCHOOL		
3	98	96	75	76	73	70
5	35	59	76	47	66	72
	DISTRICT AVERAGE			STATE AVERAGE		
3	82	80	68	86	84	70
5	49	61	76	60	68	80

PROGRAM COSTS

The implementation of the Accelerated School Model presented in this case study was partially funded by a grant. Approximately $30 per student was allocated to the school to assist with staff development expenses and materials to enrich the curriculum and to provide additional time for teachers to meet. In addition, the grant paid the expenses of the training and facilitation by university personnel. However, the cost is somewhat modest compared with the remediation costs normally incurred by districts (see Lyons and Beaver, this volume) and the almost incalculable costs associated with student dropout and failure to become contributing members of society. Economic analyses indicate that it costs much less to pay for education now than to pay later for public assistance to the unemployed or for the results of crime associated with school dropouts (Levin, 1989).

Nevertheless, the goal of ASM is to enable teachers and administrators to restructure their curriculum, instruction, and organization with little added cost by reallocating existing resources. Training a core group of teachers and administrators who will later train their colleagues reduces expenses considerably. In addition, schools may vary in their need for financial and technical assistance. For example, one highly successful Accelerated School implemented the model without receiving formal Accelerated School training, additional funds, or initial follow-up assistance (Texas Research League, 1991). The principal of the school, after reading Levin's articles about ASM principles and practices, engaged teachers in the restructuring and implementation processes described earlier. As a result, the school has documented achievement gains in all areas and positive attitudes of teachers, students, and parents toward the model after approximately four years.

CONCLUSION

Considerable time, money, and effort have been devoted in the past five years to the development and implementation of programs to restructure for educational improvement. In particular, school reform movements have targeted the problems associated with students considered at risk of failure in school and in the workplace with limited success (Cuban, 1989). The Accelerated School Model is an approach to the reform of curricular, instructional, and organizational practices that targets retention of disadvantaged students in school and elimination of the achievement gap by the end of elementary school as primary goals. Emphasis on reading, writing, and language are integrated across all content areas. Active learning, heterogeneously grouped classrooms, student–student and teacher–student interaction, and emphasis on higher-order thinking predominate. Using the inquiry process, teachers, parents, staff, and community members work together to define strengths and challenges, identify priorities, and implement various solutions to concerns and deficiencies identified during the taking-stock process. The process is relatively slow, requiring five or six years before ultimate goals are reached (Levin, 1990).

Evaluation of the implementation and initial results at Urban Elementary are promising. Prior to implementation, results of a survey administered at the end of the summer training session indicated that 75 percent would consider the program successful if the model enabled them to maintain unity of purpose, work cooperatively, feel ownership and responsibility for their actions, and take risks for student growth. The remaining 25 percent measured success in terms of observable student outcomes. Initial results suggest that all criteria for program success are evident to some extent in the beginning stages of implementation. In the words of one teacher:

> I see my class in a different light . . . more motivated. I see my students more excited about learning and I find I am teaching through my students' interests. I see that what my students and I have framed as intended outcomes are becoming real outcomes. Our cadres have helped create a stronger sense of shared responsibility for the school and students in the school. I guess what I'm trying to say is that we're moving closer and closer to our vision.

Acknowledgment: The authors gratefully acknowledge the assistance of Margaret Ferrara in the collection of qualitative data on the implementation of the model.

REFERENCES

Cuban, L. (1989). The "at-risk" label and the problem of urban school reform. *Phi Delta Kappan, 70*, 780–784.

Ferrara, M. (1992). *Cadres within the Accelerated School process: Looking within and beyond.* Paper presented at the annual meeting of the Southwest Educational Research Association, Houston.

Fisher, D., & Fraser, B. (1990, April). *Validity and use of the School Level Environment Questionnaire.* Paper presented at the annual meeting of the American Educational Research Association, Boston.

Fraser, B. J., & Fisher, D. L. (1981). Using short forms of classroom climate instruments to assess and improve classroom psychosocial environment. *Journal of Research in Science Teaching, 23*, 387–413.

Hopfenberger, W. S. (1990). *Accelerated school training manual*. Stanford, CA: Stanford University.

Hopfenberger, W. S., & Levin, H. M. (1993). *The accelerated middle schools resource guide*. San Francisco: Jossey-Bass.

Knight, S., & Stallings, J. (1992, April). *Examining the effects of the Accelerated School Model on teacher and student perceptions and behaviors*. Paper presented at the annual meeting of the American Educational Research Association, San Francisco, CA.

Levin, H. (1987). Accelerated schools for disadvantaged students. *Educational Leadership, 44,* 19–21.

Levin, H. (1988). *Toward an evaluation model'for Accelerated Schools*. Stanford, CA: Stanford University.

Levin, H. (1989). Financing the education of at-risk students. *Educational Evaluation and Policy Analysis, 11,* 47–60.

Levin, H. (1990). *Building school capacity for effective teacher empowerment: Applications to elementary schools with at-risk students*. Stanford, CA: Stanford University.

Levin, H. (1991a). Getting started. *Accelerated Schools, 1,* 12–16.

Levin, H. (1991b). What are Accelerated Schools? *Accelerated Schools, 1,* 10–11, 14–15.

McDill, E., Natriello, G., & Pallas, A. (1985). Raising standards and retaining students: The impact of the reform recommendations on potential dropouts. *Review of Educational Research, 55,* 415–434.

National Commission on Excellence in Education. (1983). *A nation at risk: The imperative for educational reform*. Washington, DC: U.S. Government Printing Office.

Newmann, F. (1989). Student engagement and high school reform. *Educational Leadership, 46,* 34–37.

Slavin, R., Karweit, N., & Madden, N. (1989). *Effective programs for students at risk*. Boston: Allyn & Bacon.

Slavin, R., & Madden, N. (1989). What works for students at risk: A research synthesis. *Educational Leadership, 46,* 4–13.

Sperling, M. (1991). Toward an interactive model of writing instruction in the Accelerated School. *Accelerated Schools, 1,* insert.

Spradley, J. P. (1979). *The ethnographic interview*. Fort Worth, TX: Holt, Rinehart, & Winston.

Spradley, J. P. (1980). *Participant observation*. Fort Worth, TX: Holt, Rinehart, & Winston.

Stallings, J., & Knight, S. (1991, April). *The Houston Satellite Center Accelerated School Project evaluation: Year one*. Paper presented at the annual meeting of the American Educational Research Association, Chicago.

Texas Research League. (1991). Accelerating remediation. *Achieve,* January 15, p. 1.

Uguroglu, M. E., Schiller, D. P., & Walberg, H. J. (1981). A multidimensional motivational instrument. *Psychology in the Schools, 18,* 279–285.

No Quick Fix: Where Do We Go from Here?

RICHARD L. ALLINGTON
SEAN A. WALMSLEY
State University of New York at Albany

In this book we have showcased a number of promising approaches to remediation of at-risk elementary students. What the projects described in these chapters—and those not reported on in this volume, such as "Success for All" (Slavin, Madden, Karweit, Dolan, & Wasik, 1993)—demonstrate clearly is that even with modest funding, it is possible to increase the reading levels of at-risk children in the elementary years and thereby reduce the number of children who fail to meet literacy standards. Intensifying remedial efforts seems to bring with it a corresponding raising of reading test scores and reduced use of retention-in-grade and special education services. The most intensive approach we know about, Reading Recovery, is also one of the very few instructional support programs to have demonstrated long-term effects on children's reading abilities. But it requires a substantial initial outlay of funds and an enormous commitment of time and energy on the part of those who adopt it.

But we have noticed some other things about the programs exemplified in this book. One is how varied their instructional practices are. Some programs (e.g., Morrow & O'Connor, Chapter 5; Hall, Prevatte, & Cunningham, Chapter 7; Taylor, Short, Shearer, & Frye, Chapter 8; Knight & Stallings, Chapter 12) offer a range of instructional practices that have been found in the research literature to be effective; others derive their approach from the work of Marie Clay (e.g., Lyons & Beaver, Chapter 6; Biggam, Teitelbaum, & Willey, Chapter 10); some are based more directly on a particular instructional philosophy (e.g., Walp & Walmsley, Chapter 9). They all seem to "work" in the sense that they reduce literacy failures quite significantly. What this says to us is that the particular instructional strategy used with at-risk children is not as important as simply attending to their

253

needs. The projects described in this book strongly suggest that any elementary school can reduce literacy learning difficulties but that some special effort will be required.

But we have some lingering concerns. One thing we have noticed is how most of these programs measure the success of their interventions in terms of how well students perform on measures of reading (standardized tests, IRIs, and so on), typically administered at the end of each year's intervention program. In those programs where raising students' test scores is a primary goal, this poses no problem. We worry that if success is measured too narrowly, we may be deluding ourselves that children who perform better on standardized tests are in fact becoming more literate, especially given the tendency for these measures to only assess a narrow band of literacy behaviors. On the other hand, so long as traditional achievement tests are used as the primary means by which the public judges success, then ensuring that children meet these demands will always remain the critical goal for remediation.

Another concern is that none of the programs discussed in this book— nor any others we have read about—achieve the goal of having every child become literate (by any definition), and it looks as though even the most intensive approaches fail to meet the needs of between 3 and 5 percent of the population. On the other hand, since failure rates run in the 20 to 50 percent range in some school districts, lowering them to even 5 percent has to be regarded as a remarkable accomplishment.

We have also noticed how difficult it is for schools to keep programs going, even if they are successful in the short term. Frequently innovative programs are introduced, are highly successful for a year or two, and then run out of steam. Thus a few students are given the intensive support they need for a year or so. Then the support is withdrawn or becomes slack again, and the students return to the very programs that failed them in the first place. We are not the first to have noticed how difficult it is to keep reforms going (Cuban, 1989; Fullan, 1991, 1993; Sarason, 1991). Unfortunately, if well-designed, intensive remedial efforts are not sustained over time, then they are of little benefit to anyone. Special intervention efforts must become part of the fabric of schools—incorporated into the belief system of teachers and administrators and fitted into the routines and organizational plans of the school district. It may well be that a relatively modest remedial program that lasts over a long period produces more benefits than a superbly designed program that lasts only a year or so.

But our major concern is that while these approaches demonstrate that it is possible, even with modest funds, to raise the literacy levels of a small number of students (e.g., Hall, Prevatte, & Cunningham, Chapter 7; Taylor, Short, Shearer, & Frye, Chapter 8), they leave open the question of whether we can make a significant dent in the numbers of children across the United States—estimated at one in four—who fail to complete school with adequate literacy abilities.

For that to occur, we are going to have to come to grips with a number of issues. The first is that we need to take a perspective on literacy difficulties that starts well before school and is sensitive to what happens beyond school. For example, we know that children's literacy experiences in the first few years of life play an important part in their eventual literacy success (Wells, 1986), yet few schools are willing to invest time and effort in preschool literacy programs or actively target preschool children whose early literacy experiences are seriously impoverished. There is a legitimate question as to whether schools should be involved in preschool literacy. Our concern is not so much who should be responsible (local education authorities, county or town agencies, or whoever), but rather that all children receive adequate preschool literacy experiences. One of the America 2000 goals is that "all children shall come to school ready to learn." The term *ready* is unfortunate in this context, implying traditional readiness skills such as auditory or visual discrimination, or gross or fine motor skills. But we need to seize this opportunity and start thinking about what literacy experiences are needed prior to formal schooling, and how we are to have children experience them. For all its faults, Head Start is one of the best early-intervention programs we know, but the quality of Head Start programs is enormously variable (Zigler & Styfco, 1993). Too often the literacy activities of preschool programs serving poor children compare poorly to programs that serve the children of more affluent families (McGill-Franzen, 1994). Frequently children from poor families have no access to preschool or attend preschools that offer relatively impoverished literacy experiences. We will need to ensure that Head Start programs are properly funded and their staff adequately trained and remunerated. These programs are much too important to staff with inadequately trained and minimum-wage personnel, and to offer meager literacy experiences for those who most need rich ones.

Second, we need to expand these early literacy programs to target parents and parents-to-be so that at least they know what literacy experiences their children need and have the appropriate materials at hand. We will need many different approaches, but they will all have one thing in common, namely, to ensure that the children themselves are exposed to appropriate literacy experiences before they come to school. Some of these experiences we will try to ensure take place at home; if that does not work, we will have to see that they take place in day care, nursery school, or Head Start settings. This is no light undertaking, because it involves the voluntary cooperation of parents and federal, state, and county agencies, as well as private day care facilities. But every child who receives adequate preschool literacy experiences through such efforts will be a child who needs less help during the school years and may, as a result, escape the fate of early school failure and long-term difficulties with literacy learning.

We have a great deal more control over children's literacy experiences and progress once they are in school. As we have discussed earlier, there are two major elements of this approach—a strong core language arts program and a well-designed instructional support program. But there is also the question of keeping track of children's literacy progress. Because most schools are organized around one-year-at-a-time instructional programs, children take a series of "field trips" with different teachers who, if they are accountable at all, are accountable only for coverage of material in a given year. They have no responsibility for children other than during the year they have them, and so no one has responsibility for the literacy experiences or the literacy accomplishments of a child across the entire elementary or secondary years. Under these circumstances, at-risk children routinely fall through the cracks. Occasionally there will be some communication between teachers or specialists along the way, but this is not likely to include a careful analysis of what the child needs in terms of literacy experiences in both regular and remedial classrooms, so that gaps can be filled in both the classroom experiences and the child's literacy abilities throughout the elementary years. Sure, we can find individual schools in which superb communication exists across a few grade levels, perhaps in one or two instances across an entire elementary school. What we cannot be assured of is that this communication will last across time (i.e., will still be in place 5 or 10 years from now), or that it exists in more than a handful of schools across the country. Improving communication between teachers and specialists both within and across grade levels should be a major goal in every school, because of the benefits that accrue to both the at-risk children and to the school. This cannot be overemphasized: If at-risk children are not allowed to fall through the cracks, we will make significant gains in the war on their illiteracy.

In general, we are skeptical about applying business models to education—educating children is not the same as manufacturing automobiles or appliances—but we could learn a lot from one manufacturing innovation, that of having teams of designers, engineers, and assemblers work on a single product from start to finish, as opposed to individuals having responsibility for individual parts. In schools, this could be accomplished by having teams of teachers and specialists who routinely follow children through the grades, ensuring that their core and remedial programs are cumulative and that current approaches build on what has taken place before. It also assumes that someone (or a group) actually takes responsibility for this monitoring, as opposed to leaving responsibility to individual teachers or to the "system" as a whole.

Schools also need to be sensitive to, and be able to adapt their programs to, the ever-changing literacy demands of the world beyond school. In many schools, simply meeting the minimal demands of standardized tests or competency measures is such an overwhelming task that it makes little sense to go beyond that. But once these minimal demands are addressed, we think schools should routinely gather information about what kinds of literacy experiences will best equip students for the world beyond school and make appropriate changes in core and remedial programs to accommodate these shifting literacy demands. Our experience is that schools are too insulated from the real world and are not sensitive to what people outside elementary and secondary education think literacy is all about. Engaging this issue in regular discussion groups that include teachers, specialists, community representatives, business people, scholars, state education staff, publishers, librarians, journalists, adult literacy volunteers, and others will help schools better understand how literacy is viewed from the outside and promote a better balance between what goes on in language arts programs and what kinds of literacy are practiced beyond school. Since literacy demands and expectations change, these discussions will have to take place on a regular basis.

But there are other issues that are important to address if American elementary schools are to be restructured to better serve all children. While the efforts described in this volume represent real enhancements of the educational effort, especially the effort to educate at-risk children, any attempt at larger-scale and long-lasting restructuring must involve consideration of these fundamental issues:

- What will be the focus of the restructuring effort?
- What sort of implementation framework will be developed?
- How will restructuring be funded?

FOCUS

"The problem with schools is not that they are no longer as good as they once were; the problem is that they are precisely as they always were, but the needs of society and the needs of students have changed significantly" (Urbanski, 1991, p. 29). We cannot continue to simply fine-tune existing programs and practices in order to address the literacy learning difficulties many children now experience in our schools. Reformulating an educational program that deals effectively with at-risk children requires a clear focus not only on the intended outcomes, but also on the quality of the literacy experiences. Recently there has been much talk about educational outcomes, as though specifying the outcomes of education will magically produce the needed reforms. The problem is not knowing what a literate child looks like—almost every teacher can tell the difference between someone who is literate and someone who is not—it is ensuring that the child actually becomes literate. Teachers know what they are aiming for, but they often lose sight of this aim, and they frequently do not engage children in the activities that will likely make them literate. One of the problems teachers face is that literacy outcomes cannot be guaranteed because children themselves play a critical role in their own literacy development, and without their consent and active participation—both of which may be withheld by children—only so much progress can be made. On the other hand, what we have students experience affects what they learn, and what we plan affects the likelihood that all children can and will elect to participate. What we need to do is increase the probability of outcomes by focusing on those experiences most likely to result in literate outcomes, rather than simply on the outcomes themselves, especially if these constitute narrowly defined literacy behaviors.

In an ideal world we would create coherent plans for restructuring programs and schools. However, as Cohen and Spillane (1992) note, fragmentation and inconsistency are hallmarks of American education whether one considers curriculum, assessment, licensure, funding, monitoring, or virtually any other facet of the enterprise. Nonetheless, while the system as a whole will always exhibit enormous confusion, that is no excuse for failing locally to clearly define what we are trying to do.

Schools exist for children, not for the benefit of the adults who work in them. Thus the focus of reform and restructuring efforts must be to enhance the benefits for children. We see benefit primarily in an academic sense, although there are a number of other roles that schools also fulfill (e.g., psychological and physical well-being). But the primary purpose of schools is educating children, and so evaluating the educational benefits that children experience as a result of reform efforts must remain the primary focus. This does not mean a narrow and exclusive emphasis on purely psychometric measures of children's academic development across time (although we can be less critical of the use of standardized tests if those measures are also balanced with broader and deeper evaluations of children's learning). But it does mean that program quality must be evaluated on the basis of the benefits children derive from that program. For instance, implementing a preschool screening that serves to deny low-scoring children entry into school when age-eligible might make teaching the primary grades easier and even raise the reported achievement levels of the school. However, denying needy children access to early educational experiences offers them no benefits.

A FRAMEWORK

Most of the efforts described in the preceding chapters are interventions that operate within the existing school organization. For instance, all focus on enhancing instruction during the regular school day. It may be time to expand our horizons and think about restructuring beyond the normal school day. These so-called extended-time efforts might involve before- or after-school activities, Saturday school, or summer school (Allington, 1993).

There are two potential benefits that extended-time models offer at-risk children. First, they expand the quantity of instruction. When we attempt to intervene during the regular school day it is literally impossible to increase instructional time. During the regular school day we might provide more intensive instruction to some children (e.g., tutorials), or furnish a bit more literacy instruction if we take away instructional time from some other area (e.g., social studies), or offer more expert instruction (e.g., specialized training of support teachers), but when all children attend school for the same length of time no additional instructional time is available. When we extend the school day, week, or year for some children we create additional instructional time. Of course, unless that time is used wisely there may be no great benefit in adding instructional time. Still, some states (e.g., Texas) are moving away from the notion that all children should attend school for roughly identical amounts of time and now require extended school attendance for elementary-aged children who are finding learning difficult.

A second potential benefit of extended-time models is the reduction in disruption of regular classroom instruction. By moving instructional support services outside the regular school day, classroom instructional programs can run without most of the interruptions that teachers most frequently complain about. Initially schools might want to simply shift special program teachers onto a flextime schedule so that at least some children can be helped outside the regular school day. However, rethinking the whole school day might lead us to consider some alternative schedules. One would be a split-shift schedule whereby classroom teachers worked with children without interruption (except for recess/snack and lunch breaks) from 8:30 in the morning until 1:30 in the afternoon. At 1:30 special-area teachers would take over the instructional responsibilities. Thus between 1:30 and 5:30 in the afternoon we would schedule art, music, physical education, and library as well as remediation and special educational interventions.

Another approach would be to integrate some or all of these nonremedial programs into the regular program, so that art, music, and library at least would be integrated within the language arts and subject areas, with additional time in the afternoon devoted to the needs of children who are particularly talented in these areas or having specific difficulties. A variation on this approach would be to devote complete days or significant portions of a day to a particular activity—such as art or music—on a rotating basis, so that teachers and children would have extended periods for these subjects on a less frequent basis, rather than brief periods on a regular basis. A curriculum based on themes or project work (Gamberg, Kwak, Hutchings, & Altheim, 1988; Walmsley, 1994) would be particularly suitable for this schedule.

Some children might attend homework assistance periods, some might be involved in drama, dance, club, or athletic activities during these afternoon or extended-day periods. Such a shift would move public elementary schools closer to approximating full workday schedules provided by middle-class day care centers and most private schools. Such a dramatic reorganization of the school day would be a huge step to even contemplate in most public schools, but given the steady increase in the number of special classes that interrupt the regular school day, it may be time to consider an alternative plan.

Another shift we think will be necessary involves the working relationships among the various teachers, administrators, and specialists in the elementary school. We need to move from a model in which each teacher works largely autonomously to an approach where far greater collaboration is expected.

Collaborative models of instruction make sense to us. But we do not imagine that such plans can simply be mandated and expected to work well. In most schools collaborative planning is a new skill that teachers must acquire—most teachers were neither hired for their collaborative expertise and experience nor evaluated on that basis after being hired. In most schools traditions will have to be renegotiated. For instance, in our experience only rarely have classroom teachers been involved in the development of the mandated Individualized Educational Plans (IEPs) for mainstreamed handicapped students. Yet it is these classroom teachers who will spend the greatest amount of instructional time with the mainstreamed student! But having classroom teachers develop IEPs collaboratively with special educators will be but one small part of the necessary collaboration in restructured schools.

Finally, we believe that while regular classroom instruction will have to change—no matter how good the instructional support programs may be, they cannot overcome weak or unfocused classroom instruction—classroom literacy instruction cannot be significantly enhanced by issuing mandates and tightening monitoring of classroom practices. The evidence available suggests to us that most teachers work hard at doing what they know. No amount of external pressure or oversight can make them more expert in their work. A framework for restructuring will need to make clear how instructional efforts will be evaluated and what sorts of assistance will be provided to assist teachers in achieving the desired outcomes. State agencies and school districts can encourage and support teachers as they commit themselves to improving their instruction, or they can attempt to control teachers with mandates, threats, sanctions, and rewards (Rowan, 1990).

But choosing to emphasize commitment strategies means involving teachers in decisions. Just as children consent to and participate in their own literacy development, so do teachers consent to and participate in their own professional development. In the long run, treating teachers as coprofessionals rather than as technicians or merely employees will probably result in more systemic and longer-lasting reforms than any mandates or new systems of accountability. One of the reasons why mandates rarely work is that teachers' work goes on in the relative privacy of a classroom, where it is impossible to monitor the day-to-day activities. On the other hand, public schools have few built-in career ladders or incentives for improvement, so that simply leaving teachers to their own devices may be a recipe for maintaining the status quo. One of the few benefits of choice is that it provides genuine impetus for reform, because if no one chooses your school, it simply goes out of business. Unfortunately, this benefit may be too high a price to pay for the problems inherent in adopting that reform.

Shared decision making in elementary schools is already proving itself to be both difficult and rewarding. It is difficult because it involves administrators losing their traditional control and teachers awkwardly gaining it. It is rewarding because it involves both teachers and administrators (and sometimes students and their parents, too) coming to terms with the realities of how to restructure elementary education in a changing world. But for shared decision making—and all the reforms we and others have been contemplating—to work, there has to be time built into the school day and into the school year. Despite public opinion to the contrary, elementary teachers already have a teaching day that is too crowded, and to expect that they take on administrative duties with no relief from teaching is simply unrealistic. Just as we have suggested reorganizing the students' day, we should think about reorganizing the teachers' day. It may be that we need to move toward a model in which the school is open not only all day, into the evening, and on weekends, but also all year, so that teachers can spend part of their time teaching, part engaged in professional development, part in administration, and part on vacation. We also need to differentiate, in terms of pay, rank, and status, between teachers who are just beginning, those who wish to stay in the classroom, and those who wish to take on more responsibilities.

FUNDING

It costs more to educate some children than others. Levin (1989) suggests that, generally, we can expect to spend about 50 percent more to educate the at-risk child. Obviously, the costs vary from child to child depending on the nature of the child's difficulties and the intensity and duration of the needed intervention. However, we currently spend additional money on the education of at-risk children, although often those funds are ill-spent (Allington & McGill-Franzen, Chapter 2; Dyer & Binkney, Chapter 3).

The various efforts described in this book all cost something additional, but costs of the intervention efforts vary widely and are not clearly related to educational outcomes. In other words, low-cost interventions sometimes work reasonably well (e.g., Taylor, Short, Shearer, & Frye, Chapter 8). However, the more expensive Reading Recovery provides the best evidence of long-term success for the largest proportion of students served. Program costs vary depending on a variety of local factors, including state and federal initiatives available to schools, local talent, and interest in competing for those funds. There are no clear patterns of funding in the projects described in this book. Many were funded from federal Chapter I money, in whole or part. Some were funded with state special initiative funds, while others were funded almost exclusively from local funds.

Too often local educational administrators suggest that reform is needed but that there is not sufficient funding available. They complain about the inadequacy of state and federal funding streams, especially, it seems, when discussing educational services for at-risk children. At times the rhetoric suggests that they believe it is a state or federal responsibility to educate hard-to-teach children. We think local education agencies have the responsibility to educate all children under the various state and federal education laws. Schools do not have limited responsibility, educating only those children who find learning easy!

If we are ever to solve the country's literacy problems, local school districts will have to assume greater responsibility for the education of all children, including the responsibility for funding extraordinary educational efforts. This will usually involve developing a convincing rationale for why funds should be allocated, along with projected costs and careful monitoring of outcomes. Without such an effort it should not be surprising that members of a local board of education or local taxpayers might balk at extraordinary expenditures for reforms.

We find it odd that school districts routinely create funding plans for capital construction and maintenance projects (e.g., reroofing buildings, resurfacing parking lots, repairing heating systems, and such items) but rarely plan or budget for long-term educational improvement and reform efforts. Perhaps schools need to follow the suggestions made by President Clinton and Vice President Gore (1992) and allocate 1.5 percent of the annual payroll to training or retraining of professional staff. Most of the cost of restructuring and reforming American elementary schools will be people costs—renewing, refreshing, extending, and enhancing the professional expertise of the teachers and administrators who carry out the daily work of educating children.

CONCLUSION

Elementary schools will change. Of that we have no doubt. They really have no choice. If they continue to ignore their role in the country's literacy problems, their problems will increase, not go away, because the public has become tired of throwing money at schools to have them produce more children without adequate literacy. At no time in recent history has there been more pressure to offer publicly funded alternatives to public schools, nor more pressure to produce "results." This is a good time to start thinking about where we want elementary education to go so that we can regain control over our literacy curriculum and begin to make significant reductions in the numbers of children who develop only minimal literacy as a result of attending the schools we currently have.

REFERENCES

Allington, R. L. (1993). Michael doesn't go down the hall anymore. *Reading Teacher, 46*, 602–605.

Clinton, W., & Gore, A. (1992). *Putting people first: A national economic strategy for America*. Little Rock, AR: National Campaign Headquarters.

Cohen, D. K., & Spillane, J. P. (1992). Policy and practice: The relations between governance and instruction. In G. Grant (Ed.), *Review of research in education* (pp. 3–49). Washington, DC: American Educational Research Association.

Cuban, L. (1989). The "at-risk" label and the problem of urban school reform. *Phi Delta Kappan, 70*, 780–784, 799–801.

Fullan, M. (1991). *The new meaning of educational change.* New York: Teachers College Press.

Fullan, M. (1993). Innovation, reform, and restructuring strategies. In G. Cawelti (Ed.), *Challenges and achievements of American education* (pp. 116–133). Alexandria, VA: Association for Supervision and Curriculum Development.

Gamberg, R., Kwak, W., Hutchings, M., & Altheim, J. (1988). *Learning and loving it: Theme studies in the classroom.* Portsmouth, NH: Heinemann.

Levin, H. (1989). Financing the education of at-risk students. *Educational Evaluation and Policy Analysis, 11,* 47–60.

McGill-Franzen, A. (1994). Is there accountability for learning and belief in children's potential? In E. H. Hiebert & B. Taylor (Eds.), *Getting reading right from the start: Effective early literacy interventions.* New York: Allyn & Bacon.

Rowan, B. (1990). Commitment and control: Alternative strategies for the organizational design of schools. In C. B. Cazden (Ed.), *Review of research in education* (pp. 353–389). Washington, DC: American Educational Research Association.

Sarason, S. B. (1991). *The predictable failure of educational reform: Can we change course before it's too late?* San Francisco: Jossey-Bass.

Slavin, R. E., Madden, N. A., Karweit, N. L., Dolan, L. J., & Wasik, B. A. (1993). Success for All: A comprehensive approach to prevention and early intervention. In R. E. Slavin, N. L. Karweit, & B. A. Wasik (Eds.), *Preventing early school failure: Research, policy and practice* (pp. 175–205). Boston: Allyn & Bacon.

Urbanski, A. (1991, October 23). Real change is real hard: Lessons learned in Rochester. *Education Week, 11*(8), 29.

Walmsley, S. A. (1994). *Children exploring their world: Theme teaching in elementary school.* Portsmouth, NH: Heinemann.

Wells, G. (1986). *The meaning makers.* Portsmouth, NH: Heinemann.

Zigler, E., & Styfco, S. J. (1993). *Head Start and beyond: A national plan for extended childhood intervention.* New Haven, CT: Yale University Press.

Index